World History of Erotic Art

Erotic Art of the West

Robert Melville

Erotic Art of the West

With a Short History of Western Erotic Art
by Simon Wilson

G. P. PUTNAM'S SONS
NEW YORK

© Robert Melville 1973

Designed by Rod Josey

Library of Congress Catalog Card Number: 72-93662

SBN: 399-11102-6

Printed in Great Britain

Contents

Has it ever been your experience, as it has mine, that after spending long hours turning over a collection of bawdy prints, you fall into a great spell of melancholy? And have you ever asked yourself the reason for the charm sometimes to be found in rummaging among those annals of lubricity, which are buried in libraries or lost in dealers' portfolios – and sometimes for the ill-humour which they cause you? It is a mixture of pleasure and pain, a vinegar for which the lips are always athirst! The pleasure lies in your seeing represented in all its forms that most important of natural feelings – and the anger in finding it so badly copied or so stupidly slandered. Whether it has been the fireside during the endless winter evenings, or in a corner of a dealer's shop, in the dog-days when the hours hang heavy, the sight of such drawings has often put my mind into enormous drifts of reverie, in much the same way as an obscene book sweeps us towards the mystical oceans of the deep. Many times when faced with these countless samples of the universal feeling, I have found myself wishing that the poet, the connoisseur and the philosopher could grant themselves the enjoyment of a Museum of Love, where there would be a place for everything, from St Theresa's undirected affections down to the serious debaucheries of the ages of ennui. No doubt an immense distance separates *Le Départ pour l'île de Cythère* from the miserable daubs which hang above a cracked pot and a rickety side-table in a harlot's room; but with a subject of such importance, nothing should be neglected.

CHARLES BAUDELAIRE,
from *Art in Paris 1845–62,*
translated and edited by
Jonathan Mayne (London, 1965)

Short History of
Western Erotic Art
by Simon Wilson

Graeco-Roman Erotic Art

The largest source of erotic themes in classical Greek art is the cluster of ideas, legends and celebrations assembled around the person of the wine god Dionysus or Bacchus. The earliest erotic scenes in Greek art, dating from about the middle of the sixth century BC, are vase paintings of Bacchic riots. These paintings depict the activities of only one group of beings within Bacchus's retinue: the satyrs, woodland creatures characterized by horses' tails and pointed ears and always shown with erect phalluses. Their natural sexual partners are nymphs and animals, creatures of the woods like themselves, and there is an Eretrian amphora in the National Museum at Athens showing a wonderfully dynamic and graceful satyr copulating with a doe, and a famous (and much less attractive) Roman sculpture of Pan penetrating a goat in the National Museum of Naples. They did not do so well with women; there are vase paintings showing maenads (women of Bacchus's troupe) rejecting their advances and, while their antics remained popular with vase painters, later vases show them reduced to buggery and fellatio and even, on a vase from the circle of the Nikosthenes painter in Berlin, to making advances to a sphinx!

The innumerable stories of the loves of the Greek gods became another major source of erotic subject matter and one of the most popular seems to have been the tale of Leda's seduction by Jupiter, disguised as a swan. The iconography of Leda's strange love can be traced back in sculpture and reliefs as far as the early fourth century BC and she is usually shown standing. The reclining Leda, with the swan between her legs, which so captivated Michelangelo, appears later, in Hellenistic art.

Once the illustration of erotic themes was established in Greek art the importance of religious and mythical motivations dwindled and the vast bulk of Greek erotic art deals with the actions of real rather than mythical people. This new iconography emerges in the late archaic period (after about 530 BC), is characterized by a particular social setting, the banquet or symposium, and, not surprisingly perhaps, appears almost exclusively on wine cups. An example is a red figure cup by the Thalia painter in Berlin, which on the outside has a frieze showing ten men and seven women in a variety of amorous attitudes: one woman is leading a man by his erect penis, one pair are copulating standing up and one man reclines between the legs of a standing woman staring intently at her vulva which he has exposed by lifting her left leg up and bending it outwards. He is evidently preparing to perform cunnilingus, something rarely depicted in Greek art. The male participants in these scenes appear to belong to the upper classes and the women are presumably high-class courtesans of elegance and intelligence. This is not always the case, however, in these wine cup friezes: a red figure cup in the Louvre attributed to the Pedieus painter shows what appears to be a brothel scene, quite different in character from the elegant orgy on the cup by the Thalia painter.

Erotic Greek vase paintings mainly depict heterosexual activities although Greek literary sources such as Plato's dialogues would perhaps lead us to expect at least a balance between heterosexual and homosexual scenes. There *are* homo-erotic scenes, such as the painting by Peitinos on a cup in Berlin of four young men delicately dallying with adolescent boys, yet even here the scene on the other side of the cup shows similar young men, this time in the company of women. There seems to be no explanation for this.

During the classical period of Greek art (from approximately 450–300 BC) the frequency of erotic representations declines, they change in character and are also found on a variety of other types of pottery besides drinking cups, as well as on objects such as mirror cases. Ancient sources also mention independent erotic paintings (probably done on small tablets) at this time.

In classical period erotic art there are usually only two participants, and whereas in archaic orgy scenes the sexual acts seem to be taking place on an impersonal, purely genital, level, in classical art there is an emotional element, an element of tenderness and feeling: the two figures are engaged only with each other, and this gives it an immense charm. In, for example, the red figure jug by the Shuvalov painter in Berlin a pretty and very young couple are shown naked, about to make love: he is sitting on a low chair, she is facing him, her arms round his neck preparatory to sitting down on his erect penis; she has leant forward so that their foreheads touch and their gazes meet in a look of ineffable bliss. The tenderness of this painting is present in perhaps even greater measure in three other extant works: a bronze mirror cover relief in Boston, a terracotta relief in Berlin, and a small, fully-in-the-round terracotta group in the museum at Delos. All show the same act, a man penetrating a woman from behind, both facing front, so that the genital areas are fully exposed, but all three show the couple kissing and this gives them a lyrical and celebratory quality.

During the Hellenistic and Roman period, frequency of erotic representation again began to rise and reached a peak under the Roman Empire. Quality, how-ever, declined and the erotic art of this period takes on a popular character since the typical vehicle became the terracotta oil lamp – a simple everyday utensil – and the various representations of the sexual act shown on these lamps amount to a catalogue of sexual positions entirely lacking the psychological element present in classical art. An exception to this is the pottery decorated with erotic reliefs made at Arezzo which was of high quality and exported all over the Roman Empire. Erotic scenes also appear extensively on Roman medallions and carved on gem stones.

A number of Roman paintings of erotic scenes have survived from the brothels in the Roman cities around the Gulf of Naples and their character as representations is similar to that of the oil lamps; they show various sexual positions. The early first-century AD frescoes in the Villa Item at Pompeii, usually known as the Villa of the Mysteries, are perhaps the most famous of all Roman paintings, but while they are connected with the phallic cult of Dionysus, they do not show any overt erotic activity. They in fact depict the rites of initiation into the Dionysiac cult and include scenes of ritual flagellation as well as the preparations for the unveiling of the phallus.

During the Hellenistic and Roman periods two important new elements were introduced from the East into the iconography of Western erotic art: Priapus, the garden god, and the hermaphrodite. Priapus was originally venerated as a grower of fruits and vines, but became enormously popular all over the Hellenistic and Roman world as a phallic deity personifying the generative power of nature.

Hermaphrodite, in Greek mythology, was the son of Hermes and Aphrodite. The nymph Salmacis fell in love with him and persuaded the gods to fuse their two bodies into one. The idea of a twin-sexed being has an obvious fascination and the hermaphrodite became a popular theme of Hellenistic and Roman art. There is an extremely erotic standing hermaphrodite in the Louvre. It has full breasts beneath a thin dress and with both hands holds up the hem of the dress at the front to expose exquisitely formed male genitals with the penis in full erection.

Finally it must be emphasized that the phallus is omnipresent in Greek and Roman art, in the ithyphallic figures on vase paintings and sculpture, in the images of the god Hermes, shaped as phallic pillars, in the extraordinary phallic monuments at Delos, which are connected with the Dionysian cult, in the Priapic shrines which dotted the Roman countryside, in the mystic ceremonies of the Roman bacchic cult in which phallic objects played an important part and in the independent phallic objects which were kept as protection against evil and bringers of good luck.

Romanesque and Gothic Art

After the triumph of Christianity in the fourth century the human figure did not completely disappear from Western art (not even in Byzantium during the iconoclastic crisis) but the nude (with the single exception of representations of Christ on the Cross) certainly did, and with it the erotic. The causes of this disappearance were iconoclasm, superstitious fear of pagan idols and a new condemnatory attitude towards the body and its pleasures which came with the collapse of paganism. When it did finally reappear in Christian art, the body had ceased to be, as it had been for the Greeks, a mirror of divine perfection and had largely become an object of humiliation and shame, on the official level at least.

In the sculptured decoration of Romanesque and Gothic cathedrals, churches and monasteries, specifically erotic themes appear in two main contexts: firstly in the didactic religious carvings found in the public and visible parts of a building, such as doorways and façades, and secondly in the less visible and accessible parts of the building where the medieval craftsman seems to have been given considerable freedom to express his own fantasy: the roofs with their gargoyles and the under-sides of the seats of the choir stalls with their misericords.

There are three major sources of themes of sexual significance found among the didactic carvings: the story of Adam and Eve, the representations of the Sin of Unchastity, and the representations of the Last Judgement which appear from the middle of the thirteenth century. The early representations of Adam and Eve tend to be totally unsensuous, being carved in a flat, stylized manner, but they are nevertheless concerned with sexuality: the knowledge gained from the fruit of the tree is the knowledge of sexual shame, and representations of the Fall also serve as a reminder of the Augustinian doctrine of original sin (Eve's sin) being transmitted by sexual intercourse which itself therefore becomes the gravest of sins. Eve is sometimes shown in isolation caressing the serpent (there is a thirteenth-century example on Reims Cathedral) and to post-Freudian eyes the serpent is a very obvious phallic symbol. Perhaps it was to the medieval mind too, since in the representations of the Vice of Unchastity woman is often shown with the devil as her lover and since the serpent of Eden was the devil the sexual implications of Eve's relationship with it become obvious. There is a twelfth-century relief at the Church of Sainte-Croix, Bordeaux, showing the devil putting his hand into a woman's bosom, and at the Chartreuse de Val de Bénédiction (Villeneuve-les-Avignon) there is a fourteenth-century relief showing a woman copulating with a goat (the devil again); and on the doorway of the Church of St Martin de l'Isle Adam-sur-Oise there is an amazingly explicit carving showing a man performing cunnilingus with his head between the thighs of a standing naked woman.

The most extraordinary representations of the Vice of Unchastity are those which show, not the vice itself, but the punishment for it which takes the form of a particularly disgusting analogy with sexual intercourse – the breasts and vulva of the women are penetrated and eaten away by serpents and toads: at Moissac there is a twelfth-century relief showing a naked woman with two serpents coiled about her, each one eating a breast, while a huge toad clings to the top of her thighs and buries its head in her vulva.

The misericords and gargoyles did not usually have a didactic purpose (they did sometimes: at Villefranche-en-Beaujolais there is a marvellous gargoyle depicting the sin of unchastity. It is a woman copulating with a goat again). As I have suggested above, in making these things the medieval craftsman was given considerable freedom to express his own fantasies and these, it is apparent, were frequently erotic or scatalogical. At the fourteenth-century cathedral of Fribourg im Brisgau, for example, one gargoyle is made from the figure of a man clinging to the parapet by his hands and feet, his body enormously elongated to form a pipe terminating in his buttocks: the water flows from the anus. Another has a naked woman sitting astride the pipe so that the water flows straight through her.

The bawdy subjects found in misericord carvings were probably mainly inspired by the Feast of Fools, a medieval festival (really the Roman Saturnalia taken over by the Christian church) during which, apparently, ceremonies of extreme licence were performed within the cathedrals. Such perhaps was the inspiration for the early fourteenth-century misericord in Chichester Cathedral which shows a fiddler pausing in his music-making to kiss a dancing woman bent backwards in an ecstatic pose emphasized by her flying garment. She bears a remarkable resemblance to the Dionysiac maenads of Greek and Roman art.

The Last Judgement is a subject which automatically involves depicting naked men and women, either emerging from their tombs or – and here there is particular scope for the introduction of sexual themes – undergoing the tortures of the damned in Hell. There are endless depictions of Hell in sculpture, in painting and in illuminated books from the mid-thirteenth century right up to the late sixteenth century when the Gothic style finally disappears. One of the earliest is in the London Psalter of *c*. 1220 (Cambridge, Trinity College): naked men and women are shown strapped together face to face while they are being roasted over a fire.

By the beginning of the fifteenth century the Gothic nude had emerged in northern European art as something quite different in character from the type of Renaissance nude being simultaneously developed in Italy. In general the Gothic nude is, in itself, more erotic than the Renaissance nude. The reason for this seems to me to be that although most Gothic nudes conform to a formal stylistic pattern (plump bellies, small high breasts and narrow shoulders) which Sir Kenneth Clark has called the Alternative Convention, they are nevertheless more *realistic* than the Renaissance nudes. Realism is the key to provoking a physical as opposed to an intellectual erotic response, and obviously the more clearly a painting of a nude evokes an actual human being the more physically erotic it will be. In this respect another crucial aspect of the Gothic nude is that both sexes are often shown with pubic hair and women sometimes have the vulva indicated as well, whereas the Renaissance nude almost without exception adheres strictly to the convention of a bland and hairless pubic region.

The Gothic nude as an independent form makes its first major appearance in painting in the illustration of 'The Fall' in the Limbourgs' *Très Riches Heures du Duc de Berry* (*c*. 1411). Here Eve appears before the Fall completely naked, and with her plump belly with its shading of pubic hair and her firm little breasts she is extremely sexy. The Gothic tradition lasts in northern Europe right up to the end of the sixteenth century and erotic themes abound in paintings, drawings, woodcuts and engravings by artists like Bosch, Bruegel, Dürer or the extraordinary Swiss, Urs Graf. But there are two artists of outstanding erotic sensibility who brought late Gothic art to a splendid climax, Lucas Cranach (1472–1553) and Hans Baldung (called Grien) (1484–1545).

Cranach painted what are arguably the most erotic independent nudes in the history of Western art and he incorporated them too into subject paintings such as the *Earthly Paradise* (Oslo National Museum) which gave the opportunity to show couples engaged in sexual play in a pastoral setting. Hans Baldung is an altogether more sinister and fascinating figure: he produced innumerable representations in paintings, drawings and engravings of woman as the personification of lust and frequently gives her Death as a companion. He is probably the originator in Western art of the theme of sexuality and death which so fascinated the Romantics, the Symbolists and the Surrealists. He was also intrigued by witches and another theme that he perhaps bequeathed to the Romantics is that of the dominant, sexually aggressive woman.

Finally, one of the great erotic masterpieces of Gothic art and one of the most compelling representations in Western art of a much painted subject is Albrecht Altdorfer's *Lot and his Daughters* of 1538 (Vienna).

Renaissance

The Renaissance nude was directly inherited as a form from classical Greece and Rome and it is largely due to the lasting prestige attached to classical art at the time of the Renaissance (powerfully reinforced by Michelangelo who in his 1504 *Bathers* cartoon established the nude as the supreme mode of expression in art) that artists ever since have been able openly to embody their erotic impulses in art at all. In this context it is important to remember that the Gothic nude was theoretically justified as an embodiment of man's sexual shame and guilt: the sense of sin so essential to the Gothic nude and which adds a strong element of the perverse to its erotic appeal is entirely absent from the classical nude which is above all an idealizing form embodying a sane, sensual and celebratory eroticism.

The female nude in Greek sculpture is Aphrodite or Venus, the goddess of sexual love, and her cult seems at first to have demanded that she be fully draped: the naked Venus is rare in Greek art before Praxiteles (mid-fourth century BC) and was introduced from the East. Praxiteles perfected the classical nude and his most famous work is the Cnidian Venus of *c.* 350 BC.

Having stressed that the classical nude is an ideal form, the question arises, can it and should it also be erotic? The Victorians, for example, including the queen herself, approved of the nude because they supposed it to be 'pure' art, free of sexual feeling, and it is clear that this view remained common until at least as recently as 1956 when Sir Kenneth Clark, writing on the nude, felt obliged to challenge and repudiate it, which he did with total effectiveness:

It [the nude] is ourselves, and arouses memories of all the things we wish to do with ourselves; and first of all we wish to perpetuate ourselves. This is an aspect of the subject so obvious that I need hardly dwell on it; and yet some wise men have tried to close their eyes to it. 'If the nude,' says Professor Alexander, 'is so treated that it raises in the spectator ideas or desires appropriate to the material subject, it is false art and bad morals.' This high-minded theory is contrary to experience. In the mixture of memories and sensations aroused by the nudes of Rubens or Renoir are many which are 'appropriate to the material subject'. And since these words of a famous philosopher are often quoted, it is necessary to labour the obvious and say that no nude, however abstract, should fail to arouse in the spectator some vestige of erotic feeling, even although it be only the faintest shadow – and if it does not do so it is bad art and false morals. (Sir Kenneth Clark, *The Nude,* 1956)

And, to return now to the Cnidian Venus of Praxiteles, Pliny in his *Natural History* (vol. 36, chapter 5) tells the story of a young man whom the Cnidian Venus 'so enflamed, that one night he hid himself in her temple and coupled with the statue, leaving on its thighs a large stain, token of his gratified passion'. We can therefore add to the canon of explicitly erotic Greek and Roman art discussed on pp. 11–13 the idealizing and symbolic erotic art of the classical nude which was passed across a gap of a thousand years to the painters and sculptors of the Italian Renaissance.

In painting, the Renaissance nude at its most warm and sensual was the creation of the Venetians, Bellini and his pupils Giorgione and Titian. Giorgione's *Fête Champêtre* is the prototype of the erotic pastoral idyll in European art while his Dresden *Venus* and Titian's *Venus of Urbino* are the first in a long line of calmly erotic nudes which culminates in the *Olympia* of Manet which so electrified the public at the 1865 salon in Paris.

In sculpture, Donatello's David (*c.* 1435), the first free-standing bronze sculpture cast since antiquity, is also unique in its erotic impact: it is an extraordinary celebration of the adolescent body.

Michelangelo's sculptures are usually concerned with the expression of power and energy but a number of his more relaxed works display an eroticism that was remarked on by his contemporaries. Examples are the so-called *Dying Slave* in the Louvre who seems rather to be swooning in ecstasy than dying, and the extraordinarily sensual 1498 *Pietà* in St Peter's. In this work Michelangelo has taken the mystical medieval concept of Mary as the bride of Christ and given it an erotic reality. Michelangelo produced at least two drawings featuring genitalia which, not unexpectedly in view of his homosexuality, show an obsessive phallicism. There is a drawing in the Doria-Pamphili collection in the Vatican of a man wearing a phallus in his bonnet as one might wear a feather, and there is an engraving after him called *The Dream of Human Life*, a complex allegory with an ithyphallic man embracing a woman, a mysterious giant hand grasping a huge phallus and a disembodied phallus floating in the sky.

Botticelli's *Primavera* (*c.* 1470–80) is the prototype of the multi-figure mythological subject painting which, as well as the independent nude, becomes a major vehicle for erotic feeling or erotic themes in Western art from the Renaissance onwards. The erotic focus of this painting is the group of the Three Graces, whose nakedness is enhanced by their transparent *draperies mouillées*. Edgar Wind (in *Pagan Mysteries of the Renaissance*) has convincingly interpreted this as an initiation into love of the central nymph, Castitas, by the other two, Voluptas and Pulchritudo. It is at Castitas that Cupid is aiming his phallicly symbolic, flame-tipped arrow.

There is a very large group of mythological subjects of this type which artists particularly exploited for their erotic possibilities. A discussion of each of them and their many representations is outside the scope of this history, but perhaps the most important erotic myths are those of Cupid and his affair with Psyche, of the life and loves of Bacchus and his troupe, of Venus and her love affairs with Adonis, Jupiter, Mars, Mercury, et al., and of Jupiter and his innumerable and exotic erotic adventures (including, of course, his seduction of Leda). Leonardo's famous lost *Leda* (*c.* 1505) is the first great Renaissance version of this erotic myth and it seems to have been intended as an allegory of the process of generation (one of his sketches of the subject appears on a sheet of anatomical drawings of sexual organs). Leonardo's *Leda* is standing, hugging the swan to her: it was Michelangelo, nearly thirty years later, following Hellenistic precedents, who put Leda on her back and the swan where it properly belongs, between her legs.

Michelangelo's Rome *Pietà* is an example of a religious work which is also erotic, and many artists who wished to express erotic feeling but who could not or would not use pagan subjects turned to Christian subjects with sexual themes or erotic possibilities. The Last Judgement is a major subject of this type and it is worth remembering that Michelangelo's version in the Sistine Chapel (1541) came under heavy attack for its nudity and was eventually mutilated in the interests of prudery. Some of the many other important erotic religious subjects are Lot and his Daughters, Susanna and the Elders, Salome, Joseph and Potiphar's Wife and Judith and Holofernes. The lives, the temptations and the deaths of the saints and martyrs also provide a major source of erotic (in the case of the deaths, sado-erotic) subject matter.

The two great early masters of the erotic mythology are Titian and Antonio Correggio, while Raphael's *La Fornarina*, an intimate portrayal of his mistress with breasts bared, is the first of a new type of painting, the erotic portrait. In 1516 Raphael also designed (they were carried out almost entirely by pupils) the famous 'secret' erotic frescoes of Venus and Cupid, Cupid and Psyche and Vulcan and Pallas for the bathroom of Cardinal Bibiena in the Vatican. In the same year he was also responsible for an ambitious cycle of frescoes illustrating the story of Cupid and Psyche at Agostino Chigi's new villa in Rome, the Farnesina.

Finally, Piero di Cosimo, that oddity among the Renaissance masters, must be mentioned. His two paintings in the National Gallery, London, *The Battle of the Lapiths and Centaurs* and *The Death of Procris*, reveal a haunting, melancholy and intensely poetic erotic imagination.

Mannerism

Mannerism is the style of the sixteenth century, the style essentially of the followers of Michelangelo and Raphael who seized on the idea of an art based on the primacy of the human figure and developed it to the ultimate limits of its possibilities. In mannerist art, painting and sculpting the human body in ever more difficult and bizarre perspectives and postures became a game played for its own sake – or rather for art's sake – and given this obsession with the body it is not surprising that Mannerist art is frequently erotic. Indeed, eroticism is one of its main identifying characteristics, and furthermore this eroticism is in general much more explicit and intense than in Renaissance art. The reasons for this are that Mannerist art was produced mostly for the wealthy, pleasure-loving royal courts of Europe whose atmosphere would encourage refined (refined in the sense of distilled, purified and concentrated) sensuality; and also that the status of the artist and of art itself had reached unprecedented heights: both Michelangelo and Raphael were given the title 'Il Divino' by their contemporaries and many Mannerist artists were elevated to the nobility. Painting was referred to as 'the noble art' by Francisco de Hollanda in his treatise on painting of 1578 where he also quotes Michelangelo as saying that 'there is only one single art and science on earth, namely that of drawing or painting from which all others stem . . .', and the word *disegno* was interpreted as Signo di Dio. The effect of this was to give the artists more freedom in their handling of commissions and it had the further crucial effect of enabling them sometimes to work for themselves, to be their own patrons, in a way that had never happened before.

The Mannerist artist, Giulio Romano, was the most brilliantly gifted of Raphael's many pupils and he created two major works of erotic art which are, however, very different in character and significance. The first of these is the Hall of Psyche in the Palazzo del Tè which Romano both built and decorated for the Duke of Mantua in 1532-4. Outstanding among the erotic groups in the hall is that of Jupiter and Olympia: Jupiter is poised between the legs of the reclining nude Olympia, his erect phallus pointing straight at her vulva: he is about to slide forward and into her. The explicit treatment Giulio was able to give this subject illustrates the freedom enjoyed by a Mannerist artist working for a princely patron.

The other great erotic work by Giulio is the group of twenty drawings of sexual intercourse which were engraved by Marcantonio Raimondi (whose talent had made him Raphael's favourite engraver) and embellished with erotic sonnets by Aretino. These works, known as the *Sedici Modi*, are remarkable both for their explicitness and for their pagan, celebratory and guilt-free attitude towards sexuality. Published in 1524 they at once became famous and much copied and imitated, and have remained so ever since, although ironically only one complete sheet and nine fragments of Raimondi's original engravings are in a known collection (the British Museum). These works must be the first 'commercial' erotica and from the time of their publication onwards an ever-swelling stream of such things flowed from the hands of the engravers. Another famous series of this type was the *Loves of the Gods* by Agostino Carracci.

Mannerism reached France in 1530 when François Iᵉ commissioned decorations for the Palace of Fontainebleau and other royal palaces from the Italians Rosso, Primaticcio and Niccolo dell'Abbate. Because of this, Mannerism in France became known as 'Ecole de Fontainebleau' and it is characterized, especially towards the end of the sixteenth century, by an elegant and ubiquitous eroticism. One work which encapsulates the whole erotic ethos of the Ecole de Fontainebleau is the famous double portrait in the Louvre of Gabrielle d'Estrée, the mistress of Henri IV, and her sister in the bath.

Among the northern Mannerists, Hendrick Goltzius and Bartholomeus Spranger produced erotic mythologies and allegories, the inventions of Spranger, who was gifted with a particularly powerful erotic imagination, often being engraved by Goltzius.

It was in Florence that Mannerism reached its most extreme development. Wartenburger in his *Mannerism* says of Florence, 'Artistic activity became quite independent of commissions, it was only used to live out personal psychological states and seems so self-centred that often it can only be explained as the manifestation of abnormal or even pathological states of mind.' It comes as no surprise then to find that it was a Florentine painter, Angelo Bronzino, who produced painting which must be the great masterpiece of Mannerist erotic art: his *Venus, Cupid, Folly and Time* in the National Gallery, London.

The Baroque

By the end of the sixteenth century, then, the nude, the mythology and certain religious subjects were firmly established as the vehicles of erotic feeling in Western art. Not that the mythological subject with nudes or semi-nudes is always necessarily imbued with erotic feeling beyond that 'vestige' of which Clark speaks. Indeed, within the major style of the seventeenth century, the Baroque, the degree and type of erotic feeling expressed vary enormously. There is the frigidity of the French Baroque, the lifeless boredom of Le Brun or Le Sueur, alleviated only by Poussin in whose work there is evidence of a powerful erotic impulse kept severely under control. The famous drawing of Acis and Galatea in the Royal Library at Windsor shows, however, that this impulse found occasional overt expression. There is the Italian Baroque, as represented by Bernini, whose *St Theresa* is a matchless expression of female orgasm and whose *Apollo and Daphne* embodies a different kind of ecstasy; a rush of pure feeling to the brain, an extraordinary frisson of delight.

And there is the northern Baroque, the fantastic celebrations of the flesh of Rubens and his followers. In Rubens human flesh blooms and proliferates, and whatever the ostensible subjects, his mythological and allegorical compositions are always about the same thing: they are metaphors for the very processes of sexuality and procreation, images of fertility and growth.

In Rubens and followers of his like Jordaens is continued the northern tradition of a realistic non-idealizing approach to the nude, and as we have seen, this permits a more direct expression of sexuality than does the classic approach. This attitude of mind also enabled Rubens to turn his attention away from mythological and religious subjects and to depict the basic sexual pleasures of peasants at a village festival in works like *La Kermesse* in the Louvre. This type of subject – festivals, tavern scenes, brothel scenes – is common in Dutch and Flemish art in the seventeenth century.

The great seventeenth-century realist was Rembrandt and his nude women appear before us as more convincing representations of a real human being than ever before in the history of art: Rembrandt's nudes appear in the erotic mythologies (*Danae, Jupiter and Antiope*) that he painted and etched, as well as in biblical subjects like *Bathsheba* and *Joseph and Potiphar's Wife*, but his most compelling erotic work is a piece of straightforward observation. It is the etching known as 'Ledikant' or 'The Great Bed' and it shows frankly and with tenderness a young couple making love in a huge four-poster bed.

Rococo

The dynamic and celebratory eroticism of Rubens was greatly admired by his fellow Fleming, the painter Jean-Antoine Watteau, who came to Paris in 1702 and soon made friends with Claude Audran, Keeper of the Luxembourg Palace, who gave him access to the great Rubens Marie de Médici cycle of paintings which then hung there. He admired but, consumptive as he was, had not the power to imitate and he looked back again, through Rubens, to Giorgione whose *Fête Champêtre* (which then belonged to Louis XIV) is the prototype of the kind of painting Watteau was to make his own: the 'Fête Galante', which is the phrase used by the French Royal Academy in 1717 to describe Watteau's reception piece, the *Departure for the Island of Cythera*. Watteau's pictures are about love, about men and women falling in love to the accompaniment of music, in a tranquil, slightly melancholy or wistful dream-like world. The trip to Cythera is, of course, a trip to visit the shrine of Venus, Goddess of Love and, as Michael Levey has remarked, the only deity the eighteenth century really believed in.

Watteau rarely painted the living nude although (rather oddly) the nude statues that appear in some of his paintings are remarkably sensual, and it was left to his follower, Boucher, the Rococo eroticist *par excellence*, to strip away from his art both the delicate psychological atmosphere and the ravishingly textured clothes and together with his pupil, Jean Honoré Fragonard, and a whole host of lesser 'galante' painters and engravers to produce great quantities of the most blatant high-class erotica in the history of Western art.

In fact, French Rococo painting and engraving, like Mannerist art in the sixteenth century, is almost by definition erotic and for much the same reasons: its patrons were wealthy, sexually indulgent autocrats. Boucher and Fragonard worked almost exclusively for Louis XV, his mistresses and his aristocratic court at Versailles. Boucher's painting of Miss O'Murphy, one of the royal harem, is far and away his most famous work. Louise O'Murphy is supposed to have been procured for Louis by Casanova himself and it is tempting to believe the claim made by the great lover (at this stage in his career a high-class pimp) in his memoirs, that he also invented the celebrated pose of Boucher's painting.

Going beyond erotic nudes like Miss O'Murphy or erotic mythologies and galanteries, however suggestive, Boucher and Fragonard also painted and drew genitally explicit erotic scenes. Photographs have survived of four paintings of this nature done by Boucher, it is said, for Madame de Pompadour: the works themselves have vanished, but there are extant many others by lesser artists (often attributed to Boucher).

The erotic engraving flourished at this period, ranging in quality from the delicacy of Boucher's engravings after Watteau down to the directness, explicitness and crudity of the anonymous plates in the first illustrated edition of De Sade's *Juliette*, published (and prosecuted) in 1797. Explicit erotic scenes appeared extensively on snuffboxes, lockets and other trinkets and the often very high-quality small terracotta groups produced by sculptors like Clodion and Falconet.

In England the major artist of the first half of the eighteenth century was William Hogarth, who adapted the delicate style of Watteau to rather more robust ends; combining it with Dutch realism he created the Modern Moral

Subject which, inevitably, frequently touched on sexual matters. Indeed, the most successful of all Hogarth's Modern Moral Subjects was *A Harlot's Progress* (in the eighteenth century, as now, sex was a sure-fire seller). However, Hogarth's attitude towards sex is that of a moralist and only in one major work does he get at all close to the atmosphere and spirit of the French Rococo painters; this is in the pair of paintings, now in the Fitzwilliam Museum, Cambridge, called *Before and After*.

Romanticism

In 1792 the Spanish painter, Francisco Goya (1746–1828) became deaf as the result of an illness. This deafness reinforced his already introspective and brooding personality and in 1796 he produced the extraordinary series of etchings, *Los Caprichos*. These were, as Goya himself said, works in which he could 'make observations for which commissioned works generally give no room and in which fantasy and invention have no limit'. This statement sums up the attitude of all Romantic artists and it marks a turning point in the history of Western art: the point at which the artist finally begins to work primarily for himself rather than for any particular patron, the point at which he begins consciously to explore new kinds of subject matter, both in the world of appearances and in the inner world of the imagination.

Goya's *Naked Maja* of *c.* 1797 is certainly a piece of observation of the kind 'for which commissioned works generally give no room'. Here is a courtesan staring directly out at the spectator with a slight smile of complicity, secure in her professional competence, available, with a neat, sexy body, the erotic impact of which Goya has completed by defying the usual convention and painting in the pubic hair.

In Goya, realism and fantasy co-exist; it is only in the 'Black Paintings' of the last years of his life that he cuts himself entirely off from the social world and gives free expression to his most private imaginings. But in the art of one of Goya's contemporaries, the Swiss-born painter Henry Fuseli (1741–1825), we can see a consistent endeavour to produce paintings and drawings in which 'fantasy and invention have no limit' but which are without any social relevance whatever, which are no more and no less than the expression of the artist's pathological obsessions. 'The most unexplored region of art is dreams,' said Fuseli, a remarkable enough statement to make in a pre-Freudian era but even more remarkable is the fact that Fuseli's art lends itself almost too readily to analysis from a Freudian point of view. A glance at Fuseli's extensive œuvre reveals two major obsessions, one with violence, conflict and death, the other with the erotic; there is *nothing* else: these obsessions correspond exactly to Freud's twin formulation of the human instincts, Eros and Thanatos.

Furthermore, Fuseli's eroticism is of an extraordinary kind; his work is crammed with hair fetishism and clothes fetishism; his women are mysterious, dominating, sexual goddesses; a vaginal obsession reveals itself in his famous series of drawings of women standing in front of fireplaces in which, as well as the fireplace symbolizing in Freudian terms the vagina, the women themselves are drawn in such a way that their whole body becomes a metaphor for their sexual parts; and in at least one drawing the woman represents not only the vagina but simultaneously and metamorphically the phallus (there are drawings by Picasso, e.g. the drawings for his *Crucifixion*, of 1929, like this). Even without the evidence of the bulk of his more explicitly erotic drawings (of which there are clearly a large number scattered about: known examples are in the Victoria and Albert Museum, London, and the Horne Foundation in Florence) Fuseli emerges as one of the most profound, complex, fascinating and enigmatic of all erotic artists.

William Blake did not share his friend Fuseli's exclusive obsessions; his was a broader vision, but his central concept of Energy as defined in the 'Marriage of Heaven and Hell' (1794) ('Energy is the only life, and is from the Body; and Reason is the bound or outward circumference of Energy' and 'Energy is Eternal Delight') seems indistinguishable from Freud's concept of libido: drive energy, the principal components of which are sexual. His work, both literary and visual, is permeated with sexual themes, from the early illuminated books like *Visions of the Daughters of Albion* (1793) and *Vala and the Four Zoas* (never published by Blake) to his last great project, the illustrations to Dante.

From the earliest phase of the movement in the late eighteenth century, neurosis and perversion are the keynotes of Romantic eroticism and reach a climactic expression in the exotic, baroque, sado-erotic fantasies of Eugène Delacroix, the greatest of which is *The Death of Sardanapalus* of 1829 (Louvre). But in the second half of the nineteenth century Romantic art changes in character: the crude energy of a Delacroix is replaced, on the continent, by the sterile, static, hothouse atmosphere of an Ingres or a Gustave Moreau, a Fernand Knopff, a Jan Toorop or a Gustav Klimt; in England, by the dreamy, almost drugged ambience of a Rossetti, a Lord Leighton, or an Albert Moore; and the eroticism becomes even more perverse and neurotic. This is particularly apparent in the work of the last genius of the Romantic movement, the English artist, Aubrey Beardsley, who takes his place alongside Henry Fuseli as one of the greatest eroticists in Western art.

The extraordinary impact of Beardsley's art is undoubtedly partly due to the fact that he invented quite new formal means for the expression of erotic feeling and was aware of this: 'fresh and original' was how he described his own work in a letter written shortly after receiving the commission which launched his glittering, if brief, career.

Beardsley created two illustrated books which are monuments of erotic art: the first was Oscar Wilde's *Salome*, published openly by John Lane in 1894, the second, Aristophanes's *Lysistrata* published 'under the counter' by Leonard Smithers in 1896. Wilde's play is about what is perhaps the ultimate perversion of all, necrophilia, and it is this, we know, which originally fired Beardsley's *fin de siècle* imagination and inspired the two most important drawings in the book, those showing Salome with the head of the Baptist. But Beardsley's major obsession was a phallic one (a total of four penises were censored out of the first edition of *Salome*, although by way of compensation the censor, John Lane, overlooked three more: erect at that – a tribute to the novelty of Beardsley's style) and it is for his phallic illustrations to Aristophanes, which are a recreation in late nineteenth-century terms of the vase paintings of classical Greece, that he is most famous in the context of erotic art.

Beardsley had many followers and imitators but only one of them, the extraordinary Graf Von Bayros, managed to go beyond him and build a unique erotic art of his own. His hundreds of erotic drawings embody a consistent vision of a kind of rococo pleasure dome with Watteauesque gardens in which gorgeous dandies and ravishing adolescent girls are depicted, in a style of exquisite refinement and remarkable formal strength, elegantly engaging in every conceivable sexual perversion.

Realism

Romanticism, as we have seen, nurtured the expression of erotic fantasy in art: the parallel tendency of realism produced artists who devoted themselves to taking a straight look at the human body and at human sexual activity.

If any artist in England inherited Hogarth's role as an observer of, and commentator on, contemporary life that artist was Thomas Rowlandson (1757–1827). Trained at the Royal Academy, Rowlandson soon abandoned oils for the more convenient media of watercolour and etching and all his life was a prolific producer of topographical, sporting, satirical, political and humorous drawings and prints. (His obituarist, W. H. Pyne, remarked that Rowlandson had 'etched as much copper as would sheathe the whole British Navy'.) When young his life style was riotous: drinking, gambling and whoring (he never married) on the fringes of the Prince of Wales set. His taste for bawdy is evident in his work throughout his career but in the last decade or so of his life, when he had emerged from a period of extreme poverty resulting from the excesses of his youth, he produced a large group of prints and drawings which deal with sexual subjects in a totally explicit way. The bulk of these erotic works is in the George IV collection at Windsor Castle and would appear to have been done for the Prince Regent; there are others in the Victoria and Albert Museum and the British Museum. They fall into two main groups: the first, and most charming, consists of works like *The Music Master*, *A Country Outing* or the scenes of soldiers whoring, which celebrate the sexual pleasures of ordinary people from all walks of life; and such works, no doubt, reflect the nostalgia of the artist for his ribald youth. However, it is apparent that this nostalgia frequently turned sour and *The Spy Glass* is a savage comment, pointed up by the bowl full of dildoes in the foreground, on the impotent lust of old men.

In 1868 Gustave Courbet published in the Paris *Courier du Dimanche* a long statement of the realist aesthetic in which he said, among other things, 'Especially, the art of painting should consist solely of the representation of objects visible and tangible to the artist.' Women were clearly among Courbet's favourite visible and tangible objects and all his paintings of them, clothed as well as nude, are imbued with a heavy sensuality. Among Courbet's paintings of women are three in particular which are deliberately erotic and one at least of these must be counted among the great masterpieces of nineteenth-century painting. This is the famous painting of Lesbian lovers known as *Laziness and Sensuality* or *The Sleepers* now hanging in the Collection of the City of Paris at the Petit Palais. This remarkable work was painted on commission for a wealthy Turkish ex-diplomat called Khalil Bey who lived in Paris and who also commissioned from Courbet a small painting of a woman's torso, the legs spread apart so that the vulva is the focus of the composition. The body above the breasts is cut off by the top edge of the canvas and the legs by the lower edge so that the effect is of a camera zoomed in on the pubic region. Khalil Bey kept this picture in a tabernacle on the outer door of which was painted an innocuous landscape of a chateau in the snow. The third major erotic work by Courbet is the picture now in the Barnes collection, Philadelphia, which is essentially a worm's eye view of the pudenda of a seated girl wearing nothing but a pair of white stockings.

The Belgian artist, Felicien Rops, has his roots in the tradition of Flemish and Dutch realism. He began his career as a caricaturist and naturalistic painter in the Barbizon manner, but became exclusively concerned with, and indeed totally obsessed by women, or rather, Woman. Working as he did in the 'minor' media of drawing and etching (of which he was a master) and distributing his work through printsellers and bookshops (he did a lot of work in the 1860s and 1870s for the famous 'underground' publisher of erotica and avant-garde literature, Poulet-Malassis, who operated from Brussels), Rops was free to produce, when he wished, explicitly erotic works for discreet sale to discerning collectors. He in fact produced vast quantities of erotic drawings and etchings and their wide distribution has ensured him a continuing notoriety as the pornographic artist *par excellence* of his period.

In the early 1860s Rops met Charles Baudelaire, who was immediately excited by his work. Not surprisingly, for Baudelaire had just written his essay on the theory of realism, 'The Painter of Modern Life', and Rops in his drawings and etchings of prostitutes and the Paris demi-monde of cafés, cabarets and brothels must have seemed to be putting into practice some of Baudelaire's own ideas on the subject matter of modern art. Furthermore, Baudelaire says in his introduction to 'The Painter of Modern Life': '... the *poetae minores* have something good, solid and delightful to offer and however much we may love the *general* beauty expressed by great artists and poets we would be quite wrong to ignore the beauty of the *particular*, the beauty of particular places and aspects of human behaviour.' Rops is the very type of the 'minor poet' who concentrates his whole vision on a particular aspect of the world, in this case human sexual behaviour.

It is a tragedy that Baudelaire died prematurely, as he did in 1867. Had he survived the following decade we might have had from him an essay on Degas's monotypes of brothel scenes, executed *c.* 1879–80, which also correspond perfectly with his theory of the particular. But Degas is no 'minor poet': in spite of the particularity of his subjects and the fact that much of his work is in the 'minor' graphic media, especially monotype and pastel, it has a seriousness and a formal grandeur that put him in the very top rank of Western artists. Had he known Degas's mature work, Baudelaire would have wept tears of joy.

In the context of the history of erotic art Degas's brothel scenes are of great importance. Over fifty are now known but there were probably many more in

Degas's studio at his death: seventy monotypes were destroyed by René De Gas before the studio sale and although Vollard denied that they were brothel scenes they almost certainly were. Some of Degas's sketchbooks have been similarly censored. Even if we accept that the surviving works are all that Degas did, we have for almost the first time in the history of post-Renaissance art solid evidence that an artist of undisputed greatness and seriousness devoted a great deal of creative effort to the frank treatment of sexual subjects and that furthermore many of these works must be counted among his masterpieces.

It is interesting that just a few years later Degas's great contemporary, the sculptor Auguste Rodin, entered a phase in his career in which the distinguishing characteristic of his work is an intense and lyrical eroticism. From the early 1880s onwards he produced dozens of groups of amorous couples of which by far the most famous is *The Kiss* of 1886.

Rodin, however, was working in the idealizing tradition of the Renaissance nude ('this son of Michelangelo', he was called in his funeral oration) and he selected his models with care. They were, as photographs of them show, usually ravishingly beautiful young women and Rodin made no bones about his attitude towards them: 'A woman undressing, how dazzling! It is like the sun piercing through clouds . . . in every model there is the whole of nature.' And the critic Gustave Coquiot wrote of Rodin: 'He is grateful to them for all the joys they give him. He tells them, "Don't hurry your undressing" and gazes with greedy and sensuous pleasure.'

The Pre-Raphaelites

In England, in the art of the Pre-Raphaelites, realism and romanticism were combined. They were inspired on the one hand by Ruskin's doctrine of 'truth to nature' and on the other by William Blake and the Italian Primitives. Pre-Raphaelite paintings dealing with sexual themes thus tend to fall into two groups: one group of works which are essentially Hogarthian 'modern moral subjects' and another, mostly emanating from Rossetti and his circle but including one of the greatest Pre-Raphaelite paintings, Millais's *Ophelia*, in which the paintings are imaginative, poetic and often dream-like embodiments of erotic fantasy.

Nearly all the Pre-Raphaelite painters attempted 'modern moral subjects': Hunt's *The Hireling Shepherd* of 1851 was intended to show how sex can be a dangerous distraction from the business of everyday life although, as Robert Melville has pointed out, its actual effect is rather different. Hunt had more success with his other major moral subject *The Awakening Conscience*, which depicts a young kept woman at the awful moment when the full moral horror of her situation suddenly dawns on her. A similar subject was treated by Ford Madox Brown in *Take Your Son, Sir!*, 1857, which shows another kept woman presenting her illegitimate child to its putative father who brutally shrugs his shoulders: the clear implication is that she and the child will shortly be on the streets: a truly desperate situation for a woman in the Victorian age. Augustus Egg's triptych *Past and Present* of 1856 deals with a slightly different but related subject: marital infidelity (of the wife, of course) and its dire social consequences, while Rossetti's *Found* of 1854 shows a young farmer bringing a lamb to market who finds his ex-fiancée, literally in the gutter, having left her village and sunk into prostitution in the town.

Millais, too, treated subjects of this type, for example in his drawing *Retribution* of 1854 (marital infidelity again, this time of the husband), but his most compelling erotic works are those like *Ophelia* of 1852 or *Mariana* of 1851 in which the erotic content is largely unconscious and which are more romantic than realistic. In *Ophelia* Millais's image is of an ethereally beautiful young girl with an ecstatic expression on her face, but the spectator's desire for her is given a perverse, even necrophiliac, edge by the knowledge that she is in fact dead. Thus the painting plays upon our erotic responses in a curious and subtle way and it is perhaps this which makes it so unforgettable to almost everyone who sees it.

In Rossetti's work of the 1860s and 1870s realism is finally left behind in his obsessively erotic depictions of beautiful, sultry, enigmatic women. For the greatest of these paintings like *Proserpine* (1874) or *Astarte Syriaca* (1877) the model was Janey Morris and it was her extraordinary looks – the long columnar neck, the sensual, thick cupid's bow lips, the superabundant crinkly hair (Rossetti's hair fetishism was remarked upon by his contemporaries) that Rossetti gave to his most disturbing creations.

Rossetti's pupil and follower, Edward Burne-Jones, developed his own dream world of knights and maidens, a world pervaded by a curiously androgenous sexuality which stemmed partly no doubt from the convention of sexlessness which the Victorians applied to the nude but which is, too, a haunting manifestation of Burne-Jones's own repressed erotic impulses.

Munch

Much of the work (specially the graphic work) of the Norwegian painter Edvard Munch reveals an obsession with the erotic. He was not, however, interested in the expression of erotic feeling as such but rather in expressing his own (very complex) feelings about human sexuality and the relations between the sexes, which he certainly saw as one of the central problems of human existence. The nature of these feelings was in fact tragic and depressive: in his work sexuality and death, passion and jealousy, love and despair go hand in hand.

In the early 1890s Munch conceived the idea of incorporating his vision into a great cycle of paintings to be called 'The Frieze of Life', which he described as 'a poem of life, love and death'. This subject matter Munch incorporated into his paintings less by direct representation than by the use of lurid or grating colour, distorted forms and free, expressive brushwork as well as by elaborately symbolic compositional arrangements. It is this which makes him one of the founders of Expressionism.

His *Madonna* belongs to the 'Frieze of Life' cycle and depicts the moment of conception (that arch misogynist and friend of Munch, August Strindberg, wrote of *Madonna*, 'Immaculate or not, it is all the same. The red or gold halo crowns the consummation of the act, the only justification of this creature's life'). There is no hint of life or joy in it, and indeed somehow Munch manages to incorporate the feeling of death into the composition, thus completing its meaning as an image of the human life cycle of desire, orgasm, conception, birth and death.

Vienna 1900-1918, Klimt and Schiele

Gustav Klimt (1862–1918) and Egon Schiele (1890–1918) are names which have a particular resonance for the historian of erotic art: as Thomas M. Messer put it in his introduction to the catalogue of the Guggenheim's 1965 Exhibition:

Preoccupation with erotic subject matter, common to both, is not in itself surprising at a time and in the very city where Sigmund Freud's discoveries originated. But Klimt and Schiele felt compelled to visualize for themselves, and inevitably for others, what had until then been relegated to a most private domain. Inevitably, therefore, clashes between a truly Freudian irrepressibility and a conventional sense of decorum had to arise. Given the charged atmosphere in which Klimt and Schiele imparted forbidden knowledge through the most explicit of art forms – the visual media of painting and drawing – the personal consequences could not but be varying degrees of disgrace, humiliation and withdrawal.

Klimt, like Munch, was fascinated by the association of sexuality and death and he incorporated this into his great tryptych of paintings (1900–1907) for the three faculties (Medicine, Philosophy and Law) of the University of Vienna, as well as putting it into his Beethoven mural of 1902 and a number of independent paintings. The paintings of 'Medicine' and 'Philosophy' caused a tremendous scandal when they were exhibited and an issue of the Vienna Secession magazine, *Ver Sacrum*, containing sketches for 'Medicine' was confiscated by the police. But it is for his wonderfully erotic drawings of the female nude that Klimt is best known outside his native city and a contemporary critic left an account of his method of making these:

... he was surrounded by enigmatic naked women who, while he stood silently at his easel, wandered up and down his studio, lazing and stretching and luxuriating through the days – yet always ready, at the artist's signal, to freeze obediently into a pose, a movement that had caught his eye ...

In 1907, at the age of seventeen, Egon Schiele, then a student at the Vienna Academy of Art, was introduced to Klimt. Klimt was enthusiastic about his work and from that time on their relationship was an increasingly close one. Indeed, Schiele sketched Klimt on his deathbed just a few months before his own premature death in October 1918.

The influence of Klimt in Schiele's work is obvious and he too painted allegorical works concerned with themes of sexuality and death. But also, like Klimt, he is best known outside Vienna for his extraordinary erotic drawings which are, however, very different from those of his teacher. They are, in the first place, extremely explicit and they also have a tense, neurotic, angst-ridden quality which, on the whole, is absent from those of Klimt. It was Schiele's reputation as a pornographic draughtsman which resulted in his arrest and imprisonment for twenty-four days in 1912 when he was living in the town of Nenlengbach near Vienna.

Schiele was the first major artist of the twentieth century to produce a large body of frankly erotic work. It is characteristic of the age that not only was he persecuted for doing this but that the work itself agonizingly reflects the profound sexual anxieties of modern man.

Surrealism

It was inevitable that, as soon as the First World War was over, as soon as artistic life had begun to function more or less normally again and as soon as the formal revolution of Cubism had been thoroughly absorbed, an art movement would appear based exclusively on the theories of Freud. In 1924 André Breton published the *First Surrealist Manifesto* in which he called for an art that came straight from the subconscious. Since for Freud the subconscious mind was dominated by two major instinctual drives, Eros and Thanatos, sexuality and death, Surrealist art would be *by definition* erotic. Breton points this out in his essay on 'Surrealism and Painting' in which he says that he has no interest in any work of art which fails to 'produce in me a state of physical disturbance characterized by the sensation of a wind brushing across my forehead and capable of causing me to really shiver. I have never been able to help relating this sensation to erotic pleasure and can discover between them only differences of degree.' Furthermore, Breton admits of no interference with the artist's total freedom to express his unconscious: in the *Manifesto* he defines Surrealism as 'pure psychic automatism by which it is intended to express . . . the true function of thought. *Thought dictated in the absence of all control exerted by reason and outside all aesthetic or moral preoccupations.*'

All the great Surrealist masters, Ernst, Magritte, Dali, Delvaux, were masters of the erotic, but once again it is in the work of a Baudelairian 'minor poet' among the Surrealists, the German-born Hans Bellmer, that we find an erotic obsession developed with the greatest intensity. In particular Bellmer developed a graphic style of great brilliance in which human sexual anatomy is detailed lovingly and with exquisite precision. Not only that, but these anatomies merge, interpenetrate and metamorphose so that the intricacies of a Bellmer drawing eventually resolve themselves into a series of convulsively sexual images.

Enormously admired by the Surrealists, while not precisely being Surrealist painters, are Balthus, the creator of hauntingly erotic images of adolescent girls, and his literary brother Pierre Klossowski who produces weird 'Sadique' erotic drawings in which the theme of sexuality and death is once again stressed.

Paralleling the sudden blossoming of eroticism in the art and literature of the Surrealist movement there is, from the mid-twenties on, a sudden surge of interest in the erotic in the work of Pablo Picasso who, while he held himself somewhat aloof from the Surrealist group, was clearly tuning in to the *zeitgeist*. This phase of Picasso's career is heralded by his great painting of sexuality and death, *The Three Dancers* of 1925 in the Tate Gallery. This is his first major work in the 'metamorphic' style which he developed and explored in the twenties and thirties. In his paintings and drawings of this period he creates complex visual puns and metaphors in which endless sexual analogies are invented, mouths are simultaneously vulvas, women's heads become phallic, whole human figures are also simultaneously both male and female sexual organs, and he invents strange, sexual monsters, perambulating sex organs who often savagely attack each other.

Spencer

At his death in 1959 Stanley Spencer was one of the best respected and best known painters in England. He was remembered for his religious paintings, his charming landscapes and for his work as a war artist. It has since become apparent that Spencer hated painting landscapes and only did so for the money they brought him and, more importantly, that the religion of his religious works was not Christianity but Spencer's own religion of sex: 'I am convinced that the physical urge in me is the very substance and core of the spiritual essence I am seeking,' he wrote in 1939. Spencer was haunted by the erotic right from the beginning of his career and there are already strong sexual undertones in early religious paintings like *The Centurion's Servant* of 1914; but it was only after he married in 1925 at the age of thirty-four and finally lost his virginity that sexuality becomes a major element in his work. At the time of his marriage he painted the great *Cookham Resurrection* which he later said was the first of his sex pictures, and his wife Hilda is its presiding deity, appearing in it no less than five times. Spencer's eroticism was essentially of a sado-masochistic and fetishistic kind, and his ambivalent attitude comes out particularly well in the portrait of himself and his second wife Patricia, *The Leg of Mutton*, where he is both a worshipper at the shrine of her body and, so to speak, a sultan contemplating an odalisque. This extraordinary painting is one of his masterpieces and as well as being a devastating piece of self-revelation has a terrific sexual impact.

In 1935 Spencer wrote: 'During the war, when I contemplated the horror of my life and the lives of those with me, I felt that the only way to end the ghastly experience would be if everyone suddenly decided to indulge in every degree and form of sexual love, carnal love, bestiality, anything you like to call it. These are the joyful inheritances of mankind.' It was at this time that he conceived the idea of the cycle of erotic paintings called *The Beatitudes of Love*. These works and other erotic paintings of the thirties he intended to be incorporated into a great scheme for a 'Temple of Peace' which was in fact to be a church devoted to the religion of sex. Spencer worked out plans for this temple in some detail: 'Along the church aisle would be twelve chapels for the contemplation of married happiness . . .' The church was to be connected to two houses which would be, in effect, sanctified brothels and the passages from them would be bursting 'with different emblems of sexual love such as clothes, scents, brushes, smart hats and jewellery. In an alleyway would be paintings of men and women in different stages of undressing, opening into a room of nudes making love or lying about.' The portrait of himself and Patricia would have hung in this temple and Spencer made drawings for many other pictures. The one of himself and a woman on a double lavatory was apparently intended to be carried out on a large scale to hang in the nave.

Pop Art and After

It was in the late 1950s and early 1960s that, after two decades of abstraction or semi-abstraction, bold figurative imagery returned to Western art in the work of the 'Pop' artists. Drawing their subject matter as they did from the sex-riddled world of advertising, comics, girlie magazines and Hollywood movies it was inevitable that there would be an immediate proliferation of erotic themes in their work. In fact all the major Pop artists have dealt extensively with the erotic: Warhol in his prints and paintings of Marilyn and other Holywood sex symbols; Lichtenstein in his love comic paintings, Wesselman in his ongoing series of Great American Nudes, some of which have the vulva exposed and interestingly treated as a formal structure; Mel Ramos, in his marvellous paintings of exotic animals in sexual situations with pin-up girls; Oldenburg in his projects for erotic monuments as well as in much of his sculpture; Jim Dine in his phallic London drawings (confiscated by the Metropolitan Police in 1966); David Hockney in his illustrations to Cavafy's homoerotic poems; Allen Jones in his girlie paintings and fetishistic furniture . . .

In the last few years there seems to have emerged a generation of erotic artists whose style, while it owes something to Pop, looks back through Pop to Surrealism and back again through Surrealism to the Romantic and Symbolist painters of the nineteenth century. Two such artists are Graham Ovenden and Barry Burman and another is Jim Leon whose lush work appears regularly in *OZ*.

There is no doubt that the increasingly relaxed attitude towards sex in the Western world in the last decade has encouraged increasingly open treatment of erotic themes in all the arts. Unless there is some kind of 'puritan backlash' this process is bound to continue and erotic art will proliferate as never before since Graeco-Roman times.

Simon Wilson
May, 1972

1 The Act of Love

The Meeting

Titian's *Bacchus and Ariadne* is probably the most dynamic account of love at first sight ever conceived in pictorial terms. The two figures involved in the encounter *3* are at the mercy of overwhelming physical sensations for which Titian has found perfect visual symbols. The iconography comes from Ovid. Bacchus is leaping from his chariot because he does not want Ariadne to be frightened by his tigers, and when he clasps her in his arms she will die in order to share his immortality. Titian, however, has concentrated all his attention on the moment of mutual 'recognition' and the erotic implications of the encounter. The story behind the picture bows to the idea of eternal bliss in heaven, but the bliss which the encounter in the picture anticipates is transient, and totally within human experience. The 'recognition' is a matter of pure sexual acknowledgement, like that unexpected meeting of glances that has rocked us all at one time or another. It is a vertiginous sensation, expressed in the painting as involuntary action. Bacchus bounds towards Ariadne before even desire has caught up with him; it is equivalent to the leap of the heart. In the same instant, Ariadne raises a hand as if temporarily blinded although the exchange of glances is becoming a fixed staring. All thought has fled and they are beyond themselves.

The painting was cleaned in 1969 and revealed the full brilliance of the pure ultramarine used for Ariadne's robe, the traditional colour for the garments of the Holy Virgin. Ariadne's vermilion scarf makes a resonant contrast to the blue of her robe, but the crimson glazes on the mantle streaming out behind Bacchus are even more intense. Immediately before the meeting, Ariadne was alone on the shore, still yearning for Theseus. She was the daughter of Minos, and when she fell in love with Theseus she gave him the thread that enabled him to find his way out of the Labyrinth after killing the Minotaur. He took Ariadne with him when he left for Crete, but later deserted her. She is not sexually inexperienced, but she becomes instantaneously innocent in response to Bacchus. Theseus is forgotten, and the virginal blue of her robe is the sign of her undivided heart. It can happen more than once – sometimes many times – in the life of a woman. Passionate love is invariably exclusive while the passion lasts.

1 (*Opposite*)
EDVARD MUNCH
The dance of life

32

2 (*Above*)
PETER BEHRENS
The kiss

3 (*Opposite*)
TITIAN
Bacchus and Ariadne

4 (*Right*)
RENOIR
Dance at Bougival

5 (*Overleaf left*)
RAPHAEL
Galatea (detail)

6 (*Overleaf right*)
FRANCESCO DEL COSSA
Palazzo Schifanoia fresco,
April (detail)

8 (*Right*)
After FRAGONARD
Eighteenth-century
engraving

9 (*Overleaf*)
Etruscan tomb drawings

(*Above*)

GUSTAV KLIMT

The embrace

(*Right*)

EDVARD MUNCH

The kiss

2 (*Below*)

EDVARD MUNCH

Moonlight

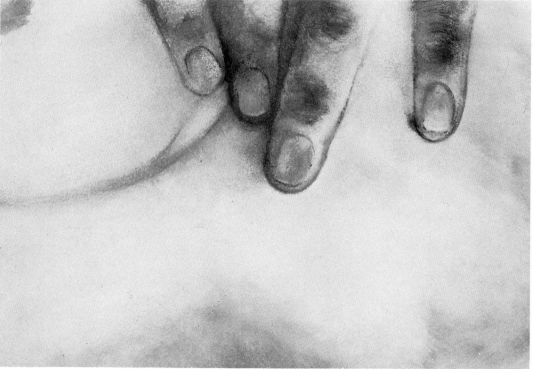

16 (*Above*)
HOLMAN HUNT
The hireling shepherd

17 (*Left*)
HAROLD STEVENSON
Caress

18 (*Opposite*)
SPRANGER
Hercules and Deianira

19 (*Left*)
EGON SCHIELE
Lovers

20 (*Opposite*)
BOSCH
Garden of terrestrial
delights (detail)

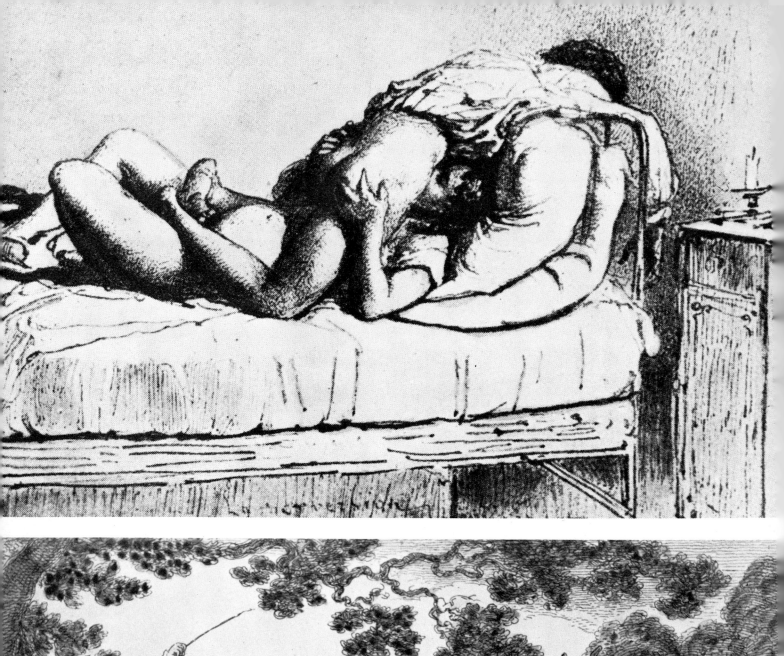

AVBREY BEARDSLEY.

24 (*Left*)
Pedieus painter
Red figure cup

25 (*Below*)
HANS BELLMER
Drawing

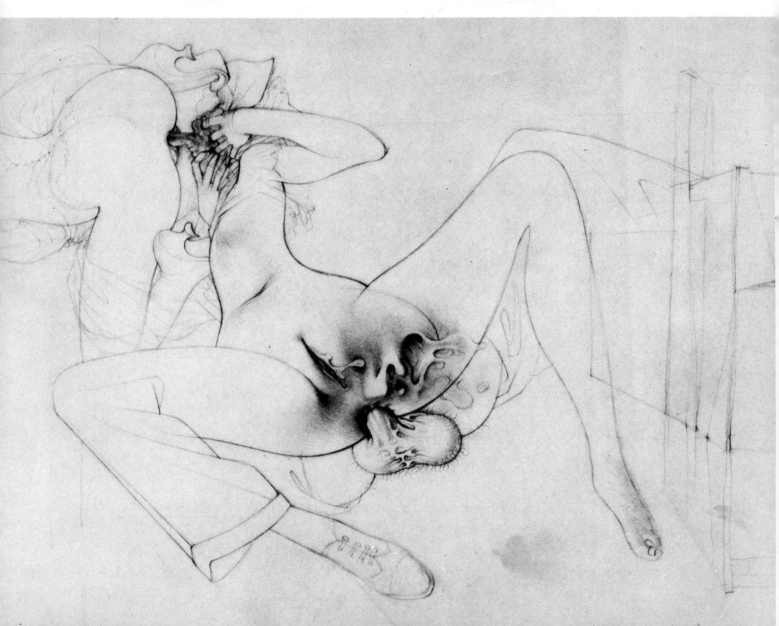

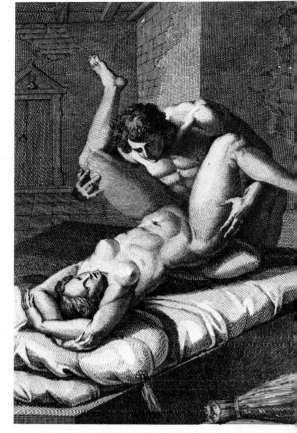

27 (Right above)
After GIULIO ROMANO
Sedici Modi engraving
no. 6

28 (Right below)
After GIULIO ROMANO
Sedici Modi engraving
no. 11

29 (Overleaf)
After GIULIO ROMANO
Sedici Modi engraving
no. 16

8 (*Right*)
After GIULIO ROMANO
Sedici Modi engraving
no. 12

39 (*Far right*)
After GIULIO ROMANO
Sedici Modi engraving
no. 13

40 (*Right*)
After GIULIO ROMANO
Sedici Modi engraving
no. 14

41 (*Far right*)
After GIULIO ROMANO
Sedici Modi engraving
no. 15

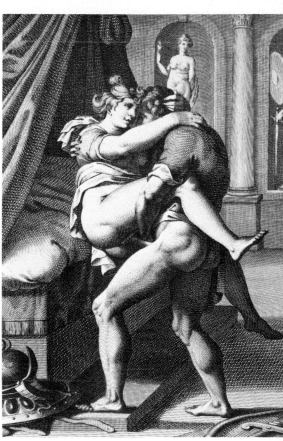

There is a sense in which the crimson mantle streaming away from the shoulder of Bacchus is even more representative of his passion than his own movements. The mantle is extremely agitated, and flutters in a fiercer wind than the leaping figure could have caused. It flutters in a wind of sensual upheaval, and the cold fire of the crimson glazes emblemizes the sudden coldness felt on forehead and wrists when the heart is overturned.

Ariadne is not frightened of the cheetahs that Titian has substituted for Ovid's tigers because she is aware of their presence only as attributes of the leaping god. Like his retinue they are pictorial symbols of his nature. This retinue of male and female votaries creates an atmosphere of sombre violence. There is a clashing of cymbals and a rattling of tambourines, but there is no gaiety in the dancing figures, and only the baby satyr, tripping along with the severed head of a steer on a string, could be called blithe. The others are intoxicated or possessed. They have torn to pieces the animal whose head is being dragged along the ground, and one of the male figures is still triumphantly waving one of its wrenched-off legs. The man just in front of him, borrowed from Laocoön, illustrates a passage in Catullus. He has girded himself with coiling snakes and grapples with them in wine-inspired bravado. Fat, drunken Silenus brings up the rear of the procession, swaying on an ass. Ariadne does not see them, but is aware of them because Bacchus is approaching her with his entire being, and all his Dionysian attributes are in his impassioned stare and in his importunate leap, which is at once tender and brutal, ecstatic and destructive. But he is irresistible, and the distance between them will be closed like a clap of thunder. Titian treats sexual passion as a disruptive force.

The Dance

The dance in which a man and a woman are allowed to press against one another, enabling the man to take mild liberties with his partner, in pursuit of pneumatic bliss, was probably a nineteenth-century innovation. Previously, dancing in couples was more a matter of stepping out side by side, with the woman's right hand held in the left hand of her partner, or of facing one another and clasping hands at arm's length. The peasants and the working people were of course dancing in couples long before the upper classes gave up formation dances, but even in Bruegel's *Peasant Dance* the couples are still side by side or facing one another with outstretched arms, though the excitement is growing and no doubt they will soon be assuming more intimate postures. There are signs in Rubens's *Kermesse* that the dancing started in the same way, but most of the couples are now intoxicated. The left half of the composition is devoted in the main to settled drinkers, but a young man is trying to persuade a girl to join him in the throng of dancers on the right by prancing in front of her. The dance is turning into an orgy, and Rubens has choreographed his couples to illustrate the moves that bring the couples in the foreground to overt love-making. On the perimeter of the throng, couples are still dancing hand in hand, but with reckless vigour. In the middle distance the men have changed their position and are clasping the women from behind, and the women are half-turned to face and kiss them. Nearer still, a woman is being bent backwards by her partner as he drives his mouth against hers, and only his supporting arm keeps her on her feet. Beside them, a man is forcing his raised leg against the back of a woman's knees, and she is beginning to topple. In the foreground, a woman has been brought down without the man taking his mouth away from hers. She is on her back and he is climbing on to her.

Dancing face to face had become generally permissible by the time Renoir's *Moulin de la Galette* was painted in 1876, but the dancing couples are in the background. His *Dance at Bougival*, painted in 1883, concentrates on one couple and *4* wonderfully conveys the intimacy of the dance. Renoir's models for the painting were his brother and the painter Suzanne Valadon, but if they were standing still and only pretending to dance, no trace of posing remains in the painting. The man has drawn the woman close to him and is looking intently into her face as if trying to make her return his stare; but her eyes are half-closed with pleasure; she is content to feel the firm pressure of his body and swing lightly to the steps his masculine assurance dictates. It is a love affair for as long as the beat of the music lasts.

The eroticism is more intense in the treatment of the central couple in Edvard *1* Munch's *The Dance of Life,* painted at the turn of the century, and the woman dominates the man. Woman has a more fatal attraction for Munch than for Renoir. The novelist Julien Green once said of the latter that his 'obsession with the beauty of human flesh is so overwhelming that it appears even in his landscapes in which the soil sometimes has flesh tints'. (He was referring of course to the flesh of the human female.) Renoir's great gifts as a painter served a naïve sensualism; there are no psychic reverberations in his paintings of the nude. They are composed of beautiful velvet rotundities like ripe peaches. The beauty of Munch's images of woman is less obvious, but his women feel and love and suffer; they are more real and more provocative. He drew and painted far fewer nudes than Renoir, and they are almost always studies of a woman who has undressed to take full possession of a man. The central figure in his lithograph *The Three Stages of Woman* is woman as temptress; with her legs wide apart and hands clasped behind her head she tempts every man who ever sets eyes on this print. She is said to be Dagny Juell Przbyszewski, who is certainly the woman in his *Madonna* lithograph and probably in *Moonlight*. She was a childhood friend of Munch's who later became his mistress. She married a Polish writer without breaking off her relations with Munch, who introduced her to Strindberg. She had a short, passionate affair with Strindberg who raged against her unrepressed sexuality in a way which revealed his latent homosexuality. He wrote that if a woman is free and has relations with other men 'she delivers my soul and transfers my love into another man, and thus causes me to live in a prohibitive relation with another man's soul or body or both. . . . This tortures me because I have always had a horror of contacts with my own sex.' Munch expressed his jealousy in his prints and paintings by casting man as the victim of woman's inordinate sexuality.

In his painting of the dancing couple, he uses the curvilinear style of Art Nouveau to create an Expressionist masterpiece. The heavy undulatory swirls of the young woman's gown, sweeping the floor, are essential to the effect of dangerous and mesmerizing power he has imparted to her. Her gown is closing round the man like a vortex. His eyes are closed, and his knees are bent not simply because he is taller than the girl but because hs is slowly being sucked down as if her gown were made of quicksand. Perhaps the most remarkable thing about Munch's approach to woman is that he never yields to caricature. He may be in a state of fear and hatred when he depicts her, but is never less than just to her loveliness and desirability.

The Kiss

7 If Gérard's *Cupid and Psyche* is supposed to illustrate the story in *The Golden Ass*, it is rather puzzling. The beauty of Psyche aroused the jealousy of Venus, who sent Cupid down to earth to make her fall in love with some hideous creature, but he himself fell in love with her, and, without allowing her to see him, kept her in a palace and visited her only in the dark, forbidding her to try to find out whether he was ugly or fair. Of course the story too is implausible because if they made love in the dark – and it is difficult to imagine why else he should visit her – she had only to caress him to realize that his face and body were as beautiful as her own. Nevertheless, her jealous sisters half persuaded her that he was a monster, so one night when Cupid was asleep she looked at him by the light of an oil lamp. Her hand shook at the sight of his beauty and a drop of oil fell on his cheek and woke him. He was angered by her disobedience and left her. She searched all over the world for him, and Venus forced her to undertake impossible tasks, but finally Cupid persuaded Jupiter to allow them to marry in Heaven. Gérard's picture suggests that the first kiss bestowed on Psyche was in the light, and therefore in Heaven.

The idea that Cupid refrained from kissing her until they were married, and then only on the forehead, may have been Gérard's way of playing safe. The picture was painted in 1798, round about the same time as David painted *La Citoyenne Crouzet*, a veristic portrait of a plump, fashionably dressed member of the new middle class, which is superbly indicative of what had happened by that time to the Revolution. Her hair hangs in carefully coiffured, careless wisps to show that she is a good Republican, and Gérard too, who was rivalled only by Girodet in the speed with which he adapted his art to political change, was still being a good Republican. The picture was intended to conform to neo-Classicism: it was to provide a thematic relief from David's severity without showing any trace of the sensualism of the pre-Revolution boudoir painters. He only succeeded in achieving a kind of frigid sugariness, influenced by the smooth marble sculpture of Canova and Chaudet. There is even a sense in which it looks like an ingenious collage which brings together studies of two quite separate sculptures, for Cupid's mouth seems to be by a hair's breadth missing its mark and gliding very slowly past Psyche's forehead. Yet, given enough determination, one can, without departing from appearances, transform the painter's indifference to the situation into an emotional problem for the figures, and compel the utter stillness of the girl and the tentative approach of the young god's mouth and hands to her cold flesh to conspire against the painter's uncaring efficiency and lend them the shyness of adolescence.

All the same, the colour woodcut, *The Kiss*, by Peter Behrens, one of the founders 2
of the Munich Secession, shows clearly enough that a lover's kiss can be reduced to pure Art Nouveau decoration and yet not look as frigid and stilted as Gérard's neo-Classicism. The lips of the two cool profiles, simplified to an androgynous neutrality, meet to form a sort of Art Nouveau brooch, and in its different way the elaborate interlace of their hair makes a single form: heavily serpentine, its coils cannot be unravelled by the eye, and the form can be read as an organic intermingling and an image of inseparability. Furthermore, as a result of the artist's rigid adherence to the flat-pattern concept, the lovers appear to be not only kissing, but rubbing noses.

Civilization would have seemed to be on the right course if the eighteenth- 8
century engraving of beautiful young lovers had been done later than Behrens's abstract of sensuous contact. Instead, it was a distillation of the frivolity of a society falling apart, a vision of sexual love as divine providence that was soon to be chilled to the bone. But although art never seems able to recapture the lyricism of another time, life can and does. Shorn of its cupids and doves, the central image in this work gathers to itself all the fleeting moments of unalloyed joy scattered through past and future centuries.

Munch's *The Kiss* brings us to a more hazardous situation. Kissing naked in 11
the dark, in front of a window overlooking a lighted street, these lovers may be able to distil this moment into pure joy when it is a distant memory, but even that is doubtful. Nothing can go wrong in the love-making of our pair of eighteenth-century lovers, but an awkwardness in the stances of Munch's figures tells us that conscience, desperation, a sense of frustration or even of despair will attend their intercourse. This is the denouement of a situation which was developing in his painting of a dancing couple, and once again the hunching of the man's back and the bending of his knees seems to make the woman mistress of the situation. This print of 1895 is a different, less furtive version of a picture painted three years earlier, in which the lovers are kissing behind a curtain. Strindberg wrote about it in the catalogue of Munch's first Paris show: 'Man gives, creating the illusion that the woman gives in return. Man begging the favour of giving his soul, his blood, his liberty, his repose, his eternal salvation, in exchange for what? In exchange for the happiness of giving his soul, his blood, his liberty, his repose, his eternal salvation.'

The Assignation

In Edvard Munch's *Moonlight*, a woman is keeping an appointment with a man 12
who has not yet appeared. The painting arouses the suspicion that she is the instigator of a dangerous liaison and is determined, come what may, to see it through to the end. She stands in front of a white fence at the corner of a Norwegian house that is probably her home, and the atmosphere is so disquieting, so Strindbergian, that one tends to jump to the conclusion that she is casting

contempt on her marriage by waiting for her lover outside the house which she shares with her husband; and the word 'casting' has probably come to mind because of Munch's strange treatment of the shadows. He shares with the early Chirico a profoundly poetic feeling for the cast shadow, and has used it here to create a sense of impending catastrophe. The woman casts a double shadow. The shadow cast on the wall assumes a phantasmal life of its own; it appears to constitute a threat to the house, and in this is aided and abetted by another shadow, cast by the woman's head, much larger but not as sharp as the one on the wall, being more a darkening of the darkness beyond the house. The woman herself is dressed in black, as if she were in collusion with the shadows. The moonlight gives her face a soft pearly radiance, but the features are indomitable, and her imperturbable recklessness charges the picture with a kind of erotic expectancy. She is a conscious breaker of taboos. This is love in a cold climate, and a fragment of Munch's vision of a world where people are totally engaged by passion and anguish, and suffer loneliness and separation with the same wholeheartedness that enchants us in *Wuthering Heights*.

Embracing and Caressing

When a naked man embraces a naked woman, whether in life or in art, no dictionary definition of the verb 'to embrace' has very much connection with the happening. The *Shorter Oxford Dictionary* daringly mentions that the word is sometimes used as a euphemism for sexual intercourse, but has no definition for the specifically erotic embrace, no phrase that describes passion rather than affection. The embrace so lyrically depicted by Gustav Klimt, and so natural to lovers, is not described by 'the action of clasping in the arms, pressing to the bosom'. One could not expect a reference to the shiver of flesh against flesh, but there could at least be some reference to the areas of pressure that distinguish eroticism from sentiment.

10

On the other hand, the definition 'to clasp in the arms as a sign of affection' is not mild enough to describe Prud'hon's *The Union of Love and Friendship*. The word 'clasp' is too strong a term for the feeble pictorial signs devised by Prud'hon to celebrate their union. Amour is another name for Cupid, and although he is usually the plump winged child with bow and arrows, he is sometimes depicted as a winged adolescent. In Bronzino's painting in the National Gallery, for instance, he is a boy who has just reached the age of puberty, and is making incestuous love to Venus. But Prud'hon, in a somewhat misguided attempt to demonstrate that the nude is a pure and noble category of art, totally free from sexuality, produced a caricature of the Cupid and Psyche theme. I suppose it could be argued that his version of their relationship is intended as play-acting for the benefit of Venus, who was so inordinately jealous of Psyche that for a long time Cupid only dared to have intercourse with Psyche in total darkness. It is more likely that Prud'hon's male figure, who is slightly older than Bronzino's Cupid but appears to be sexually retarded, is intended to personify Spiritual Love. By giving him Cupid's wings he has created an iconographical confusion: 'Love'

13

keeps the union cool, and the situation leaves the wingless but riper figure of 'Friendship' in a state of enforced virginity. Not surprisingly, she could equally well personify Melancholy, and say with Violette Leduc: 'My sex pleads.'

An erotic embrace that pretends to be serving some other purpose is superbly depicted in Holman Hunt's *The Hireling Shepherd*, a painting which approaches   *16* greatness because the artist achieved the opposite of what he consciously intended. If Hunt himself had not written an explanation of the picture no one could have guessed that he strongly disapproved of both characters, condemning the girl for waywardness and the shepherd for neglecting his flock. Adopting a heavily sarcastic tone, he added: 'My fool has found a Death's Head Moth, and this fills his little mind with forebodings of evil, and he takes it to an equally sage counsellor for her opinion. She scorns his anxiety from ignorance rather than profundity.' But the moralistic conception has not been translated into persuasive pictorial terms; on the contrary, the painter has given the couple a lovely, Palmeresque 'ripeness is all' setting that turns his symbols against his conscious intentions. The landscape details become laudatory symbols of the girl's physical attributes in the manner of the Song of Solomon, and the artist's own sensual interest in her is disclosed by a curious detail: a swirl of embroidery on her tight-fitting blouse enables him to linger over the mound of one breast, and he then gives her shoulder the same caressively spiralling treatment, as if he were seeking compensation for not being able to get at her other breast by inventing a surrogate. The Shepherd discloses no sign of superstitious dread, and it is clear that he is showing the moth to the girl as an excuse for brushing against her and putting an arm round her shoulder. She, for her part, is too intensely aware of his physical presence to be interested in his find. It is a situation that gives the death's head moth the significance of a winged phallus.

The sea-maiden who is wading through the water alongside Galatea's sea-shell chariot, in Raphael's painting of the most famous of the mythological Nereids,   *5* has been seized by a merman, fish-shaped from the middle down. The model for this maiden, if there was one, came from a lower class than the girl who posed for Galatea, but she is much more fascinating. She shows the self-possession of a girl who is used to such sudden assaults. The merman's abrupt change at the waist from human male to fish is not very convincing; the substance of his lower half is a soft green jelly and the sea-maiden is probably well aware that he has no means of having intercourse with her. Nevertheless, the act of encirclement is boldly possessive, and the veil billowing out from the sea-maiden's hands is an acknowledgement of the stirring contact.

The Antwerp Mannerist, Bartholomeus Spranger, who became court painter to Maximilian III in Vienna and, later, to Rudolf II in Prague, was a master of the slender excuse for painting the female nude in provocative poses. His *Vulcan*   *14* *and Maia* presents a very unlikely bedroom scene between the fire-god and the earth-goddess. Vulcan is depicted as if he were a desperate old man imploring a young woman to let him make love to her. Even if he were simply a lustful old man and not a fire-god, his desperation would scarcely make sense, for the young woman has every intention of being taken. Her outrageous posturing and the eager thrust of her belly announce a state of sexual readiness more intense than his own. He is trying to arouse a woman who is already aching for intercourse.

18   The same painter's *Hercules, Deianira and the dead centaur Nessus* is only slightly less implausible. Hercules had already secured Deianira for himself by winning a wrestling match with a river-god, but when he came with her to a flooded river he sought the help of the centaur Nessus to carry her to the other bank. Not unnaturally, the centaur's contact with her nakedness filled him with desire for her, and Spranger could have made a more impressive account of the situation by depicting Hercules killing the centaur as he was trying to rape her. As it is, the centaur lies dead, and Deianira seems to have embarrassed Hercules by jumping uninvited into his lap. To judge from the absence of any sign of desire or even pleasure on his countenance, he is badly in need of the dart that Cupid (putting in an unexpected appearance) has hopefully discharged at him. It would seem that our hero, who once took the fifty daughters of Thestius in a single night, is not in the mood for loving.

Spranger devised his pictures like a film director committed to the star system. The classical themes are vehicles for his female nudes, who are unashamedly projected at the spectator. He was an expert eroticist, and the male figures play an undistinguished role in his pictures in order to give his patrons the feeling that they would make bolder partners for his ever ready nymphs.

Baudelaire has likened intercourse to an administration of torture or a surgical operation, but in heterosexual love-making it is often the one who plays the part of torturer or surgeon who does most of the groaning and gasping. Some men make much of the agony of intercourse, but although in the drawings of George Grosz and Hans Bellmer the faces of copulating males are frequently contorted by an insane ferocity, the hopelessness that can overtake a male at the moment of orgasm has never, as far as I know, been adequately depicted, and it is only in the work of Schiele that the gauntness and suffering of a male nude sometimes clearly associates itself with the aftermath of sexual intercourse. In his intimate

19   and tender study, *Lovers*, the woman is trying to console a man whose anguish arises from the horror of the return to the self.

Harold Stevenson's contributions to the art of the evocative fragment include

17   a painting of fingers on a breast which fills a large canvas with female flesh. The limits of the breast, imposed by a curved line, convey the sense of a ball floating in a cloudiness of the same substance without beginning or end, as if the artist were thinking of the flesh of woman as a substance pervading the universe, and from this point of view the painting could be an attempt to produce a figurative equivalent of certain aspects of Abstract Expressionism. As long as one steers clear of value judgement it can even be seen to have a certain conceptual relationship with Tintoretto's magnificent *Origin of the Milky Way* (in which the milk spilt from Juno's breasts forms the stars and planets) and with the wonderfully simple abstract in which Hans Arp emblemizes the expanding universe as a double stream of whiteness issuing from a floating amphora open at both ends.

Francesco del Cossa's young lovers are in a garden of terrestrial delights where the company is less experimental in its pursuit of pleasure than in the picture by

6   Bosch painted at a somewhat later date. A detail from the fresco of April painted by Cossa for the Hall of the Months in the Palazzo Schifanoia in Ferrara shows the lovers surrounded by a group of young musicians who are watching the progress of the youth's attentions to the maiden with keen interest and approval. A kneeling girl is plaiting a garland for the lovers, and the scene has the engaging air of a spontaneously ceremonious observance of the call of spring. The maiden is wearing a gown very similar to that of the Madonna in Piero della Francesca's *Madonna del Parto*. The fastenings on her tight-fitting bodice are almost identical with the Madonna's; there is the same pleating at the waist and the same long slit just below. By sharing an iconographical detail, the two images are brought into an unexpectedly intimate relationship. The Cossa fresco was painted some twenty years later than the Piero, but the widening of the slit in the maiden's gown caused by the insertion of her lover's hand takes a place in the life cycle that presages the widening of the slit in the Madonna's gown, which is caused by pregnancy.

No one will ever provide an entirely satisfactory interpretation of Bosch's *Garden of Terrestrial Delights*, but one of many possibilities which has not perhaps received as much attention as it deserves is that the garden is the setting for a multiplicity of sexual dreams determined by erections during sleep. None of the neat little figures of the naked males swarming in the garden shows an erection, but one has only to study the picture for a very short time before realizing that there is a prevailing atmosphere of tumescence. There are few hiding places in the garden, and the curious conduct of the figures seems to be due to the frustration of the instinct, deep-seated enough to influence dream-behaviour, that causes men and women to seek privacy for the act of love. The figures make countless moves towards intimacy, but their endlessly frustrated search for secrecy leads them to adopt grotesque makeshifts and absurd substitutes, never adequate enough to result in copulation. A not unrelated phenomenon in dreams is the series of obstructions encountered by the sleeper whose bladder is on the point of emptying itself. He dreams that he is going frantically from one public lavatory to another, only to find all the urinals occupied or too exposed to the street. Such dreams serve to preserve the sleeper's continence until he wakes and staggers out of bed to take conscious control. One important difference between the sensations that signal the approach of enuresis and the sensations that precede what are called nocturnal emissions is that the latter do not wake the dreamer before the ejaculation occurs; continence is not preserved. Nevertheless the dream images assume the same frustrated character until the very moment of emission; this is because the dreamer is dealing with an actual sensation and is unable to transform it into the quite different sensation which accompanies insertion into a vagina. Nowhere in Bosch's garden is sexual intercourse depicted, and only in one scene is there an indication that intercourse has taken place. Bosch perhaps included it to provide an obvious clue to the nature of the satisfaction being sought by all the figures, and it is not without significance that it is the only scene in which a couple has found anything approaching a satisfactory hiding place. The two figures have inserted themselves into a gigantic, slightly open oyster, and we are given a partial view of the back of one of them, and two pairs of feet. The oyster can be considered as a symbol of the vagina, and the pearls that are rolling out of its shell are even more explicitly symbols of sperm, and to ensure that no one is left in doubt, Bosch has placed the biggest pearl between the legs of the partially exposed figure, as if it has oozed out from between the couple.

20 In another scene some naked human figures are riding on huge birds floating impassively in shallow water. A white man and a black girl are seated on the back of a huge duck which is flying just above the water, so swiftly that it would have passed the other birds in a flash if it had been going anywhere. The man is touching the cheek of the negress, and the floating birds are providing them with an illusory screen. But there will be intercourse only if there is a nocturnal emission. The white male will enter the negress at the moment of ejaculation. Their loving will be marvellous but gone in a flash. In the next moment the sleeper will awake and be lying in his bed, shaken and sad, bereft forever of his blue-black girl.

Fellatio

The Surrealists, who have an unblemished record as advocates of a permissive society, issued a manifesto called *Hands of Love* in 1927. It was a protest against the harsh and ignorant findings of an American judge in a divorce case which involved a world-famous comedian. The manifesto had this to say about fellatio: 'There is something comic about considering abnormal, *contra naturam*, perverted, degenerate and indecent the practice of fellatio. If the free discussion of mores could be reasonably undertaken, it would be normal, natural, healthy, decent to dismiss the suit of a wife of having *inhumanly* rejected practices so general and so utterly pure and defensible!'

The dictionary definition of fellatio is 'a sex perversion involving oral stimulation of the penis', but the use of the term 'perversion' to designate all sexual practices other than the insertion of the penis into the vagina is quite ridiculous, and the meaning of the term 'fellatio' has in any case broadened to include any pleasure afforded by the sucking or licking of the sexual parts of both men and women.

In this connection, Henry Spencer Ashbee, the nineteenth-century bibliographer of erotica who seemed to share the Victorian horror of 'perversions', admired Rowlandson for never overstepping 'the bounds of what is manly and natural' in his erotic drawings and prints. 'He is never crapulous,' he continued, 'never anti-physical (if I may be permitted the expression); and I know no single specimen of all his numerous productions in which filthy, revolting or unnatural actions are portrayed.' He means that Rowlandson's bawdiness was always connected with heterosexual intercourse, and he would not have considered any of

22 the goings-on in Rowlandson's lively drawing of 'rural felicities' to be perverse. I am treating the activity of the male figure in the foreground of the drawing as an example of fellatio because he appears to be on the point of behaving like Charlie in *The Boudoir*, a pornographic novel published in 1860. Peter Fryer has mentioned that the pornographic literature of the second half of the nineteenth century 'literally swarms' with Charlies, and the ubiquitous Charlie is on his knees 'paying his devotions to that divinely, delicate-looking, pinky slit. His tongue divided its juicy lips, searching out her pretty clitoris, which at once stiffened under the lascivious osculation. It was more like a rabbit's prick than

anything, and his fingers could just uncover its rosy head as he gently frigged it, sucking at the same time.'

Some of Rowlandson's erotica is more brutish than this example, but there was no streak in him of the malevolence that characterizes so much of Gillray's bawdy. Even in his treatment of an innocuous theme like *A March to the Bank*, an engraving in which he tilts at the practice of sending a detachment of soldiers to form a nightly guard at the Bank of England, Gillray introduces a note of insensate, but admittedly comic, violence. The soldiers, marching two abreast, mercilessly trample passers-by underfoot. Fat women sprawl on the ground with their legs in the air, displaying their drawers; a man holds on firmly to the crotch of the prettiest one, pretending that panic has made him unaware of what he is doing; an eel from an upturned fishbasket takes a nip at the genitals of a prostrate child.

Apart from the curious rag of an arm hanging limply over the bedrail, and the claw-like fingers of the woman's left hand, the study of fellatio by the nineteenth-century Rumanian artist, Michael Zichy, is well-drawn and strikingly natural. The man is supporting himself by pressing his knees against the mattress, on *21* either side of the woman, and his legs are curled snugly round her belly. He has drawn himself towards the top of the bed, with his head beyond the rail, to enable the woman to put her face between his thighs. Both of them can sustain their postures without difficulty. In another drawing by Zichy the roles of the man and woman are reversed. The man is standing, with one leg on the bed, and bending low, with his head and shoulders between the woman's wide-open legs. The same commode and candlestick as in the companion drawing are beside the bed. There is no attempt in either drawing to suggest pleasure or excitement, but the arrangements look so practical and domestic that they have the ring of authenticity. One is afforded intimate glimpses of the private life of what one feels must be a married couple.

Something approaching a feeling for sculptural form gives the drawing of fellatio attributed to Aubrey Beardsley a fascinating stateliness, and it would not *23* be difficult to think of it as a marble monument erected in Athens to commemorate the end of hostilities between the women, under the leadership of Lysistrata, and their menfolk, if only the young man's proud testicles looked a little less like balloons. This drawing is not included in Brian Reade's authoritative book on Beardsley. I see no reason to doubt that it is by him, but I have not seen the original, and the only reproduction I have been able to find is in the German periodical *Der Amethyst*. It is one of five drawings by Beardsley reproduced in the issue for January 1906 and is there described as an unpublished drawing for *The Lysistrata*. Perhaps Beardsley decided not to include it in the book, published by Smithers for private distribution in 1896, because it makes the men appear to be the victors.

Brian Reade states that Beardsley studied Greek vase painting in 1894 at the British Museum, and he considers that the Lysistrata drawings 'reflect something of the Greek vase spirit, including the bawdiness, without perhaps much of the spontaneity of Greek draughtsmanship'. It is certainly true that the delightfully crisp line of the figure-drawings on a Greek red figure cup, depicting two *24* acts of fellatio, treats the practice with a more spirited charm than the Beardsley drawing. The trio on the left make it reasonably clear that fellatio was a preliminary to full intercourse, and not an alternative. It seems unlikely that the man whose penis is being sucked by the woman kneeling on the table will forgo the pleasure she is affording the man at the other end, and will expect to change places with him in due course. The practice of fellatio is more effectively demonstrated in the fragment in the centre of the illustration. If one can assess the situation by the way in which the man is grasping his penis, it would appear that he intends only its head to enter the woman's mouth, and it provides another reason for supposing that if an ejaculation occurs it will be considered preliminary to a further ejaculation in the vagina. Fellatio would not be an entirely satisfactory substitute for ordinary sexual intercourse unless the entire length of the penis passed between the woman's lips and its head pressed against the back of her throat as described in *Story of O*. This aspect of fellatio would give the woman a passive role, unless there was room for the tongue to come into play. From the male point of view, its unique feature would be the opportunity to ejaculate against the back of the woman's throat and thus ensure that the sperm was absorbed by her body instead of trickling out of it.

25   The fellatio in Bellmer's drawing, frightening, but brilliantly depicted, is a visionary version of the same desire to effect a penetration approximating to total invasion. The penis and scrotum have become an independent biomorph, seemingly inexhaustible. The woman has achieved an impossible paroxysm and her thighs are wearing her eager face. Vagina and mouth have already been invaded, sperm pours out of the open mouth and drips from the vagina like tears from a closed eye. Now it's the turn of the anus, and with no other orifice to offer, the woman glazes it with her remaining eye. The biomorph plunges into both, emblemizing blinding passion. It is a man's vision of course. A woman's vision of inordinate passion might take the form of a castration.

The Penetration

The sculptor Joseph Nollekens (1737–1823) owned a set of the *Sedici Modi* prints engraved by Marcantonio Raimondi after drawings by Giulio Romano. They depicted twenty different ways in which a man might have intercourse with a woman, and Pietro Aretino wrote a sonnet to accompany each plate. Sixteen of the engravings were in circulation in 1524 and the complete set was published with the sonnets three years later. They have been known ever since as Aretino's Postures.

The Marcantonio prints were already extremely rare when Nollekens acquired his set in Rome. It may even have been the last surviving set; but it didn't survive for long. His biographer, J. T. Smith, recorded how they came to be destroyed:

... it so happened, as he was glancing at them one day, that his Confessor came in, who insisted upon their being put into the fire, before he would give him absolution. ... Upon Nollekens being asked how he, as an artist, could make up his mind to burn them, he answered, 'The priest made me do it': and he was now and then seen to shed tears for what he called his folly.

He was what Rowlandson would have called 'a sufferer for decency'.

Nollekens maintained that at one time he lent the entire set to his friend and fellow Academician, Richard Cosway, who wanted to make tracings of them, and when he was told that Cosway denied that he had ever borrowed them, he exclaimed: 'He's a damned liar! that everybody knows; and I know this, that I could hardly get them back again.' If Cosway made the tracings, they have not survived, but it is said that some of the eighteenth- and nineteenth-century copies used in reprints of the *Sonetti* were based on tracings.

As far as is known, not one set of the original engravings now exists. One would have thought Marcantonio's great reputation as an engraver – Raphael gave him many designs to engrave – would have given the *Sedici Modi* some protection; and one can be certain that most of the destruction was the work of priests and sanctimonious widows.

David Foxon, in his *Libertine Literature in England 1660–1745*, refers to a late sixteenth-century edition of the *Sonetti* with woodcut illustrations more closely related to the Marcantonio plates than any of the subsequent copies, and he reproduces nine engraved fragments of the *Sedici Modi* in the British Museum, of which four are attributed to Marcantonio. The nine fragments are pasted on to a single mount, and Foxon has re-arranged them in the reproduction to show that two of the Marcantonio fragments are from plate no. 11. The engravings of the Aretino Postures reproduced in this book are late copies and lack the gracefulness and technical refinement of the fragments; but although there are evident changes, plate no. 11 depicts a similar posture. The man in the copy has become beardless and his head is less deeply ensconced between the woman's raised legs; and whereas the woman in the original has raised her head to watch the proceedings, the woman in the copy has the tense look of a victim and her gaze is unfocused; but in both the fragment and the copy the man is standing and the woman is on her back with a cushion under her buttocks. The bundle of twigs in the foreground of the copy, which seems to indicate that the woman has been whipped, may not have been present in the original.

The fragments leave the impression that Marcantonio's treatment of the postures was warmer and less strenuous than that of the copyist. In these later engravings there is for the most part an atmosphere of cold efficiency and an almost total absence of communications between the participants. The men are extremely solemn, and they dedicate themselves to the act of penetration as if it were a task involving tricky technical problems. The postures are not particularly grotesque, and none of them would make insertion impossible; but there is no doubt that some of the positions adopted by the men cannot be sustained without a good deal of concentration. It is evident, for instance, that if the standing man in plate no. 10, who has raised up the woman from a prone position face downwards on the ground, intends to maintain his stance up to the point of orgasm he will have to control a natural inclination to grope for the woman's breasts as his excitement mounts; otherwise he will collapse on to her back. But the situation depicted in this plate has a certain charm. It is clear that the lovers have gone to the solitude of a wild seashore with the definite intention of adopting this posture, for they have thoughtfully provided themselves with a tasselled cushion just large enough to keep the woman's elbows off the rough ground while she is upside down.

26, 28
27–45
28
37

There are not really twenty postures. Plate nos. 11 and 18 depict virtually the same posture from different viewpoints, and the same is true of nos. 3 and 5; 13 and 14; 18 and 12. But it is noticeable in each case that one aspect of a posture is rendered more effectively than the other. No. 18 for example is more powerfully erotic than no. 11 because it conveys a greater sense of violence and violation. The man drives into the woman with rousing implacability, and the woman responds with a splendid abandonment to despair, as if imagining herself to be Lucrece. Perhaps the most erotic of all is no. 15, where the man and woman achieve a kind of equality in the love-bout. The situation in no. 18 lends credence to the notion that in sexual love the man violates and the woman is violated, but the situation in no. 5 gives it no support. The woman standing with legs frenetically wide apart, one hand darted between them to grasp the man's penis and urge it into her vagina, the other unheedingly grasping the man's hair to keep her steady on her feet, is magnificently possessed and possessive; but the man, too, lying on his back with hands pressed hard against the mattress and all his body muscles stiffened for the galvanic jerking which will start as soon as his penis is sheathed, is no less ferociously involved in the action. The bare room with its one theatrical drape and its peeling wall, suggestive of a secret basement in a gothic novel, is an appropriate setting for their delirium.

No visual account of sexual coition could make a sharper contrast to this study of sexual pleasure than the famous anatomical drawing in which Leonardo shows the penis of a hemisected man inside the vagina of a hemisected but more sketchily treated woman. A note in the Windsor catalogue describes it as 'a remarkable instance of the way in which Leonardo struck at the centre of any problem which interested him', but I find it rather curious that he did not choose for his demonstration the more natural and more customary reclining position. Certainly it would have offered no problems that he could not have solved. He perhaps chose to have his figures standing in order to remove his anatomical study of the act even farther from its emotional and erotic associations. Nevertheless, the faintly indicated nether limbs are not sectionalized, and the fact that the man has one leg between the legs of the woman reduces the dehumanization of their contact. Another odd feature of the study is the man's hair, slightly drawn, straggling prettily alongside his exposed backbone. Two sections of a penis at the bottom of this sheet show the separate tubes for semen and urine, and remind us as effectively as the agony of the romantics and the humour of cynics that we make love with our excretory organs.

In this connection Rowlandson, in one of his piercingly observant studies of the behaviour of rough soldiery, presents the comic counterpart of that cry of disgust in Baudelaire's *Intimate Journals*: 'There are only two places where one pays for the right to spend: women and public latrines.' The drawing is one that Ashbee failed to notice in his descriptive list of Rowlandson's erotica. The soldiers have crowded into a small room to await their turn with a plump prostitute pressed back against a piece of furniture. The soldier whose turn has come has not bothered to remove his pipe from his mouth, and reminds one that Flaubert won a bet that he could keep his cigar alight whilst lying over a whore. Another soldier who has undone his breeches evidently expects to replace the pipe-smoker when he comes out of the woman. Behind him, a soldier has dropped his breeches to empty his bladder and is urinating onto the floor. A soldier drinking wine is feeling his over-long penis with his hand. Ashbee complained that most of the penises drawn by Rowlandson are too long and unnaturally tapered at the end; the second stricture does not apply here, but it is surprising in the circumstances that all the penises on view are limp. The drawing has a crude vitality and evokes a nauseating stench compounded of tobacco smoke, sweat, urine and semen, but we need not suppose that the soldiers would have wished the situation to be otherwise. After all, the author of *My Secret Life* – remarkably sensitive to the eroticism of the sordid – stifled his fear of the pox at the dazzling prospect of following a sailor into a street-woman and bathing his penis in the hot wet sperm before it had time to trickle away.

The first entry in Ashbee's list of 'amatory and obscene' etchings by Rowlandson describes *A Music Master Tuning his Instrument*. 'A young man is reclining on his back upon an old-fashioned harpsichord with two thick books supporting his head. One girl, naked with the exception of her shift which is rolled up round her waist straddles across him; they are in the act; whilst another girl, standing at the end of the harpsichord, is tickling the man's testicles with her right hand, and performing a kindly office for herself with her left. The drawing is good and the attitudes quite possible; the posteriors of the girl who is mounted on the man are very attractive!'

My impression is that the couple are about to engage in intercourse and that the other girl is not tickling the man's testicles but assisting the initial act of penetration. It is said that camels cannot mate without the helping hand of the camel breeder, and although a man and woman do not need the assistance of a third party (Rowlandson's drawing is pure luxury) it is a fact rarely acknowledged that the penis is usually guided into the vagina by hand. In the *Sedici Modi* series there are three clear instances in which the woman is performing this task. Two of these engravings depict the woman over the man; in the third, where the man is over the woman, it would be more customary for the man himself to do the guiding.

A drawing by the Australian artist, Brett Whitely, has to stand for a host of drawings by twentieth-century artists who feel that the spontaneity of the sketch _54_ evokes the impetuosity and ardour of love-making more effectively than a considered statement. It is true that Eric Gill's careful and graceful drawing has _49_ considerably less verve than Whiteley's, but the interlocking of the forms is more satisfactory and the linear precision gives its romantic gravity an emblematic charm.

Picasso's technical spasms threw up devices and emblems which create great comic poetry. The parts of the two gorgeously absurd figures in an outline drawing of intercourse do not make an organic whole; they are quite separate _55_ and complete in themselves but they are nevertheless dependent upon one another for the positions they assume and maintain. The woman is extravagantly abandoned and the man intent on his workmanlike task, which has become somewhat analogous to filling a jar from a wine skin. It's the kind of drawing that should be engraved on the walls of caves to enable future generations to realize that archaic twentieth-century man made sympathetic magic to increase the flow of oil and wine.

The frieze above the principal fresco in the outer chamber of the archaic
9 Etruscan Tomb of the Bulls in Tarquinia includes an erotic group in which a
kneeling man makes a couch of his back for a woman who then has only to raise
her buttocks a little to be at the right height to be linked to a standing man by
the long red hyphen of his erection. It is not in the least romantic but it has a
friendly, high-spirited look due to the lively, economical line and the warm earth
colours. It would seem to reflect the Etruscan custom of pre-marital prostitution.

On the same wall there is another erotic scene with only two figures. These
two scenes are separated by the image of a charging bull which probably sym-
9 bolizes virility. The female figure is bent over and the male figure is standing
behind her, inserting his penis between her buttocks. The man's head is turned
away as if he may be keeping a sharp look-out for intruders, and since Etruscan
women were expected to be faithful to their husbands the scene possibly depicts
an illicit encounter. If both figures had been male it would have made an interesting
comment on the principal fresco, which treats an incident in the Trojan War:
Achilles awaits the son of Priam who is approaching a well to water his horse,
and the outcome of the meeting will be that the young man, after refusing to
yield to Achilles's caresses, is hugged to death.

A man taking a woman from behind is depicted in many other frescoes and
mosaics at Pompeii and Naples and in innumerable works by the Greek vase
painters. I do not know whether it was simply a useful convention for showing
the penis entering a woman or a generally accepted sexual custom. It is a highly
ambiguous position because it is impossible to tell whether the penis is entering
the vagina or the anus. Women are said to feel that the posture reduces their
role in intercourse to that of a mounted bitch, and whether or not they obtain
pleasure from an anal insertion seems to be an open question. In this connection,
the only discussion of it known to me is in the form of a rather sad poem, printed
in 1856 in London, which claimed to be a 'suppressed Poem by Lord Byron,
never before published', in which the cause of his separation from Lady Byron
is attributed to his technique of love-making when she was far gone in pregnancy.
His problem starts at the eleventh line:

> I burn to press thee, but I fear to try
> Lest like incubus my weight should lie;
> Lest from the close encounter we should doom
> Thy quickening foetus to an early tomb,
> Thy size repels me, whilst thy charms invite;
> Then, say, how celebrate the marriage rite?

His suggestion for the celebration takes the form of an elaborate simile and he
argues that by her silence she consented to 'enact the Ganymede', meaning that
she agreed to play the part of a catamite.

> Quick from my mouth some bland saliva spread
> The ingress smoothed to her new maidenhead . . .
> 'Tis true, that from her lip some murmurs fell –
> In joy or anger, 'tis too late to tell;
> But this I swear, that not a single sign

Proved that her pleasure did not equal mine.
Ah, fatal hour! from thence my sorrows date:
Thence sprung the source of her undying hate.
Friends from her breast the sacred secret wrung,
Then called me monster; and, with evil tongue,
Mysterious tales of false Satanic art
Devised, and forced us evermore to part.

46 (*Opposite*)
DALI
Average atmosphero-
cephalic bureaucrat in the
act of milking a cranial harp

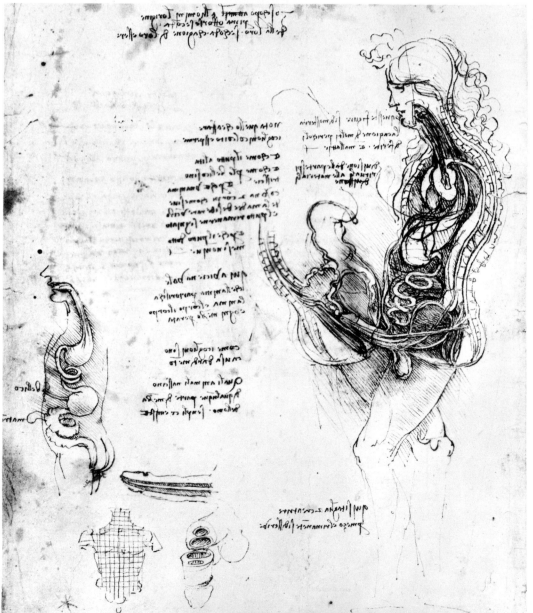

54 (*Above*)
BRETT WHITELEY
Untitled drawing

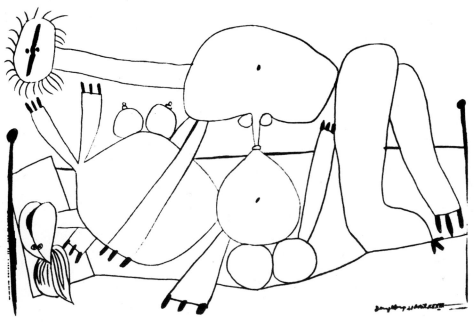

55 (*Left*)
PICASSO
Two figures

56 (*Opposite*)
BOSCH
St John the Baptist in the
wilderness

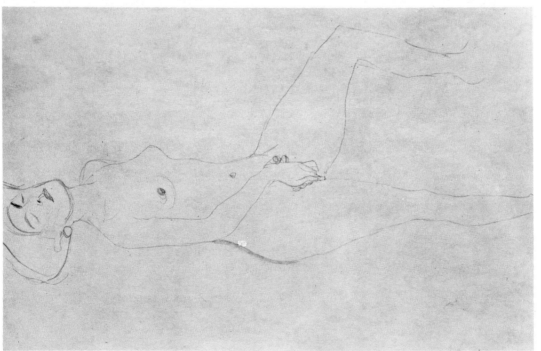

61 (*Above*)
EGON SCHIELE
Reclining woman

62 (*Right*)
GIORGIONE
Sleeping Venus

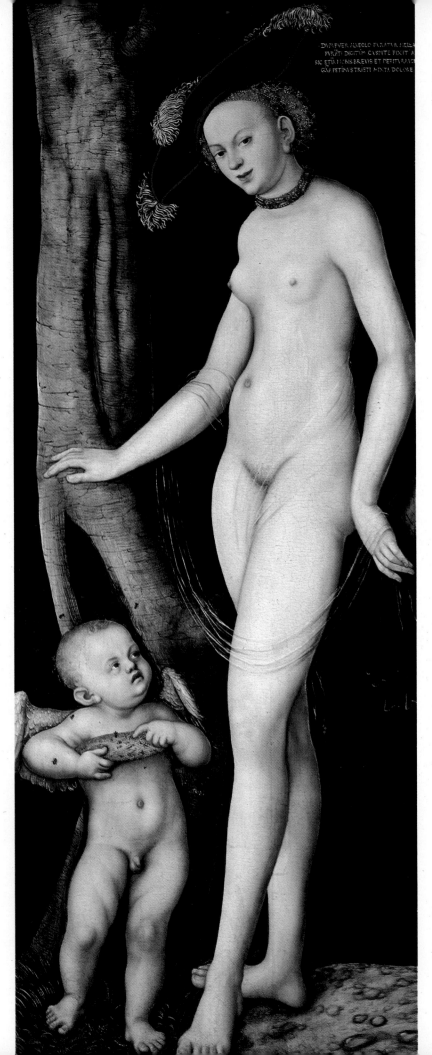

64 (*Right*)
GUSTAV KLIMT
Friends

65 (*Overleaf left*)
DALI
Study for weaning of
furniture nutrition

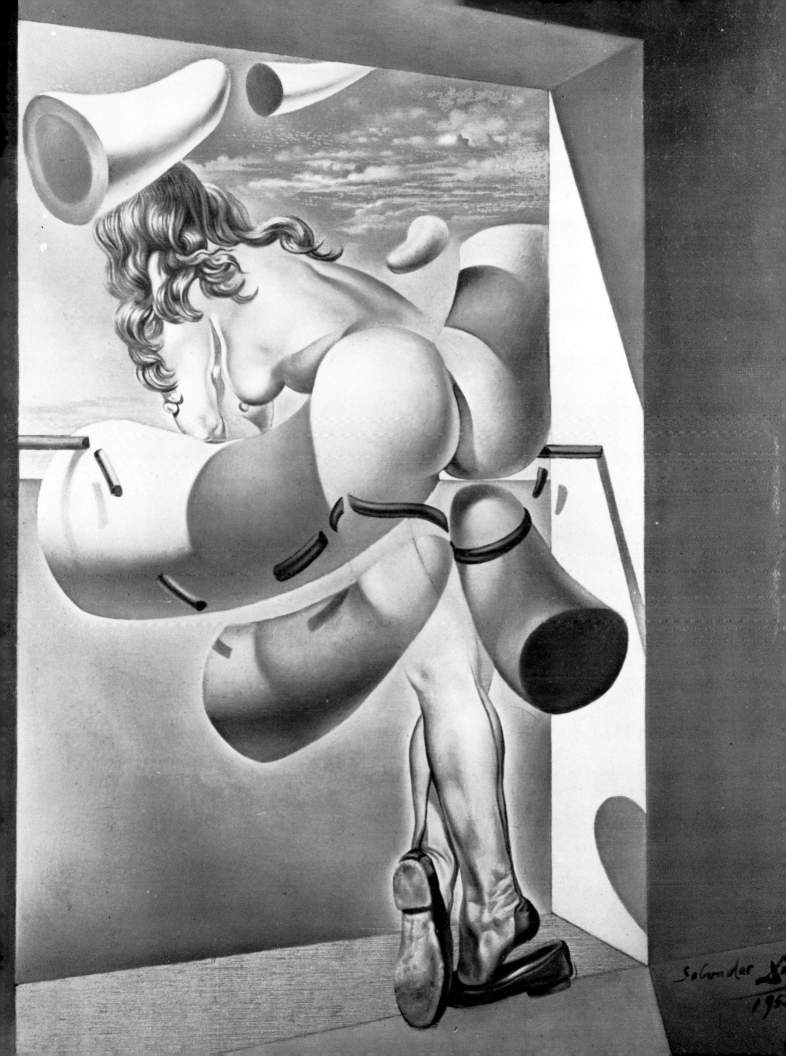

66 (*Previous page*)
DALI
Young virgin auto-
sodomized by her own
chastity

67 (*Below*)
GUSTAV KLIMT
Danae

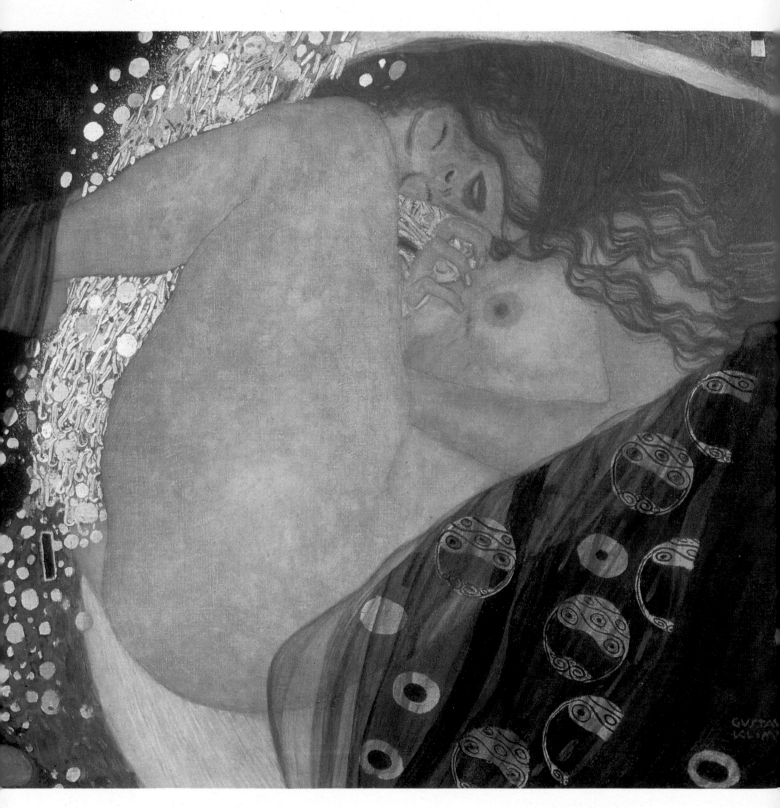

(*Right*)
PIERRE KLOSSOWSKI
Nude with rat

9 (*Right*)
BALTHUS
The guitar lesson

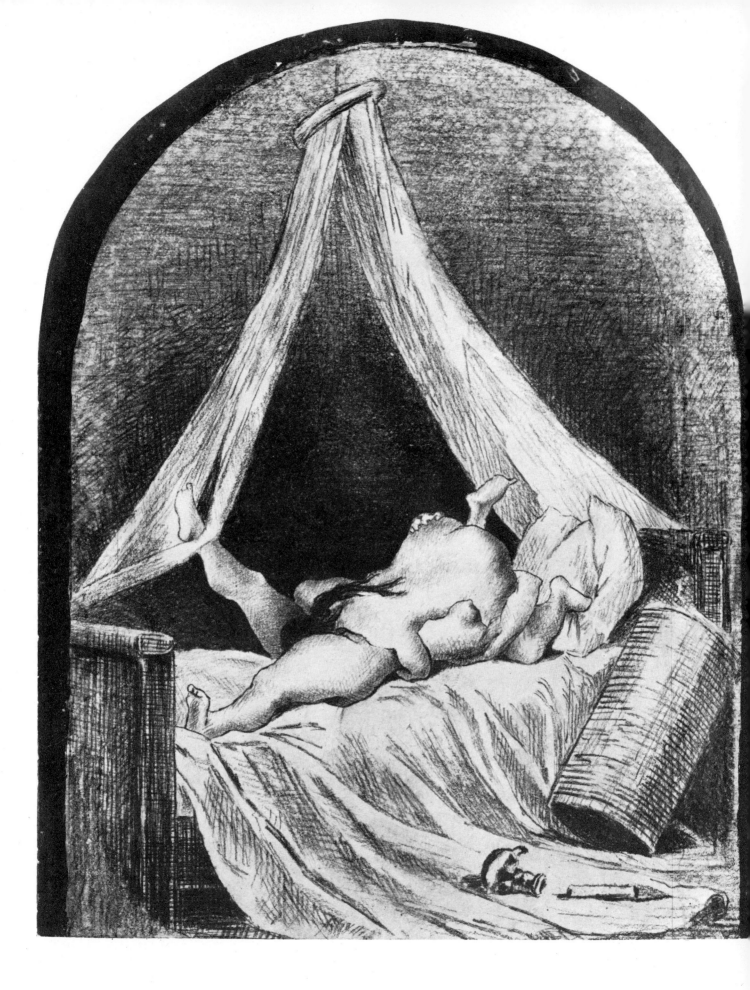

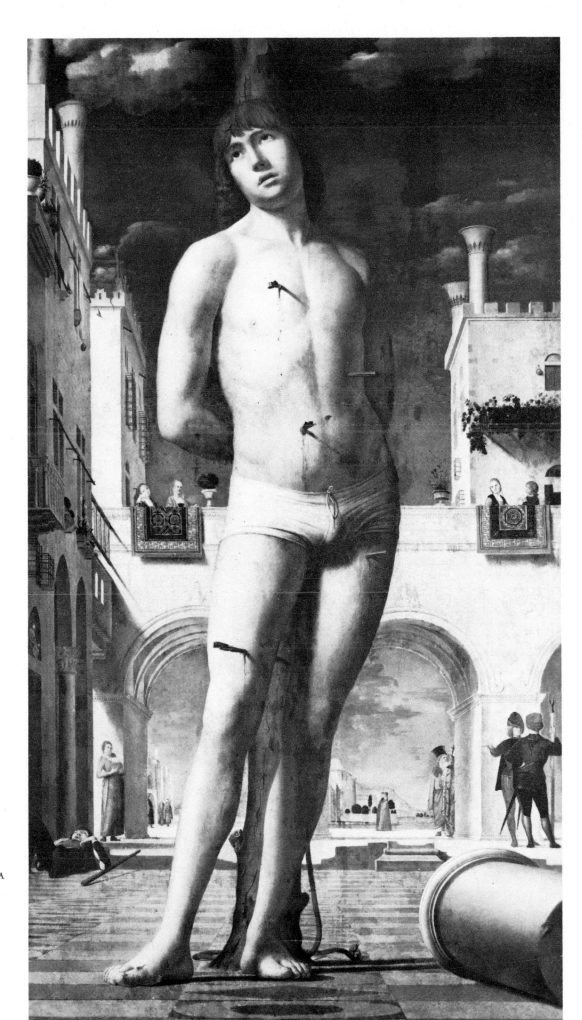

72 (*Opposite*)
Artist unknown
Late nineteenth-century
study

73 (*Right*)
ANTONELLO DA MESSINA
The martyrdom of St
Sebastian

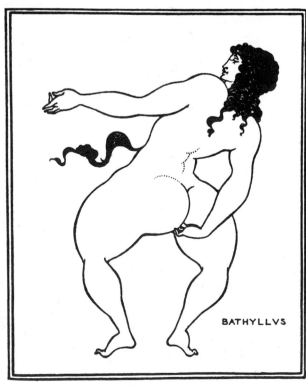

74 (*Above*)
Artist unknown
Twentieth-century study

75 (*Far left*)
BEARDSLEY
Bathyllus posturing.
Illustration for sixth satire
of *Juvenal*

76 (*Left*)
BANDINELLI
Hercules and Antaeus

77 (*Opposite*)
OCTAVE LASSAERT
Well! Don't be cruel (*Ne
fais donc pas la cruelle*)

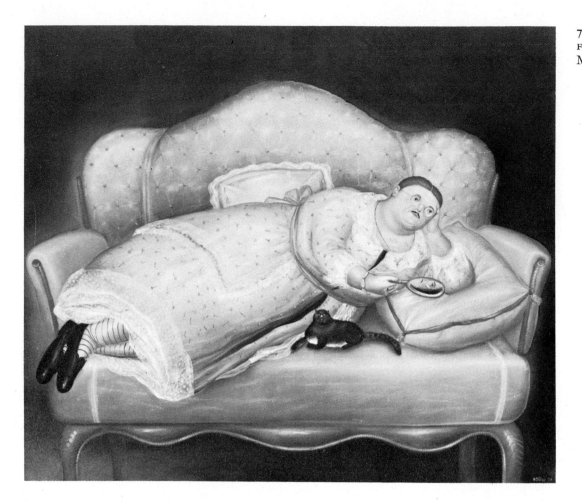

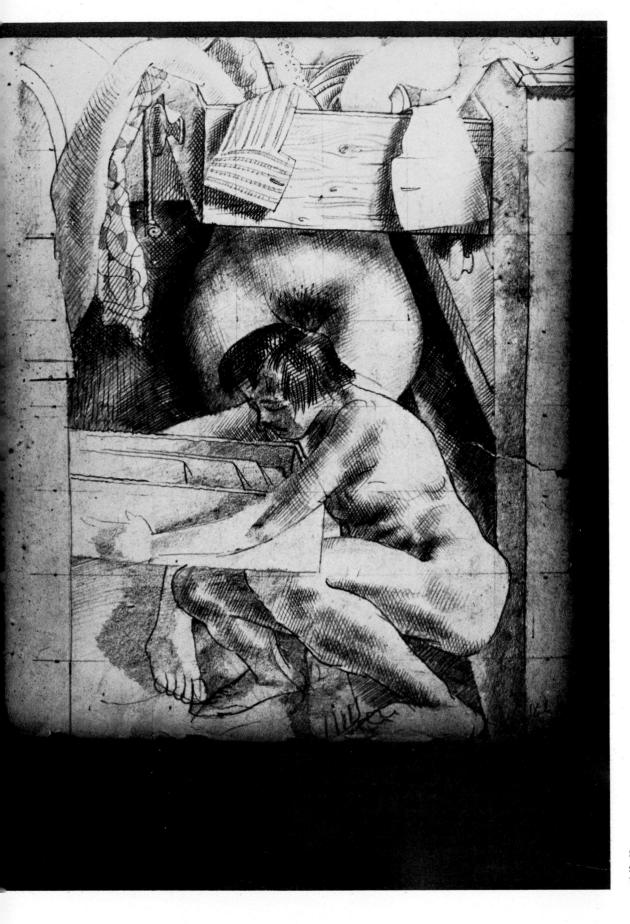

82 (*Left*)
STANLEY SPENCER
Untitled drawing

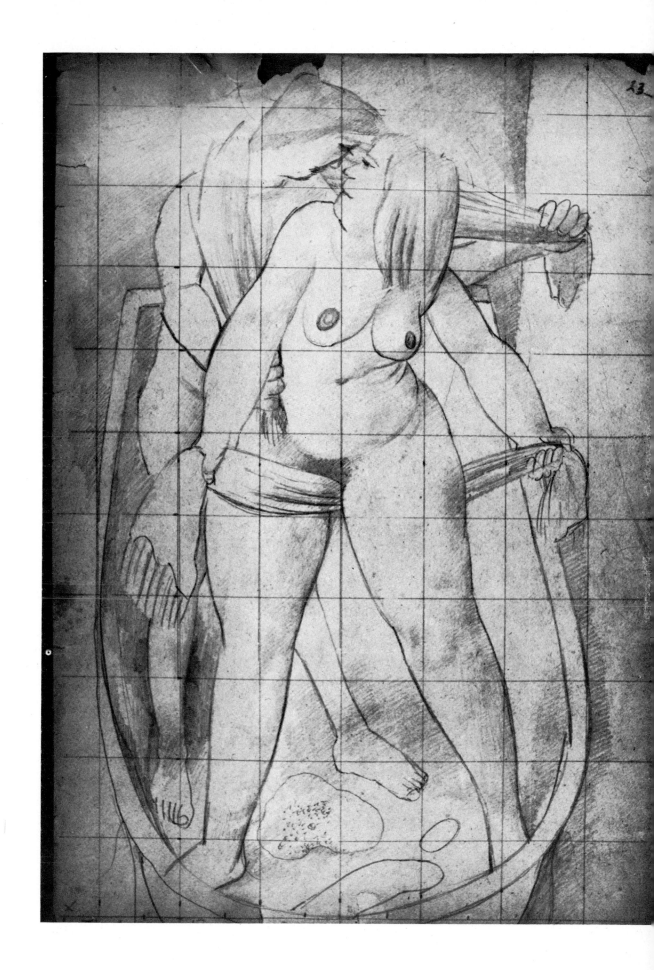

83 (*Right*)
STANLEY SPENCER
Untitled drawing

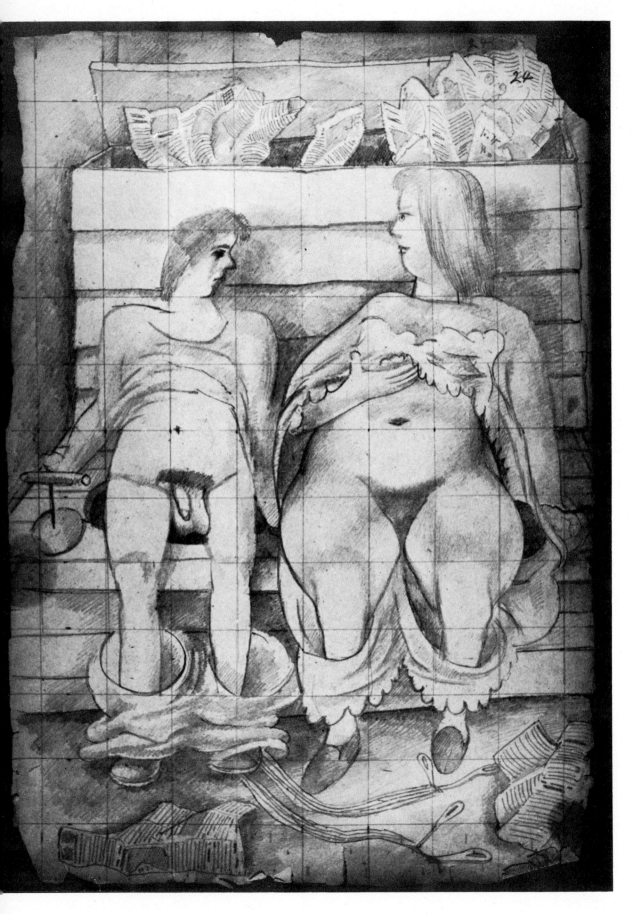

84 (*Left*)
STANLEY SPENCER
Untitled drawing

85 (*Right*)
STANLEY SPENCER
Untitled drawing

86 (*Above*)
ALTDORFER
Lot and his daughters

87 (*Left*)
FRANÇOIS DE TROY
Lot and his daughters

88 (*Opposite*)
BOSCH
Garden of terrestrial
delights (detail)

2 Varieties of Love

Masturbation

Sade's confident assumption that 'as soon as one can say to oneself, "Here am I, alone, to all intents and purposes at the end of the world, far removed from prying eyes", all obstacles and restraints are swept away' allows neither for belief in an all-seeing God, nor for the restraining influence of a built-in conscience. All the same, it is true that the sense of being entirely free from human company, especially in the open air, can sharpen the thirst for erotic adventure. André Breton spoke for most men when he said that he longed to meet a beautiful naked woman in a forest at night, but if Sade meant what he said, and was not carrying a beautiful, naked, tied up woman over his shoulder, he could only have had in mind the freedom to explore at leisure the pleasures of masturbation.

It is still the generally accepted view of masturbation that it is an adolescent substitute for intercourse and that when practised by adults is more often a sign of deprivation than of perversity. The culmination is supposed to leave the subject shamed and depressed, and before *Portnoy's Complaint* was published, writers who touched on the subject invariably equated the self-induced ejaculation with frustration. In the well-known scene in *Ulysses* in which Bloom, with his hands in his pockets, watches a lame girl on the beach, Joyce's terse description of the dismal aftermath leaves no room for eroticism: 'Mr Bloom with careful hand recomposed his wet shirt. O Lord, that little limping devil. Begins to feel cold and clammy. . . . Still you have to get rid of it some way. . . . Up like a rocket, down like a stick'.

Because masturbation is familiar to most of us only as a poor substitute for copulation, it is considered to be too shameful for direct representation. It is said that the Viennese artist, Egon Schiele, made some drawings of himself in the act of masturbating and that when they were exhibited he was sentenced to a term of imprisonment for outraging public decency. I have not seen any such drawings by him, but I think he would be as likely as any artist to treat the subject without a sense of shame and without fear of consequences. Schiele, who died in 1918 when still a young man, was one of the brilliant end-products of the enlightened conservatism of cosmopolitan Vienna; the Vienna of Sigmund Freud, whose discoveries about the instinctive drives have transformed the world; the Vienna of the novelist Arthur Schnitzler, for whom sin and guilt were obsolete terms; and the Vienna which witnessed in the paintings of Gustav Klimt the last marvellous flowering of Art Nouveau. His drawings were always the outcome of decisions taken in the presence of the model, and his nude and semi-nude studies convey a sense of disclosure, due in some measure to his treatment of the crotch as the 'hot stinging centrality' of the human figure (to borrow a phrase from D. H. Lawrence). His self-portraits leave a very powerful impression of a man passionately scrutinizing his own mirror-image. They bring to mind the mythical Narcissus whose fruitless attempts to consort with his own reflection led to despair and death.

When the preferred and chosen object of a man's desire is his own body, the practice of masturbation acquires the status of a perversion, with a name drawn from classical mythology. But when painters take Narcissus as a subject, and depict a beautiful youth gazing into a pool, the result tends to be symbolically innocuous. Unlike the stories of Leda and the Swan and Europa and the Bull, which enable painters to glorify bestiality without actually depicting how the swan and the bull effect entry into the women, the Narcissus story seems only to yield a pictorial hint of incipient homosexuality, and we have to look elsewhere for an indirect treatment of masturbation that reflects its erotic potency. I think it is to be found in some works by the fifteenth-century painter Hieronymus Bosch which celebrate the lives of the hermit saints.

The Christian hermits must have been peculiarly aware of that aspect of the solitary life which Sade described in the passage quoted at the beginning of this chapter. Underneath the desire to devote themselves entirely to the worship of God, which drove them into the desert and other lonely and inaccessible places, there would have been, perhaps, an incapacity to relate to other people; an obsessive belief in Original Sin; an acute and self-absorbed sense of the shamefulness of being in the flesh. In isolation, removed from all prying eyes except those of their all-seeing God, it could have seemed to them that it would be no offence to expose themselves to him since it had been ordained by him after the fall that the erogenous parts of the body should plague the spirit of mankind for all time. The humble demonstrations of their vileness would in any case be accompanied by counter-demonstrations in the form of constant prayer and bible-reading, designed to make them worthy of God's ultimate grace. In such circumstances the avoidance of temptation may have been reduced to a behavioural technique for refraining from voluntary emissions. It would put them in somewhat the same situation as those holy women who are said to have gone to bed with men in order to preserve their chastity under the most hazardous conditions. One false move would land them in Hell instead of Heaven. The lives of the hermit-saints must have been packed with holiness and erotic excitement.

I must admit that the idea that they were leading rich, full, adventurous lives would not have occurred to me if I had not been subverted by some of Bosch's masterpieces of hallucinatory realism. Little is known about him except that he lived all his life in S'Hertogenbosch, a town in north Brabant. He is thought to have been a recluse, and if this was so he was peculiarly qualified to appreciate not only the taste for solitude that lay at the heart of the hermit-saint's vocation but the special circumstances which could provoke and sustain an acute inclination towards masturbation.

In the paintings of *The Temptation of St Anthony*, the solitary figure of the saint is placed in an extensive landscape and surrounded by a small army of weird personages and animated objects seemingly unconcerned with the saint but engaged in meaningless activities designed to arouse his curiosity and take his mind off his devotions. He makes the correct finger signs for invoking divine protection but even these gestures of rejection tend to become questionable amidst the welter of makeshift allurements and emblematic erections.

The most obvious symbol of a hermit-saint's obsessive awareness of his own penis is not in one of the St Anthony pictures but in a *St Jerome in Prayer*, where the saint, clad in a white shift, hands clasped in prayer, lies uneasily across a stone slab. Behind him, a fallen tree trunk has sidled up close. It's like a nightmarish reptile, with a gaping mouth and a dead branch for a crest. The saint must be aware of its presence because he has flung his cloak over it. By draping the log with the saint's garment and leaving part of it exposed as if it has thrust itself out of the folds, Bosch has rather maliciously made it serve as an attribute of the saint, like the instruments of torment which accompany portraits of the martyr-saints. Another astonishing painting which symbolizes a saint in meditation and a state *56* of erection is *St John the Baptist in the Wilderness*. The symbol of the penis is an imaginary plant, one of Bosch's marvellously inventive contributions to the botany of sexual day-dreaming. Shameless, irrepressible, casually spilling seed on to itself, it rises up between the head and feet of the saint, hiding his middle from view.

Bosch painted three versions of *The Temptation of St Anthony*: the famous hinged altarpiece at Lisbon, a side panel of a triptych at Venice and a small oil in the Prado. It is in the Lisbon version that we find the most ingenious and elaborate groups of phantasmogorical situations. Bosch is not concerned here with the problem of how to depict the hermit's resistance to temptation: he concentrates on the task of devising tableaux of sexuality which are at once shameless and shameful, ugly but inviting, frighteningly absurd yet recognizable as caricatures of the hermit's desires. He is reconstructing in concrete symbols a mind entering into collusion with specific parts of the body. The hermit's mind has been set alight, like the burning house in the background of the altarpiece, where demons float in the smoky glow like the ashes of its consumed contents.

In a side panel, a naked woman appears at the entrance of a makeshift tent formed by a cloth hanging from the branch of a pale, phosphorescent tree rooted in a pool of shallow water. She would seem to be the one normal object of desire, but Bosch has put no emphasis on this figure; and she plays only a minor role in the creation of an atmosphere of enticement. Her hiding place is as tempting as the woman herself, her feet in the pool serve to indicate its shallowness and mark it as a place to wallow in.

The use of draperies to hide and reveal the inhuman forms ensconced in their folds achieves an effect of casual immodesty, and the creatures which dangle fortuitous objects from their beaks and snouts imitate the masturbator's tendency to use his out-thrust penis as a bracket. Nor is the anus forgotten. Of the many grotesques scattered throughout the altarpiece that offer their rears for contemplation, I need only mention the kneeling idiot whose raised buttocks form the entrance to a cottage, the ostrich-like bird with bejewelled hindquarters, the earthenware pot with a narrow mouth which forms the rear of a large rodent, and the man with a dead branch poking out of his anus. The human fragment sitting placidly on the ground with a dagger in its belly is a reminder that a masturbator with sadistic tendencies turns on himself and treats his penis and anus as victims as well as collaborators.

The chronicles of the hermit's life state that a ray of light from Heaven finally scattered the demons. Bosch knew all the details of the St Anthony story, and this is a scene which he could have depicted with ferocious verve. Instead, he chose to make a mock of the idea of the hermit's release from temptation by parodying the pictorial convention which allows a heavenly host to sit in the clouds: the hermit has been raised into the sky by a host of triumphant demons. Supported by his tempters, he is depicted in a sensual sprawl, as if absorbed by the giddy sensation, giving himself utterly to the ecstasy of the uprush. It has the finality of an orgasm.

In the loneliness of the mind where no prying eyes can observe the processes of visualization, in the silence of the studio where, like Rilke at Duino, the artist can hear the sounds of his own body, the dream of the sweeping away of obstacles and restraints becomes imperious, and it is then that figures, objects, concepts, works of art, anything and everything begin to turn into 'uncanny signs' and are ready to abandon their restricted, prudential and orderly uses to become, in Shelley's phrase, 'vitally metaphorical'.

It is perhaps significant that those pubescent girls who are said to be in some mysterious way responsible for the disquieting and inexplicable activities of poltergeists invariably live in out-of-the-way places. Dorothea Tanning, the American wife of Max Ernst, has shown a special tenderness for these 'electric' girls whose inner turmoils seem capable of rocking the house and sending the crockery flying. In some of her earlier paintings she has given us delightful glimpses of their fabulous pleasures. Haunting empty corridors and landings, controlling the main arteries of the house like those witches who tie knots in the tubes of the human body, they disclose their exorbitance in the most playful ways: the paroxysmal pleasure of reaching up to tear down the wallpaper brings a burst of flame; the inconsequential dragging of a huge flower to the top of the stairs whips up their hair. As an issue of tumescence, the destructive force of poltergeists bear a certain resemblance to those promptings of vitality which set boys dreaming of flooding the world with a single emission.

In this connection, Salvador Dali has recounted in obsessive detail a dream-plan for an inundation which came to him when he was a student at the School of Fine Arts in Madrid. In the sculpture class at the top of the building he turned on the tap over a large basin and began to mix fine sculptor's plaster with the water. He kept the tap running, and the milk-white liquid overflowed on to the floor and by the time he had used four sacks of plaster the entire floor of the sculpture class was awash.

'As it was greatly diluted with water, the plaster took a long time to dry, and thus was able to flow under the doors. Soon I could hear the sound of the cascade which my inundation was producing, flowing from the top of the stairway all the way down to the entrance hall. The great well of the stairway began to reverberate with such cataclysmic sounds that I suddenly realized the magnitude of the catastrophe I was producing. Seized with panic I dropped everything and left, ploughing my way through the plaster and getting frightfully bespattered. Everything was unexpectedly deserted, and no one had yet discovered what had happened. The effect of that whole great stairway inundated by a river of plaster majestically pouring down was most startling, and in spite of my fear I was forced to stop to admire this sight, which I mentally compared with something as epic as the burning of Rome . . .'

Dali himself made an interesting analysis of the dream and came to this characteristic conclusion: 'The plaster flood was thus nothing other than the ermine mantle of my absolute monarchy solemnly spreading from above, from the summit of the tower of the sculpture class, over everything that was below.' None of his paintings connected with the theme of masturbation is conceived with quite the same grandeur. One of them, *The Great Masturbator*, is less intransigent than its title, and the symbolism seems to me to be too private or too arbitrary to establish an effective visual relationship to it. One of the small peripheral images – a floating devil's head with a bright red sausage between its teeth – seems to be a sort of Struwwelpeterish illustration of what can happen to anyone caught in the act (one thinks of the scissors man who snips off the thumbs of the boy who will not stop sucking them). The dominant image is of a huge sleeping face balancing on its nose, and its neck has turned into the bust of a woman with long Art Nouveau tresses, and an arum lily, symbolic of both sexes, between her breasts. It suggests that he is connecting the Great Masturbator with Hermaphrodite.

Dali's explanations of certain paintings in which the sexual connotations are uncomfortably evident provide the imagery with an alibi. This is the case with the remarkable painting called *Average Atmospherocephalic Bureaucrat in the Act of Milking a Cranial Harp*, in which the symbolism is so transparent that the image comes very close to being a realistic representation of the act of masturbation. (His explanation, made long after the event, is merely facetious. It appears in Robert Deschanes *The World of Salvador Dali* and Dali says that it illustrates the idea that 'a theocracy ought to employ bureaucrats for lyrical purposes, as harpists for example.') The cranial harp, a huge, soft, boneless extension of the man's head, is an ingenious invention which operates as a simple substitution for penis and scrotum, and as a visual pun on the idea of a man playing with his own 'instrument'. The limpness of his boneless extension has been associated by some of Dali's critics with the idea of sexual inadequacy, but if they suppose that he was unconsciously 'giving himself away' I think they are mistaken. Dali is very familiar with the writings of Freud, and at the time the picture was painted most of his ideas arose from an eccentric and poetic response to psychoanalytical studies of dreams.

Dali has deliberately and brilliantly evoked the atmosphere of an anxiety dream to provide, paradoxically enough, the conditions in which all obstacles and restraints are thrown away. The man is out in the open, in daylight, clad only in vest, socks and suspenders, and he is perched on the edge of a tall building without safety rails. Yet he fingers and explores the soft cranial extension without any sign of fear or shame because he is entirely alone. The man is middle-aged; the condition of his 'harp' suggests that it has been in constant use for a long time, so it is possible that it no longer responds immediately to the player. I think perhaps that in this case Dali's use of a crutch to support the limp extension is intended as a precautionary measure and represents a signal-anxiety; which according to psychoanalysis enables the ego to take defensive action against primary anxiety. The painting is a fine example of Dali's ability to make his symbols provide a lucid account of what they signify. The subtle intermingling of night dream and daydream is a profound poetic achievement and the repulsiveness is brought to terms with the silence and stillness and late afternoon sunlight to create an image characterized by exceptional erotic veracity.

The *Dresden Venus* by Giorgione, reclining and perfectly at rest, inaugurated *62* a new approach to the female nude. Her hand covers her pubic hair, but whilst remaining a gesture of concealment it is no longer the classical gesture of modesty. The hand lies there easily and naturally, and it is intended to convey the impression that it is a normal and habitual position for the hand to adopt when a woman is lying down. It serves a convention of pictorial seemliness by concealing the sexual fleece, but undermines the convention by depicting hand and fleece in intimate contact. The fingers curve inwards and their tips cannot be seen. Very soon afterwards Titian copied the position of the hand with remarkable exactitude in his *Venus of Urbino*. There is no suggestion that it affords Venus any excitement; it is for her simply a comforting contact; but it is inextricably involved in two noble images of a woman on good terms with her own body. For paintings of the nude in which the hand is in contact with the pubic hair, this relaxed, concealing device remained the rule for a very long time. It was still operative in Manet's *Olympia* and Renoir's bathers. Even in the libertine atmosphere of Beardsley's illustrations for the *Lysistrata* the hand pretends to be a shield, and only in the sheet called *Two Athenian Women in Distress* is there a hint that the hand of one of the women is verging on a more active contact.

It was left to twentieth-century artists to acknowledge that a woman has in her own hands a means of giving herself sexual pleasure. In a drawing by Gustav Klimt the hand is, pictorially, a shield for the pubic hair, but it is evident from *60* the expression on the woman's face that her hand is identifying the source of all her anguish and pleasure. Klimt was in a sense the last representative of the Aesthethic Movement. In the first two decades of the century he was making brilliant contributions to an outmoded ideal of feminine beauty in the only capital in Europe, Vienna, that could afford him the luxury of seeming to be shockingly advanced. According to a Viennese eye-witness, he was surrounded in his studio 'by enigmatic naked women who, while he stood silently at his easel, wandered up and down his studio lazing and stretching and luxuriating through the days – yet always ready, at the artist's signal, to freeze obediently into a pose, a movement that had caught his eye and tempted his sense of beauty to seize it in a quick sketch'. His star pupil, Egon Schiele, brought to this dreamy, beauty-sodden conservatory of sensitive plants a fiercer linear gift and a more passionate interest in feminine sexuality. At the height of his short and stormy career he was jailed for a month for exhibiting drawings which depicted masturbation, but there is no

61 record of the sex of the figures exhibited, so his study of a girl fingering her vulva may have been one of the offending sheets.

65 Dali's sketch of a woman lying on her back, with only thighs, legs and hand visible, looks tentative, but is really a much more powerful study of female masturbation than the Schiele drawing. He seems to have felt himself into the situation and identified with the woman. The perceptual experience registers so strongly that, regardless of whether one is a man or a woman, it is like a remembered physical experience.

The same artist's comically named *Young Virgin Autosodomized by her own*
66 *Chastity* is primarily an illustration of a complicated idea not easily convertible into a visual image. Dali's explanation of it could be described as usefully confusing. 'The horn of the rhinoceros,' he says, 'is in fact the horn of the legendary unicorn, symbol of chastity. The young virgin can lean on it and play with it morally, as was practised in the time of courtly love.' Pictorially, he has associated the horns with the girl's buttocks and the upper half of her legs. The magnifications stand for her total preoccupation with her backside and define the area of fantasy. The monstrous preparations for the invasion of her anus are her daydreaming, and he makes us voyeurs of the invisible by brilliantly indicating that as far as appearances go nothing has changed; she is a perfectly normal-looking girl, leaning on a rail and gazing quietly at the sea. It is also a reminder that it is one of the pleasures of the masturbator to show the upper part of his or herself respectably at a window whilst exposing the sexual parts just below the window frame, out of sight.

I find it rather curious that Beardsley, with his free approach to illustration, did not seize on the opportunity presented by *Lysistrata* to introduce the dildo into the activities of the female figures. It was a proper occasion for the women to give a demonstration of their sexual independence and exacerbate the frustration and indignation of the men. Considering the very striking erections he bestowed on the men, it is difficult to believe that diffidence could account for the omission. He must have known Rochester's comic poem about the dildo, and if only it had occurred to him to arm Lampito or Myrrhina with this ladies' companion in a 'plain leather coat' he might have gone on to illustrate the incident in Pall Mall:

> A rabble of pricks who were welcome before,
> Now finding the Porter denied 'em the door,
> Maliciously waited his coming below
> And inhumanly fell on Signior Dildo.
>
> Nigh wearied out, the poor stranger did fly,
> And along the Pall Mall they followed full cry;
> The women, concerned, from every window
> Cried, 'Oh! for heavens' sake, save Signior Dildo!'
>
> The good Lady Sandys burst into a laughter
> To see how the ballocks came wobbling after,
> And had not their weight retarded the foe,
> Indeed 't had gone hard with Signior Dildo.

The rat in Pierre Klossowski's drawing is, I think, being invited to play at being a dildo. It wouldn't be surprising if the woman were telling the little creature in plain fur coat that a tasty morsel was concealed somewhere on her person.

Lesbianism

Michel Leiris, intent on self-exposure, confesses in *L'Age d'Homme* that he has only to crush a fly to prove to himself that he is a sadist, or drain a glass of liquor to feel like one of Dostoyevsky's heroic drunkards. Reaching for the sublime by such petty means seems to him to be despicable, and he likens himself to the *petit bourgeois* who thinks he is Sardanapalus when he visits the brothel. But the faculty of living by the inflationary correlative is an invaluable aid to erotic pleasure; the man who can feel, if not show, that when he engages with a prostitute there is no difference between him and the King of Nineveh summoning his favourite slave girl is to be envied rather than despised. In any case, I suspect that the whore's client who identified with Sardanapalus was Leiris himself and that, being sensitive to painting, the name was evoked by Delacroix's picture of the concubines chained to the king's couch to die on his funeral pyre. Also, since Leiris is essentially a man of letters, he is almost certainly familiar with Baudelaire's attempt to correlate Delacroix's gifts with those of Montezuma, 'whose hand, with sacrificial skill, could immolate 3,000 human creatures in a day'. His *petit bourgeois* has an admirable awareness of the transforming magic of names.

I put more trust in names than definitions, and one of the sexual deviations, about which I know next to nothing, has a particularly beautiful name that adds lustre to its mysteries. The definition is 'female homosexual'; the name is 'Lesbian'. It associates all women who fondle one another, the deserving and the undeserving alike, with Sappho, one of the great love poets of the ancient world, whose birthplace was the island of Lesbos. Incidentally, the meaning of words can be changed and enriched by the magic of an image: Courbet's famous picture of Lesbians (which was hidden away in various collections for many years, but now belongs to the city of Paris) is known as *The Sleepers* but Courbet entitled it *Laziness and Sensuality*, and perhaps his title should never have been dropped, for Courbet evidently had nothing but admiration for the laziness and sensuality of his two beautiful women and as long as the picture bore its original title the figures were personifications of Virtues.

It is one of the 'platforms' of the women's liberation movement that the clitoris is more sexually sensitive than the penis and that the rubbing of the penis against the walls of the vagina is a very hit-and-miss way of exciting it. The first of these claims may never be proven, but the other is probably true, and it has always been known that many women pretend to have an orgasm at the same time as the man to help him maintain his delusions of adequacy. In the circumstances, it is surprising that there are not more Lesbians than male homosexuals. But the future is full of promise: 'Sappho' may become the most popular of all 'Christian' names for girls born of artificial insemination.

Most of the direct drawings of Lesbians have been made in brothels, where, it is said, Lesbian relationships afford the girls some excitement after long hours serving the customers. Toulouse-Lautrec spent much time with the girls 'after hours', and made some fine but not particularly erotic studies of girls in bed together. Jules Pascin was another artist who was a privileged observer of the private lives of prostitutes and made some tender studies of them. The softness and smudginess of his line seems to have introduced a tinge of melancholy into
71 his drawing of two Lesbians, but the situation he has depicted may account for the silence that has sprung up between them. The seated girl has evidently made a suggestion that does not come as a shock to her friend, but she is the younger of the two and the proposal has silenced her only because it will involve her in practices outside her experience.

70 The two girls in a drawing by Dali, who have left a naked man to his own devices, present an idealistic vision of the vertiginous encounter of equals. The girls are so equal that they could be identical twins, and so perfectly proportioned for intimate contact that they can lean backwards to bring their sexual fleeces together without their nipples losing touch. No doubt they would be kissing as well, if they had not been thrown by contacts brimming with promise of frenzies to come

72 A drawing crude enough to make a suggested attribution to Rops quite fanciful nevertheless creates a vivid impression of the kind of mutual frenzy likely to overtake Dali's two girls. Again, it is a partnership of equals, and the situation here is so obviously possible that it suggests that some Lesbian practices may be totally free from the vestigial prostitution of one of the partners that haunts the intercourse of married couples. (This drawing could be more plausibly attributed to Durandeau than to Rops. It bears a striking relationship to the central image in Durandeau's *The Nights of Monsieur Baudelaire*, lithographed in 1861 and reproduced in Lo Duca's *A History of Eroticism*.)

Proust overstated the case against Mlle Vinteuil when he described her treatment of her devoted father's photograph as 'sadistic'. On the day she returned from his funeral she placed the photograph on a table beside the sofa to 'witness' her sexual activities with a girl friend, and she succeeded in inducing her friend to spit on the portrait. Her behaviour is not sadistic, but Proust's sense of the erotic value she conferred on the profanation of her father's image is unerring. He describes her 'sort' as being 'so purely sentimental, so virtuous by nature, that even sensual pleasure appears to them to be a privilege reserved for the wicked. And when they allow themselves to enjoy it they endeavour to impersonate, to assume all the outward appearance of wicked people, for themselves and their partners in guilt, so as to gain the momentary illusion of having escaped beyond the control of their own gentle and scrupulous natures into the inhuman world of pleasure'.

This 'inhuman world of pleasure' is marvellously evoked by Balthus in his image of another kind of Lesbianism. The regular music lesson has often enough provided the perfect atmosphere and setting for the ripening of a love situation between an adult and a minor, and between less likely pairs. Even in those staid Dutch interiors where the teacher is a young man and the pupil a matron there is
69 always an undercurrent of incipient dalliance. The child in the Balthus painting

is to some extent a victim. But she has found means on more than one occasion to intimate to the butch Lesbian who teaches her that she adores her. I surmise that at the previous lesson she was aware that their relationship was coming to a head, for on this day she has left her drawers in her bedroom, without knowing precisely why. Her teacher's aggressive attack on her modesty approaches sadism, but she is not being physically maltreated and will certainly survive the psychological shock – may even be feeling humbly grateful to find herself the object of desire.

Homosexuality

I think of St Sebastian as the patron saint of homosexuals, but as far as I know it has never been suggested that the saint himself was homosexual. He barely exists historically, but his image had great popular appeal, and he was one of the saints whose intercession was sought in times of plague. He was a Roman martyr and is said to have been buried on the Appian Way late in the third century. It is known that by the middle of the fourth century he was already venerated in Milan, and it is likely that his cult was encouraged by St Ambrose who became bishop of Milan in 374. It is not without significance that St Ambrose was a persuasive advocate of virginity; his cause would certainly not have been diminished by presenting Sebastian as a beautiful young martyr who had had no carnal knowledge of woman. It is the Presentation of the Virgin transferred to the male sex.

It may be no more than a legend that his execution was carried out by archers, but it is as a young man pierced by arrows that he is almost always represented. The piercing by arrows is not unimportant to a consideration of St Sebastian as an appropriate 'protector' of homosexuals. It can be thought of as the work of Cupid in a particularly malevolent mood, and a portent that he will be penetrated by other males; but there is no need to bring Cupid into the situation. The arrows are important as a way of emphasizing St Sebastian's submissive attitude towards stronger males. He is on display like a woman. The Renaissance masters invariably treat him as a young man much concerned to maintain a graceful appearance. His body is more important than any sign he may give of courage or pain, and the image is more powerful when there is no sign of either, when there is no obvious reaction at all to the piercing, but only a slight tilt of the head and an engaging hint of melancholy. In other words, his martyrdom is to be a substitute for the female nude, a beautiful docile object. From this point of view, the Pollaiuolo *St Sebastian* in the National Gallery is a superb demonstration of a young man submitting gracefully to the brutal activities of other men. He is as much the centre of attraction as Cora Pearl, reclining naked on a sofa, surrounded by admiring gentlemen friends on one of her famous Sunday morning receptions. Yet, the image is more potent when the archers are not seen. Botticelli's Berlin *St Sebastian* looks as if he has gone of his own accord to stand in front of the execution tree. If he has been bound, it is at the wrists, and they are behind his back. He has one of the loveliest faces ever bestowed on a man by a painter, and he gazes as if he contemplates his own image in a mirror, as if absorbed by the mystery of his own existence.

Mantegna's images of the saint are less successful because they are not allowed to be objects of desire. In both the Vienna and Paris versions the face is tense with suffering and it is evident that Sebastian is heroically determined not to cry out. The painter is too anxious to draw our attention to the cruelty of the piercing and the sadistic relish with which the archers have aimed at causing maximum pain. In the Vienna version it seems clear that they started on the legs and slowly and deliberately worked their way upwards until finally an arrow entered under the right cheek bone and came out in the middle of the forehead. Even Grünewald resisted the temptation to pierce the saint's face. Vittoria's marble effigy in San Salvatore, Venice, is another example of an over-demonstrative treatment. The figure writhes in agony and although only one arrow has been aimed at the saint, it has buried itself in the right nipple, and one seems to hear an echo of the applause and laughter that greeted the archer's choice of bull's-eye. This is the effigy of a man being murdered, and it is far removed from Botticelli's image of a man aware of himself as a beautiful object, emblematically transfixed by his own passivity. But it is the Dresden *St Sebastian* by Antonello da Messina that is the perfect image of a man exerting what might be called an active and vital passivity. Painted after he arrived in Venice in 1475, an invented architectural background retreats swiftly in steep perspective from the marvellous figure of the saint, abandoning him utterly to our hushed regard. If ever a male figure had an excuse to be narcissistic, this is the one, for it is difficult to imagine a body that could interest him more than his own. The background is a sort of brilliantly conceived stage-set, and the distant figures engaged in their own affairs are not as far off as they seem; the nearest of them, lying in dream-like remoteness in a corner of the piazza, is a clothed, foreshortened male figure, asleep, with knees raised and legs wide open in unconscious abandonment. The saint presents himself to us with pensive aloofness, and his monumental isolation suggests a ceremonious performance. The trickle of blood running into the waistcloth from the arrow in his stomach is a ravishing glimpse of his interior life. One is reminded of Genet's definition of the soul as 'that which escapes from the eyes, from the tousled hair, from the mouth, from the curls, from the torso, from the penis'. The saint's genitals press against the waistcloth and if the cloth were loosened a little, the penis would rise, but not so much as a masochistic response to the piercing as a sign of sexual self-esteem. He offers us pure male appearance; and as Sartre has deduced from Genet's definition, the soul is the visible body.

Having argued that the arrows in St Sebastian's body simply emphasize his submissiveness, it follows, I think, that certain representations of the male figure present this submissiveness without their aid. An example is the figure of Mars in Botticelli's *Mars and Venus*. Venus's femininity is in a sense nullified because Mars asleep becomes the object of desire. Divested of his armour by baby satyrs, he is on naked display, and Venus, fully clothed, must be considered to have been temporarily demoted as the representative of the female principle; she contemplates instead of being contemplated. Mars, defenceless in sleep, becomes the object of homosexual love. He is there for the taking, but Venus can only expect him to wake and resume the role of taker. Another example is Michelangelo's *Dying Slave*, in the Louvre. This carving is sometimes interpreted as a personification of the soul enslaved by matter, and as such a Christian symbol of paganism. Opulently naked and magnificently carnal, he offers no resistance to interpretations of this kind, but the aggressiveness which is an attribute of male animality is not present; he is as defenceless in his nakedness as the Cnidian Venus, whilst being a much more sensuous offering. It is possible that he is intended to symbolize the yielding up of the soul in death, but what we see is the yielding of the flesh of a beautiful young man, whose eyes are closed in sign of total surrender.

Considering that St John the Baptist was revered as the forerunner of Christ, his treatment in two Italian masterpieces is, to say the least, curious, and one is entitled to wonder whether Christ would have been baptized with water if either of these two versions of the Baptist had performed the ceremony. Leonardo's *St John* was the last painting to have come entirely from his hand. He has bestowed on the saint his final version of the enigmatic smile, and according to Pater it 'set Théophile Gautier thinking of Heine's notion of decayed gods who, to maintain themselves after the fall of paganism, took employment in the new religion'. St John could be wearing vine leaves in his hair, and ivy could be twined round his cross to turn it into a thyrsus; but he is not of the same order of being as Michelangelo's *Bacchus*, swaying in drunken vacancy. He is a Christianized Bacchus, and his smile is filled with a guilty but complacent knowledge of evil. Iconographically, his only connection with the Baptist is his reed cross. In all other respects, he is the effeminate Dionysus with the luxuriant hair, whose attribute was a sacrificed goat. His finger does not point over his shoulder to indicate that one will come after. It may not be pointing at all but simply thrusting up into the dark. It contains a hint of the meaning of that giant finger poking up through the roof of a house in one of Magritte's textbook illustrations of Freudian symbolism.

Leonardo's *St John* was a precedent for Caravaggio's equally unconventional treatment of the Baptist in the Capitoline picture; but the audacity is of a less intellectual order. The lamb which is one of the saint's iconographical attributes has been replaced by a ram. The sprawling youth, who has the loose sweetness of a professional bum-boy, could have come from a bad home in the slums of any big city, and he knows how to make his nakedness both insolent and provocative. It is not a self-portrait because Caravaggio was at least twenty-three years old when he painted it, but it has the look of a mirror image. He has arranged his legs so that he can catch a glimpse of his genitals, but he is actually looking at the reflection of the ram nuzzling up to him like a stand-in for all the adult males who fall in love with his body. He looks as if he might be the same sort of beautiful delinquent as Giacomo Salai who at the age of ten went to live with Leonardo and who in spite of being a lazy, greedy, insolent, thieving good-for-nothing remained in Leonardo's household for many years. Caravaggio's young man would not have been above associating with Salome in order to make a male protector jealous but the artist himself must have had protectors in high places to get away with naming him the Baptist. A banner reproducing this image should have been held high in the procession of homosexuals which, Genet

52

claims, went to the site of a street urinal which was demolished by Spanish insurgents in 1933.

It was near the harbour and the barracks, and its sheet-iron had been corroded by the hot piss of thousands of soldiers. . . . The faggots were perhaps thirty in number, at eight o'clock, at sunrise. I saw them going by. I accompanied them for a distance. I knew that my place was in their midst, not because I was one of them, but because their shrill voices, their cries, their extravagant gestures seemed to me to have no other aim than to try to pierce the shell of the world's contempt . . . when they reached the harbour, they turned right, toward the barracks, and upon the rusty, stinking sheet-iron of the pissoir that lay battered on the heap of dead scrap-iron they placed the flowers.

75   Beardsley's *Bathyllus Posturing* is one of two drawings which he based on Juvenal's mention in the Sixth Satire of an effeminate young man who danced the part of Leda in a ballet. In the other drawing the swan takes Bathyllus to be a woman and is flying directly towards the crotch, and Bathyllus hides his genitals with a gesture of mock modesty. *Bathyllus Posturing* is the second movement in the dance; the swan is not depicted, but the dancer is inviting him back with a hand signal in which one finger stands up like an erection; he fingers his behind with the other hand, to show the swan (who is Zeus, the supreme god of the Greek heaven) where he should make for.

Oscar Wilde, the most famous of Beardsley's associates, maintained that 'one should either be a work of art or wear a work of art' and in two very camp wood-cuts of a pair of young male lovers, by an anonymous twentieth-century artist, 74 the boys wear their genitals like pretty artefacts. The artist does not subscribe to Leonardo's absurd contention that the members employed in the act of copulation are so ugly that it is only the beauty of human faces that saves us from extinction. (It is suggested elsewhere in this book that Leonardo may only have had in mind the vagina and the anus.) Certainly there is nothing ugly about the testicles and penises of the two boys. They nestle like fruit in a delightfully spiky foliage which suggests that the artist had it in mind to improve on the charming treatment of the pubic hair in Pollaiuolo's famous engraving known as *Battle of the Naked Men*. The woodcut which depicts the foremost standing boy in the clasp of the other demonstrates Sartre's point that in the homosexual act the penis of the boy who plays the feminine part hardens only to give the one who enters him a better grip; it also provides a neat illustration of Proust's use of the word 'clamp' for penis.

In works of art which depict, as St Paul remarked of the Romans, 'men with men working that which is unseemly, and receiving in themselves that recompense of their error which was meet', the situation is invariably treated, even in the more permissive times, as a combat. The intimate contact of two male bodies has to appear to be either a fight or a wrestling match. Contemporary artists favour the latter, but I take as my example a fine drawing by the Renaissance 76 sculptor Baccio Bandinelli, which depicts the struggle between Hercules and Antaeus. Antaeus was a giant, so he must be the figure with head thrown back. The contact between the two men is most pronounced where the two bellies meet. The treatment of the face of Antaeus is ambiguous; the expression can mean either agony or ecstasy. It is as ambiguous as those words of St Paul's – 'receiving in themselves that recompense of their error which was meet' – quoted from the

117

Authorized Version. If the two naked figures are obtaining unadmitted pleasure from their contact, their recompense for working at one another must be two jets of sperm mingling on their bellies.

Transvestism

The lithograph by Octave Lassaert entitled *Ne fais donc pas la cruelle* was mentioned   *77*
by Baudelaire. He said that it was 'a lithograph which expresses one of the great truths of wanton love – though unhappily without too much refinement. A young man disguised as a woman, and his mistress, dressed as a man, are seated side by side on a sofa – the sofa which you know so well, the sofa of the furnished lodgings and the private apartment. The young woman is trying to lift her lover's skirt. In the ideal museum of which I was speaking, this lewd sheet would be counterbalanced by many others in which love would only appear in its most refined forms.'

I think 'lewd' is too harsh a term for this print. The drawing is certainly commonplace, and the situation has been somewhat distorted by Lassaert's anxiety to make it clear beyond all doubt that the figure in the stovepipe hat is a woman; but I feel sure that he intends the exposed breast to be seen only by us; it is like an aside in a play. There is a charming aspect to the relationship between the two figures. It is the woman, of course, who is saying 'Don't play the heartless one' – and the attempt to intensify pleasure by an exchange of roles has been unexpectedly delayed by the man's spontaneous gesture of modesty. Even if he is only pretending, it is an interesting observation on the artist's part. Lassaert's draughtsmanship is uninspired, but it has at least the negative virtue of leaving the psychological realism intact.

Botero's *Melancholic Transvestite*, resting in his private sitting-room, is the   *78*
whoremaster depicted in the brothel scene in fig. 141. He has been looking at himself in a hand-mirror. He has seen there his short hair parted down the middle, his spectacles and his small neat moustache. It is a comic *vanitas*. It was not the implications of transience that he found, and he is not reflecting on time; he came face to face with his absurdity and is reflecting on his loneliness. I think it is a daily event; I think he falls into a fit of depression every time he retires to his private room. I do not think he has much of a sex life. He is probably ashamed of his penis but we have seen that he is fond of his girls, and I have no doubt that he would like above all things to be able to be a lesbian. It is a comic picture, but also a very sad one, for to quote Baudelaire once again, 'love is the sole thing that merits the putting-on of fine linen.'

Domestic Eroticism

In spite of evidence to the contrary, I think of the figures in Rembrandt's famous *Ledikant* etching as a married couple making love in their night shirts. Christopher   *80*

White in his admirable study of Rembrandt as an etcher has no doubt at all that it is a representation of two young people having intercourse outside wedlock. He points out that 'the young man's feathered cap is hung on one of the bedposts, with all the panache of the seducer, while an empty glass and plate on the bedside table signify that a little feasting has served as prelude.' In which case, they are down to their shifts, but apart from the man's cap no other items of discarded clothing are in sight. Yet the evidence of the feathered cap seems conclusive, and the implication is either that the girl's family is out of the house and not expected back for some time, or that she is a prostitute. I suppose it is the fact that the embracing figures form an unromantic huddle that gives me the impression that they are a married couple. It is as if they are set in their ways and unconcerned about appearances. A 'seducer' might be expected consciously to preserve some remnant of his 'panache'; this young man has lost all his swagger. He has crept between the girl's legs as sluggishly as schoolboys creeping unwillingly to school.

It is not the sort of scene that Rembrandt would be privileged to observe directly, and it is presumably based on memory and visualization. White maintains that the date of the etching, 1646, coincides with the interval between the death of Rembrandt's wife Saskia and the arrival in his household of Hendrijke Stoffels 'to assume the former's role in all but name', so the subject possibly has a compensatory significance inspired by a longing for sexual intercourse; it would explain why in one respect his sense of reality may be somewhat in abeyance. If one is expected to think that intercourse is actually taking place – and the contented look on the girl's face suggests that it is – the couple are performing a physical miracle. The man is kneeling between the girl's legs; she would have to raise her thighs high off the bed to enable him to enter her, and it is clear that she is not doing so. In the positions in which they are depicted, the girl would not be looking blissful; her face would be more likely to express her concern to get into a better position to receive her lover. The etching does not disclose Rembrandt's usual desire to achieve total conviction; he has not even bothered to delete one of the girl's two left arms, and I think that the etching primarily served a different need.

79   Something about Michael Zichy's study of domestic fellatio suggests that he was familiar with the *Ledikant* etching. The treatment of the pillows brought down to the living room from the bedroom is not unlike that of the fat pillow which supports the head of Rembrandt's female figure, and the position of the legs of Zichy's husband-figure almost reproduces the way in which hers are disposed. The rather noticeable fact that the man continues to smoke his pipe suggests that his wife's attentions have become habitual and emphasizes that atmosphere of unromantic domesticity which I find in the Rembrandt etching.

A remarkable series of drawings by Stanley Spencer reveals a deeper concern with the erotic aspect of marriage. Spencer was a highly gifted artist, but his eccentric and sometimes fearsomely grotesque figuration makes it difficult to place him in relation to English art. His work seems to have no correspondence with that of his contemporaries, but I think that perhaps he had a certain affinity with Samuel Palmer. His art bears not the slightest formal resemblance to Palmer's, but the work of Palmer's Shoreham period is the visible trace of a bid to introduce a poetic principle into daily life, and in his paintings and drawings he treated the

Shoreham valley as an outpost of paradise. A passage in Maurice Collis's biography of Spencer suggests that he thought of Cookham, the village in which he spent most of his life, in much the same way, although it is certain that they had radically different ideas about paradise and that Palmer would have been horrified by Spencer's frank sexuality. Collis says that from 1910 onwards, Spencer's paintings were always attempts to 'transcend reality and present a homely golden age, where heaven and earth interpenetrated in the way they do in folklore, scriptures, fairytales . . .'. He began to paint overtly erotic pictures in 1937, and Collis remarks that by that time he was 'sure that sex was all-important, that his dream of peace and love could best be expressed through sex, and that sacred and profane love were identical, so that by indulgence in sex both peace on earth and knowledge of God could be attained'.

Collis wrote his biography of the artist after undertaking, with the help of his daughter, the enormous task of sorting and making sense of thousands of sheets of notes written by Spencer over a period of many years. The notes include elaborate plans for a building dedicated to religion and sex, to be decorated by his own paintings. 'A church and a house combined would perfectly fit the mixture', he noted. There would be doors directly opening from the bedrooms of the house into the church, and along the church aisle there would be twelve chapels containing paintings designed for the contemplation of marital happiness. A passage lined with paintings of men and women in different stages of undressing would open into a room of nudes making love or lying about.

Some aspects of Spencer's sense of marital bliss are expressed in a number of unusual drawings in Lord Astor's collection. They succeed in conveying his delight in sitting or standing about in close proximity to his wife. A bedroom scene shows a naked couple in a very confined space between two chests of drawers, rummaging for underwear; and the bulging thighs of the woman form *82* a massive halo for the head of the crouching man. In another drawing they have been sharing the bath and have remained in it to dry themselves. The towel which *83* the woman is drawing backwards and forwards between her legs is evidently rubbing against her vulva; her open and obvious self-stimulation lends a curious interest to his own note on the drawing: 'It suggests to me, as far as gestures are concerned, and in one sense as far as the nude and desire element is concerned, an Annunciation scene. I could easily give the girl a long dress. The position of her legs is right for the Virgin.'

Two drawings which depict the couple on a two-holer at the bottom of the *84, 85* garden look rather like two frames from a comic strip, but a newer system of flushing in the drawing which I take to be the second one suggests that it might have been done considerably later than the other. The figures make an intransigent contribution to what Lord Clark calls the alternative convention to the classical ideal: in *The Nude* he gives as an example the naked figures of men and women in Rogier van der Weyden's *Last Judgement*, who look like 'roots and bulbs pulled up into the light'. This striking phrase has the same ring as the strangest passage in the sheaf of love letters Spencer addressed to his wife Hilda after she was dead:

An old old toad, which has never seen the light and has from early childhood always been hidden in the dark interior, slowly emerges from under the dank leaves. Its head, no

91, 92 (*Above and left*)
PIERO DI COSIMO
Battle of the Lapiths and
the Centaurs

93 (*Opposite above*)
BOTTICELLI
La Primavera

94 (*Opposite below*)
TITIAN
Sacred and profane love

5 (*Previous page*)
GON SCHIELE
Woman

6 (*Opposite*)
OTTICELLI
Abundance

7 (*Above*)
ORENZO LOTTO
The triumph of chastity

8 (*Right*)
IM DINE
ondon no. 2

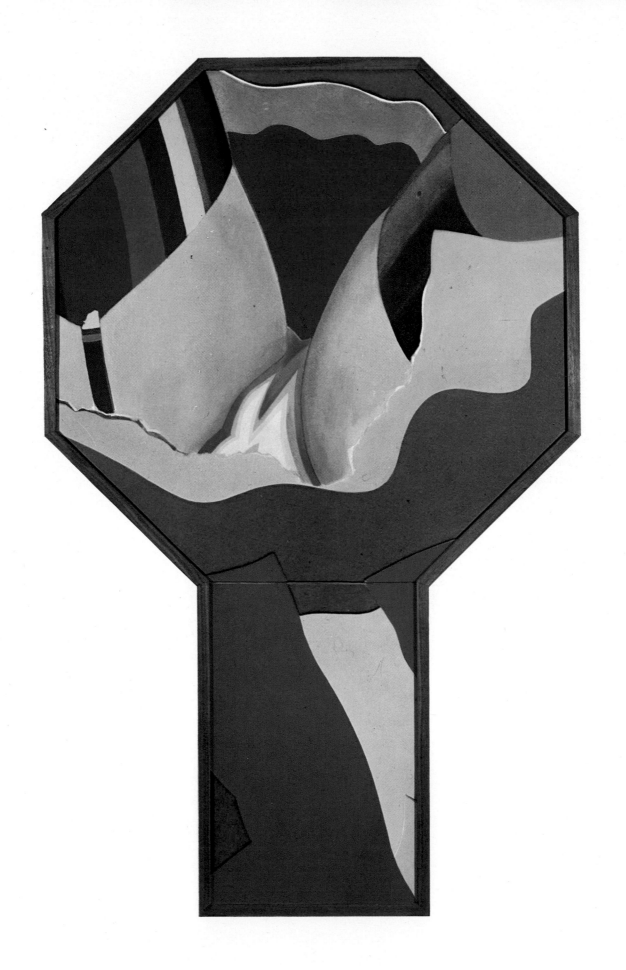

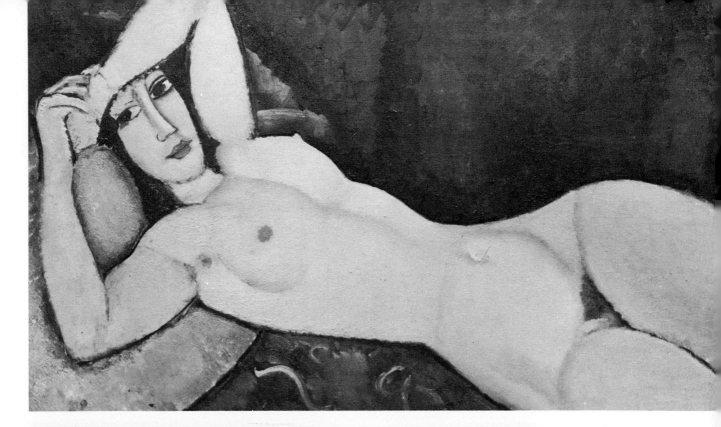

106 (*Above*)
MODIGLIANI
Reclining nude

107 (*Left*)
INGRES
Interior of a harem

Clandum erat ma
lum. Translateur.
En ceste partie du
seruie commence le
.vj.e liure qui est de dictz et des
fais dignes & memoire de la
cite de romme et des estrangiers
Onquel apres ce que valerius es
.v. liures precedens a determi
ne des virtus et des operations
vertueuses. En ce .vj.e liure il de
termine des vices selon ce quil
a promis ou prologue du pre
mier liure. Et que ceste

continuation soit raisonnable se
peut apparoir qui considere les
matieres des .v. precedens. Car
ou premier il a traictie du culti
uement suuy. Ou second il a deter
mine des choses qui appartienent
a la vertu de prudence. Sicomme
sont les institutions de anciene
la discipline de cheualerie ou
militaire le droit de triumpher
Ou tiers il a determine de
fortitude et de vertu qui a luy
appartiennent comme sont patt
ence et constance. Ou quart il

112 (*Opposite*)
Sixteenth-century MS
Illumination

113 (*Right*)
BOSCH
Garden of terrestrial
delights (detail)

114 (*Below*)
ALFRED STEVENS
The bath

Coment liziart poiſt congiet de la amoy

115 (*Above*)
HANS BOCK
The bath at Leuk

117 (*Opposite above*)
DE BRY
The jester's bath

118 (*Opposite below*)
MAX BECKMANN
Resting woman

116 (*Left*)
Twentieth-century MS
illumination

NON PROBAT EX CEREBRO LASCIVA PVELLA PRIAPVM

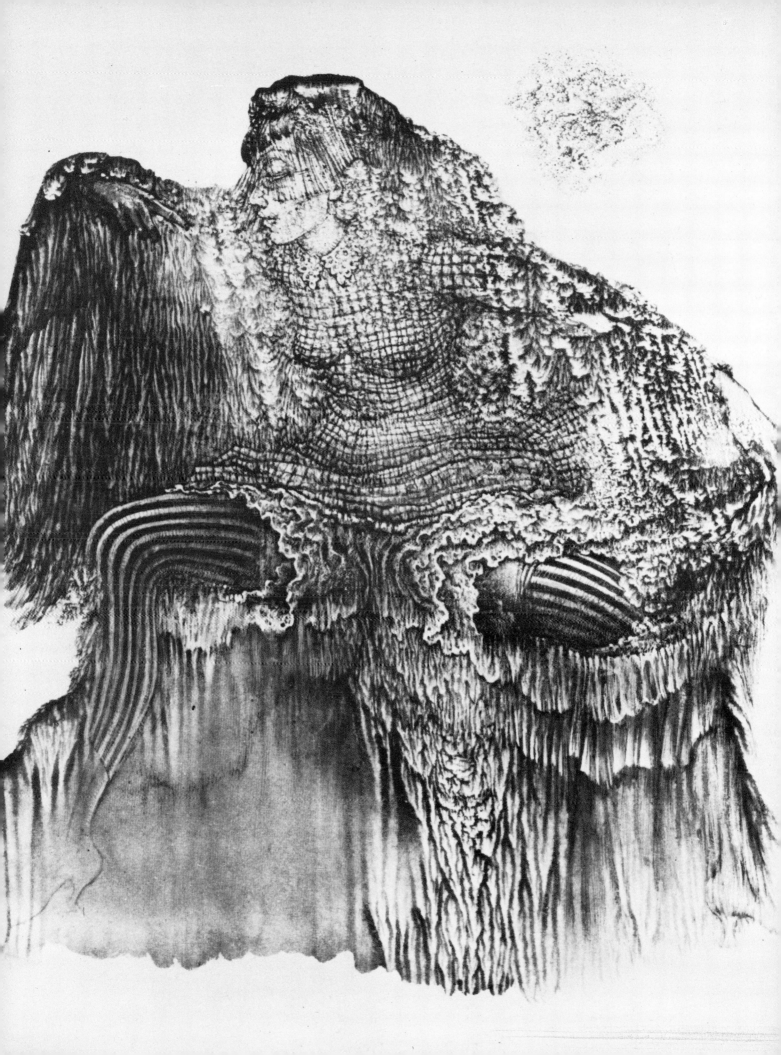

light-seeing or way-finding, is hard to recognize as a head. Ungainly, but oh! it's a you-shape. It is astonishing that it creeps towards me.

The details in these scenes in a primitive rural lavatory are of the slice-of-life kind. Torn newspapers to wipe on; the man's trousers pulled down to the ankles with the braces still attached to the rear buttons; the woman's lace-edged drawers not entirely dropped, as if she might be sitting on the back of them because the wooden seat is cold; their vests pulled up deliberately to expose their pale bellies. They are using the lavatory as a love-seat, and it is likely that they have sat together there many times before, to escape for a while from the rest of the family. Everything about these drawings is unattractively comic and deplorably ugly, and yet one feels that they have been conceived in a magnificently dauntless spirit. This couple is well aware of the imperfections of the body, but also of its power to transport, and however often they witness the phenomenon of erection they will never lose their sense of the wonder of it.

Collis suggests that some of Spencer's paintings disclose a masochistic approach to women: 'In most of *The Beatitudes* the man is small like him, and is shown abasing himself before large and ugly women . . .' In the painting called *The Leg of Mutton*, the Spencer-like figure, quietly contemplating an unclassical nude clasically posed, is not inexpressive of worship. She is *Venus Vulgaris*, and the worship is of the flesh. The man is not abasing himself; his own flesh confers equality, and his genitals are exposed without humility. The window and the fragment of wall decoration in the background suggest that they are in a church and may indicate that this is the day of rest from the toil of intercourse; but since Spencer was convinced that his 'sexual urge was the very substance and core of his spiritual essence' he would more likely have thought of Sunday as the proper day and a church interior the ideal setting for intercourse, and the limpness of the male figure's penis may be due simply to his fear that by flaunting the public moral code of his day he might be deprived of his freedom. The leg of mutton in the foreground, lying beside the woman, must have had a fairly specific meaning for Spencer, and it is probably no accident that it is one of the most popular Sunday joints. Being part of a sheep, it may even have been intended to emblemize the Lamb of God at the marriageable age, and, as such, an apt and succulent replacement of the wafer used for the vicarious cannibalism of the communion service. I do not think that he would have been revolted by the idea of eating his wife. His letters to her after her death were more erotic than when she was alive, and a ritualistic act of cannibalism might have quietened his spirit, for it would have represented their ultimate intermingling, and freed him from solitude.

The seductive art of Correggio, with its softly modelled forms and its gracefulness and refinement, is the antithesis of Spencer's work, but they share at least an unqualified delight in the flesh. In the lovely *Madonna della Cesta*, the Christian theme is used to celebrate the erotic relationship between a mother and her male child. The woman spreads the half-naked child across her lap to display with dreamy pride the physical attributes of the fruit of her womb, and it is not surprising if one finds in his involuntary exhibitionism an intimation of the images of insoucient boys to be painted by Caravaggio, whose aim, according to Burck-

53

81

hardt, was to show that sacred events unfolded in the same ways as in the alleys of Italian cities.

Incest

For European artists, the story of Lot and his daughters has always been the archetypal example of incest, but in the past any attempt to illustrate the central situation could have been undertaken only in secret; and now that it can be treated openly, the very few good story-tellers among our painters have not, as far as I know, taken up the theme. Yet probably only the comic realism of Rowlandson could have done justice to the idea that when first one daughter and then the other went into Lot whilst he was in a drunken stupor and had intercourse with him, 'he perceived not when she lay down, nor when she arose.' It is not likely that they would have got the slightest spurt out of an old man who was so far gone as to be unaware that his sexual organs were being meddled with; but with a print in mind called *The Miser* which was much admired by Huysmans, one can see how Rowlandson might have treated the situation. One of the daughters would be on her knees beside her insensible father, rolling his limp penis between the palms of her hands, and the other daughter would be standing with her chemise raised high, waiting to settle herself over his erection.

The painters had to concentrate on the scene in which the daughters pour wine, but in order to make it clear that the intention was to get themselves impregnated by him there had to be some indication of their shamelessness, and they were usually depicted with bared breasts. However, the only possible reason for deliberately exposing themselves in front of their father would be to put temptation in his way, and it would have made no sense if he had been unresponsive, so he was invariably depicted in a state of eagerness.

It was one of the favourite subjects of the eighteenth-century French painter, Jean-François de Troy. He used it merely as an excuse to paint luscious, semi-draped female figures, and he turned Lot into a man in the prime of life who could afford two lovely mistresses. But the devaluation of the incest theme was perhaps immanent by the time Jan Mandin painted his mild version of the wine-pouring convention. The German master Albrecht Altdorfer conveys much more powerfully the sense that a forbidden but irresistible act of intercourse is about to take place. The figures are now intransigently naked and Lot has compelled himself to become consciously evil to ensure that the act of transgression is not frustrated. His firstborn is ensconced between his thighs. They are not talking, and it is clear that the young woman has slotted her eyes in her father's direction in response to the hardening of his penis against her flesh. It is the longed-for signal. She will turn now, to let it rise and invade her. Beyond the trees, the younger daughter awaits her turn. Far off, the cities of Sodom and Gomorrah are lost and damned. But expectancy is reborn in the misdemeanours of the saved.

Of all the versions of *Lot and his Daughters* known to me, the one I admire most seems to lend incest the virtue of a necessary ritualistic profanation of sexual sanctions. It is the brilliantly coloured, marvellously detailed panel in the Louvre attributed to the early sixteenth-century Dutch painter, Lucas van Leyden. The burning cities on the banks of a broad river dotted with sinking ships and the fire and brimstone still pouring out of Heaven, are important aspects of the composition, for Lot and his daughters, and the encampment they have made on the opposite bank of the river are illuminated by the apocalyptic light of the fires. In the middle distance, Lot and his daughters, accompanied by an ass, are seen as small dark silhouettes escaping across the river by a narrow bridge, leaving behind them the figure of Lot's wife, turned into a pillar of salt. (Lot's wife was punished because she looked back with regret at the burning cities, remembering the good times. In any case, it was useful to dispose of her; she might have made it difficult for her daughters to have intercourse with her husband.) In the fore-ground they have set up their camp, consisting of three small pavilions. They are well supplied with food and wine. The sharp contrast between the bright colours of their clothing and the nearly black shadows in its folds make the colours look hot and angry. The longest of the pavilions is blood-red in colour and it makes a dramatic background for Lot and one of his daughters seated just outside. Lot is pressing his face against his daughter's cheek and clasping her hand. The other daughter is pouring wine from a plump flagon into a slender jug.

If, as the elder daughter declared after the destruction of Sodom and Gomorrah, there was not a man on earth to go in unto her and her sister except their father, it was God who created the situation which made incest inevitable. As human beings, if not as God's children, transgression is demanded of them by the calamity which lights up their faces. They do not need to be demonstrative. The light from the flames stands for the exhilaration of their guilt. God has rescued three fire-worshippers.

The Living Chain

The situation in which several people are linked together in sexual intercourse has not, as far as I know, been the subject of a serious work of art. There were obvious social reasons for not treating the subject in the past, but there were Renaissance and Mannerist painters who could have solved its figurative problems with great felicity, and in our own time the frieze-like serial composition of Picasso's *Guernica* is ideally suited to the theme.

The theme has of course been treated in pornographic literature. It is described in its simplest and crudest terms in *The Romance of Lust*: 'So to five women we thus had six men, and eventually a very handsome young priest, debauched by others, joined our party, and we carried on the wildest and most extravagant orgies of every excess the most raging lust could devise. We made chains of pricks in arseholes, the women between with dildoes strapped round their waist, and shoved into the arseholes of the man before them, while his prick was into the arsehole of the woman in his front.' This passage is quite remarkable for the absence of variety in the nature of the contacts. It merely describes a series of anal insertions, and the women, with their dildoes, are treated as poor substitutes for men. (The start of a simple homosexual chain is treated rather more vividly by the author of *The Amatory Experiences of a Surgeon*, in a passage purporting to be a reminiscence of his college days:

next they proceeded to annoint it with some pomade, and one of the biggest boys presenting his bottom as he stooped forward on a chair, they made me shove into him till I was fairly in, the delicious warmth of the tight sheath which held me was so exciting that without further instructions I fucked him as naturally as possible, clinging tightly to him with my arms, and thoroughly enjoying it ... the captain of the class, a fine handsome youth of eighteen, attacked me in the rear, but being well lubricated, although the pricking pain attending his first insertion was rather sharp, he was soon in full possession, and my double position of fucker and fuckee soon drove me almost mad with delight.

There are many other descriptions of multiple intercourse in pornographic books, but they are invariably verbal fantasies inaccessible to pictorial representation. Some miniatures in eighteenth-century lockets, or snuff boxes, painted by *89* someone more talented than the average pornographic illustrator, convey a sense of the problems involved in establishing an unbroken heterosexual chain in which the genitalia are fully engaged. Only two of the miniatures contain five figures or more. In one of them five figures are close together, but the chain is broken; one couple is not in vital connection with the other three figures. In the other miniature there are seven people, and of these, two are separated from the others; they are standing near the door and perhaps the male figure, who appears to be some kind of priest, is a newcomer being welcomed by the naked woman. The other five figures can be said to form an unbroken chain, if we allow for the fact that the exposed penis of the bearded, priest-like figure at the head of the divan is simply being fondled by the woman next to him; it does, however, seem likely that he will ejaculate into her ringlets or on to her face. The woman is receiving a man into her vagina, and the next woman in the line has pulled up the man's shift to insert a finger into his rectum; she in her turn is about to be taken from the rear by the male who is the last in the line. One supposes that the only reason why his penis is still exposed is to provide a full view of his erection; the only doubt about his intention is whether he intends to effect an entry into the woman's rectum or by-pass it for the vagina. A not uninteresting aspect of the tableau is the fact that only the women are naked. The men are clothed, but are wearing gowns instead of coat and breeches (presumably to avoid the vulgarity of the open fly). But the gowns have to be pulled up to expose the genitals, an action which lends the exposure a sense of revelation, like the drawing aside of a curtain. I have seen no better attempt than this to depict a living chain; but it is evident that it would require a greater and more imaginative draughtsman than this anonymous miniaturist to fetch the theme out of the underground drawing-rooms of pornotopia.

Considered as an extravaganza of erogenous bodily entanglements, the subject has immense possibilities, and there were two fifteenth-century painters of genius, who in other circumstances, might readily have accepted its challenge, and even at times seemed on the point of rising to it. Their paintings tended to involve human bodies in a kind of communal intimacy that sometimes brought them to the verge of erotic hyphenation.

One of the masters was Hieronymus Bosch, and in the centre panel of the triptych in the Prado called *The Garden of Terrestrial Delights,* his interest in the communal intimacy of naked bodies reaches its highest pitch. It will always remain an enigma because no one will ever know whether he intended it as a vision of the good life or a sermon against sensuality. Wilhelm Fraenger in his *Millennium of H. Bosch* claims that Bosch was a member of the heretical Brethren of the Free Spirit (a sect which is said to have practised ritual nakedness) and that *The Garden of Terrestrial Delights* was commissioned by the Grand Master of the sect, Jacob von Almangien, as propaganda for free love. It is a delightful idea, but other researchers say that there is no evidence that the sect existed during Bosch's lifetime or that its supposed Grand Master was ever a member. Charles de Tolnay has expressed the more generally held view of what Bosch intended. 'The artist's purpose,' he says, 'is above all to show the consequences of sensual pleasure and to stress its ephemeral character.' It is likely that this somewhat dogmatic statement is near enough to the message Bosch intended the picture to convey to his contemporaries; in the right wing of the triptych is a scene in Hell and no doubt it was to be read as a warning to the figures in the centre panel that if they didn't change their ways they would be damned. It cannot carry such a message for us. We acknowledge that sexual pleasure is ephemeral; we know too that it is endlessly renewable and that there is compensation for its disappointments in erotic fantasy. Erotic fantasy was the rich source of Bosch's innovations and marvellously patient execution; not even the fear of Hell could turn him away from it, and there is a sense in which he turned Hell itself into a sado-masochistic garden of delights.

58, 88   The centre of the triptych is a sort of erotic carnival; a gathering of pearly white anatomies involved in a host of temporary alliances. It is a remarkable composition in which seething little groups of male and female figures are spread across the entire surface. Certain landmarks and architectural features give the composition a centre, but it is a centre that is not acknowledged by the throng of figures and those at the far corners of the panel are still at the head of the concourse. Giant fruits, seashells, floating balls and transparent globes aid the highly gregarious play. People eat their way into the giant fruits and turn them into communal love-nests; they burst others to watch the seeds pour out and use smaller fruits as fancy headgear. They band together to squeeze into huge oyster shells or equally huge conches and other bands carry them about. Compact bevies of girls with long golden hair stand in a central paddling pool, and men joy-riding in close formation on all kinds of four-legged creatures move round the pool. Smaller groups carry large fish about or get together under glass domes or simply sit and lie about in casual association. There is much straddling of legs and raising of knees and buttocks and touching of cheeks, shoulders and bellies; but there is no observable touching of breast or pudenda and no acts of copulation, and however intimately the figures embrace, no penis ever stiffens. Deep

88   inside the garden, a particularly curious game is being played. From the inside of a tight ring of kneeling figures, facing inwards with heads touching the ground and backsides raised high, there emerges the belly and widespread legs of a male figure who is evidently standing on his head. Birds sit about expectantly on the backs of the kneeling figures and one of them pokes an inquiring beak between a pair of buttocks. Ostensibly, the tableau has been arranged to present the

balancing act of a mermaid with a very long tail, who is reclining above the group, supported by the feet of the man who is upside down, but the faces of some of the kneelers peer out at us as if, like the birds on their backs, they await a happening of another kind, and it gradually dawns on the spectator that all the activities in the garden are a kind of prelude; the silence before an orgiastic storm.

Don Felipe de Guevara, writing forty years or so after the painter's death, remarked that, whilst not denying that Bosch was peculiar in that he painted wondrous persons and strange situations, he thought it a mistake to regard his work as something outside the rules of what is taken to be natural, and he praised Bosch for his care and restraint. Nowhere is his care and restraint more evident than in *The Garden of Terrestrial Delights*; but it is the restraint that is unnatural. Bosch exercises his power over the people with the implacability of a sorcerer. They are under a spell. The happenings for which they came together are being withheld. They have been denied the tumescence and orgasms which would be the natural and inevitable outcome of their physical entanglements. But we can be sure that Bosch himself visualized all the potentialities of the situations he himself created.

Certain battlepieces seem ripe for conversion into scenes of multiple sexual intercourse. The polite battle between Greeks and Amazons on the Achilles-Penthesilia sarcophagus, where there is more grappling than killing and Achilles himself seems to be supporting a swooning Amazon, is a fairly obvious example. But it is also an example of Roman academicism, and it is in a much more vital and violent battlepiece, *The Battle of the Lapiths and Centaurs* by the fifteenth-century Florentine master, Piero di Cosimo, that the living chains conceived for the presentation of a bizarre affray come to the verge of compound sexual intercourse. *91, 92*

On grounds which suggest only that Piero di Cosimo did not hide his likes and dislikes and could not bear to be interrupted when working, Vasari has made him out to be a preposterous eccentric. If Vasari's account of him is true – and there is no other – Piero would shut himself away for days on end, living on hard-boiled eggs of which he cooked fifty at a time to save trouble and expense. He found it irritating to have assistants round him; could not stand the crying of children or the clanging of church bells; hated doctors and chanting monks, and was enraged by flies. He marvelled at everything produced by nature, loved a good downpour of rain, let his garden grow wild because he preferred it that way, and went for long walks by himself. The crowning evidence of his utter eccentricity was his refusal to admit a priest to his death-bed.

Piero was as original and inventive in his way as Bosch, and was famous in his own time as a designer of *Trionfi* processions. Vasari gives a vivid hearsay description of his most popular 'triumph', a *Triumph of Death* designed for the carnival in Florence in 1511. A huge black cart drawn by oxen and loaded with coffins over which towered a figure of King Death, carrying his scythe, was followed by a cortège of horsemen wearing black tights painted with white bones to give them the appearance of skeletons; from time to time other skeletons rose up out of the coffins and chanted dire warnings to the revellers that they too would one day be like them. But he himself had no fear of death and was anything but a religious fanatic. He went on painting his pagan mythologies when other painters, frightened by Savonarola's rise to power, were frantically destroying all such evidence of their sinfulness. He believed neither in the Christian conception of the origin of mankind, nor in the neoplatonic doctrine that the universe was unified by a metaphysical force emanating from God. He abandoned the idealization of the figure for a more realistic approach to the human body; his figures tend to be short, plump and tough; they look neither noble nor spiritual, but they are intensely alive.

His art reflects the spirit of *De Rerum Natura*, the great didactic poem which Lucretius addressed to Venus, as the creative force of nature. The poem expands the Epicurean doctrine that every event has a natural cause, and that the soul, being composed of material elements, dies with the body. It gives a remarkably acceptable account of the origin of the human species and attributes the development of primitive man and the birth of civilization to man's use of natural resources and his own powers of invention.

Piero painted a number of enchanting allegorical panels fancifully devoted to the Lucretian view of mankind's progress, beginning with hunting scenes in which man recognizes no fundamental difference between himself and the other animals; he fights and mates with them and brings monsters into the world which are part man and part beast. They are followed by scenes in which men are making crude dwellings and domesticating animals, and in which Vulcan symbolizes men as toolmakers. Finally human life becomes festive with the discovery of wine and honey.

His *Battle of the Lapiths and Centaurs* is set in the period when man's indiscriminate mating with animals brought forth monsters. The Lapiths have been surprised by Centaurs in the midst of a picnic and are being belaboured with their own vessels. In the foreground there is a marvellously affectionate scene depicting a Centauress embracing her dying lover and giving him a final tender kiss. The fact that the Centauress belongs to the wild band that has started the fight implies that Piero is concerned not only with the poignancy of death but with the sensual complexity of the beings involved in the affray. It is another aspect of it that the heat of the battle has brought Centaurs and Lapiths together in an intimacy only one remove from orgiastic sexual intercourse.

The four figures on the left-hand side of the picnic carpet are inextricably plaited together in an extended wild embrace, and the soft, smooth, plump muscularity of their arms bears a curious resemblance to an intertwining of snakes. Their reptilian appearance brings *Laocoon* to mind, a sculpture now less venerated than it used to be, perhaps because it has to carry as a sort of sub-meaning, more obvious to us than the ostensible one, the representation of man's struggle to control his sexual appetites. In its turn, this view of the snake as the unruliness of the penis brings to mind a charming account of the first men and women in the mythology of one of the Indian tribes of Brazil. In the beginning men were asexual and only the women desired copulation. To afford them satisfaction the Creator provided a snake, which was in fact a penis half a mile long. The men became jealous and the snake was killed, so the Creator cut its body into pieces and distributed them among the men as individual penises.

Another group of figures in Piero's painting, farther to the left but nearer to the foreground, is without weapons, and the ferocity of the participants could equally well be a fury of desire. The male Lapith who is being hugged by the female sustains her in a position suitable for easy access; the Centaur's hand is between her thighs; the male Lapith who has leapt on to the Centaur's back is probably biting, but might be thrusting his tongue into the Centaur's open mouth. (Incidentally, although the genitals of the Lapith are covered by a dangle of beads, Piero has indicated the fine hairs on the scrotum to assure us of its presence.) Piero held the Epicurean view that pleasure, partly equated with the absence of pain, was the only good, since it was the only good known to the senses. He would have approved of the hippy exhortation to the world to make love not war, and I think he would have preferred his wonderfully interlocking bodies to be a living chain dedicated to Eros.

3 The Object of Desire

The Sacred and the Profane

The pagan mythologies of the Renaissance painters present iconographical problems which are sometimes solved to everyone's satisfaction, but these solutions and explanations are rarely involved in our reasons for admiring one picture more than another. Art historians as erudite and sensitive as Panofsky and Wind frequently confront us with illuminating hypotheses, but even when they tease out a meaning that seems incontrovertible, it is not always a meaning which touches us as deeply as our own unschooled response to the painting. In their pursuit of meaning they sometimes evaluate the figures in a way which may be necessary to their elucidation of the artist's intention but irrelevant to what keeps the picture alive in our century.

93 In his account of the literary influences on Botticelli's *Primavera*, Professor Wind has convincingly argued that the Zephyr–Chloris–Flora group on the right represents an Ovidian metamorphosis. Zephyr, with swollen cheeks, breathes his passion into the awkward, primitive figure of Chloris and she is immediately transformed into the marvellously beautiful figure of Flora, striding into the foreground of the picture. Wind further argues, no less convincingly, that the decorous dance of the three Graces on the left represents a more elevated phase in the metamorphosis of love, and that in contrast to Flora, who 'firmly and jubilantly treads the earth', the central figure in the dance 'turns her back to the world and faces the Beyond'.

The figure standing between the two groups is Venus, and her gown covers a belly as gothicly bulbous as the belly of Van Eyck's Eve. She is evidently a version of the goddess of love, conditioned by Christianity. Wind says that 'the concept of a beneficent, peaceable, guarded Venus was one of the more refreshing paradoxes of neoplatonism', and the Venus in *Primavera* is mildness personified. She would be the Holy Virgin, swollen by the divine foetus, if it were not for the absence of a halo. It seems, therefore, that for didactic reasons much of the spontaneous life of the Venus and the dancing group was deliberately drained off by the painter. He was under no such constraints when creating the less elevated figure of Flora, and in the outcome she has so much more presence that she takes pictorial precedence over all the other figures. She has adopted the stance of a sower and has lifted her gown to cradle the flowers she casts on to the air. The position of the hand that supports the lifted drapery recalls the classical gesture of modesty but disappears equivocally into shadow. Pictorially, the painting celebrates the triumph of Flora. In what appears to be a slightly desperate attempt to undermine the compelling attraction of this figure, Wind suggests that her face has the 'sturdy air of a country bride', but she is in fact the image that gives the picture all its magic and mystery. Younger and more ravishing than the Mona Lisa, she has the same kind of beauty, 'wrought out,' as Pater said, 'from within upon the flesh, the deposit little cell by cell, of strange thoughts and fantastic reveries and exquisite passions'. She is potentially the central figure of the composition; one more imperious stride will put her in front of the mild, repressed figure of Venus.

She will always belong to the living so for the time being she belongs to us. The metamorphosis of wild and stumbling Chloris into Flora represents, in the language of the present, the transformation of sexuality into eroticism. Since we acknowledge no life beyond the grave, she stands for all that we are determined not to renounce. She is what the poet Eluard meant when he said of woman, 'you are horizon and presence.' She represents the only beauty that can be both contemplated and possessed, and in this sense she is a sacred personage.

Botticelli succeeded in making the contrast between sensuality and spirituality apparent in the delineation of his figures, and if we could discount the lyrical eloquence that took possession of his account of Flora, our preference for her might simply be due to the fact that the neoplatonic doctrine of love finds no echo in our experience.

On the other hand, the figures in Titian's mythological paintings, although scarcely less involved in neoplatonic doctrine than Botticelli's, provide us with grounds for preference. In the painting which is called *Sacred and Profane Love* 94 there is nothing to choose between the two female figures except that one is draped and the other is not. The terrestrial and celestial symbolism is weak. Even Panofsky was hard put to it to squeeze enough symbolic significance out of the objects and landscape features to support his contention that the nude personifies sacred love. The Victorians, with their tendency to equate nakedness with indecency, thought the draped figure more seemly and therefore more spiritual. But Panofsky's researches into the neoplatonic concept of the double Venus leave little doubt that Titian's picture is intended as a demonstration of Ficino's idea that love is an 'innate and uniting force that drives the higher things to care for the lower ones'. Titian's draped figure is seated at a lower level than the nude and takes no heed of her companion, but the nude gazes down intently at the draped figure; she is evidently the one who 'cares' and therefore the 'higher thing'. Yet when all is said and done, the pictorial contrast is simply between a draped and an undraped figure; there is every reason to suppose that if the one were divested of her finery her form would rival the other in beauty, and it seems clear that the iconographical aspect of Titian's picture is a matter of compositional devices. His primary concern in all the mythological works was to create an ideal version of natural woman. It is an image that served all his purposes and remained warmly desirable in every situation. She represents a point of equilibrium in Western man's approach to woman. She is perceived with a generous and rational passion. She represents the sheer goodness of the flesh. Beyond that point, art began to tremble, to set aside the landmarks, to yield to vertigo, to deviate in order to intensify woman's erotic attributes.

The Triplicity of Venus

Amidst the complexities of Renaissance iconography, one can discern two mutually exclusive aspects of nakedness in the treatment of Venus. One aspect represents celestial beauty, the other represents the exposure of the body for sensual reasons alone. Between them is a clothed Venus who is a combination of these opposites; she is in the flesh but has 'honourable and praiseworthy' aspirations.

The celestial Venus was not born of woman but sprang directly from the sperm spilt into the sea when Uranus, the God of Heaven, suffered castration. The naked figure in Botticelli's *Birth of Venus* is the celestial goddess based on the classical convention known as the Venus Pudica but infinitely more fragile than the Hellenistic versions which have survived, and so lightly poised that she seems to be floating. She has risen from the sea on a large shell and a pair of zephyrs blow her towards the shore, where a personification of the season of spring is waiting to cast a mantle over her nakedness. This is somewhat confusing, because once she is clothed she will surely become the Venus who was born in the natural way and was the daughter of Jupiter and Juno. But there is no doubt that this example of beauty unadorned, sharply defined yet ethereal, is intended as the celestial Venus.

The draped Venus in the same master's *Mars and Venus* is honourably and praiseworthily preparing Mars for love-making. Mars, presumably battle-weary, is fast asleep and Venus has entrusted four baby satyrs with the task, which they have evidently enjoyed, of divesting him of his armour. They have already exposed his magnificent body and are now playing about, and we can be sure that it is not the baby satyrs but the painter who has covered the god's genitals with one of those rumpled cloths which were so dear to still-life painters. When he awakens, his nakedness will make him eager to possess Venus, who is wishful of being loved, but soulfully; she will see to it that they copulate with decorum. The picture was probably commissioned to commemorate a marriage and seems to prophesy that the woman will be the dominant partner. Her motto could be Make Love not War, but she is singularly unseductive for a goddess of love, and ironically enough it is the depiction of Mars that provides the painting with an erotic element.

Botticelli was so steeped in the neoplatonic conception of the draped Venus (human but chaste) that he seemed unable to make her attractive. His Flora in *Primavera* and his superb drawing of a draped female figure personifying Abundance carry infinitely more conviction as the goddess of love. The figure of Abundance is almost frighteningly beautiful and the child she holds by the hand is appropriately sinister, as if he might be a corrupt and wingless Cupid who uses poisoned arrows. The form-caressing folds of Abundance's garment are so filament-thin that the mere pressure of her figure against the air as she walks forces the fabric between her legs and turns the parts of her body into separate delectable parcels. In this sense, she foreshadows Jim Dine's drawing of a gift-wrapped penis and Dali's *Spectre of Sex Appeal*. (Dali explained his somewhat macabre personage, composed of neat bundles of bones and bags filled with softer parts, by suggesting that the woman of the future would probably be able to satisfy her exhibitionism by detaching various parts of her anatomy and passing them round to be admired separately.) In the profoundly erotic atmosphere of Botticelli's drawing, his delicate, phantasmal, yet curiously obtrusive, study of a cornucopia – the conventional attribute of Abundance – seems less symbolic of the womb than of the vagina.

98

Titian associates the Eve in his *Adam and Eve* with Venus by giving the serpent the head of Cupid, but we only know that the association is with the sensual Venus and the 'lower' nakedness because Eve has yielded to temptation.

The nakedness that symbolizes total concern with sexual pleasure is represented with delightful circumspection by the Venus in Lorenzo Lotto's *Triumph of Chastity*. Chastity is fully clad of course, and even wears a cap with a long back flap to hide her tresses; but a charming detail is the little stoat in its white winter coat which lends its emblematic support to her and stands protectively astride her breasts. Incidentally, the role of the ermine as a symbol of chastity in the well-known Hatfield portrait of Elizabeth I is more ambiguous. It stands on a table with its forepaws on the queen's sleeve and fixes its gaze on her face as if imploring her attention. In the Lotto picture, Cupid has evidently shot an arrow in Chastity's direction; she has snatched up his bow to beat him with it, and with her other hand she pushes Venus away. Venus carries a box of toilet articles and presumably intended to show Chastity how to make herself look more presentable. She takes the rebuff philosophically, like the door-to-door salesman who sometimes gets the door slammed in his face, and with an arm round Cupid she drifts gracefully away. She does not make the conventional concessions to modesty but her nakedness is not provocative. On the contrary, she is rather reserved, and it is not the absence of garments but the wearing of jewellery that identifies her as the goddess of physical love. The ribbon and pearls in her hair, the necklace and the pretty armlet indicate that she is proud of her nakedness. The decoration of her body implies erotic liberation.

97

Erotic Liberation of the Nude

There was a touch of slyness in Titian's attitude to erotic subjects. It was no doubt encouraged by his friend and mentor, Pietro Aretino, who, as exemplified in the following extracts from two of his letters, was a model of two-faced morality. The first is from a letter to the surgeon Battista Zacchi:

I renounce the bad judgement and dirty habit which forbids the eyes to see what pleases them most. What harm is there in seeing a man on top of a woman? Must the animals have more freedom than we? It seems to me that the you-know-what given us by Nature for the preservation of the species should be worn as a pendant round our necks or a badge in our caps. It has created you, one of the first living surgeons: it has made me . . . it has brought forth . . . the Titians, the Michelangelos . . .

The second extract is from a letter to Michelangelo, written after Aretino decided that it would be good policy to make himself a leading figure in the public outcry against Michelangelo's *Last Judgement*:

> . . . even in lascivious and immodest matters I use well-chosen and decorous words and speak in terms both chaste and above reproach. And you, with a subject of such glorious history, display angels and saints without a vestige of earthly modesty and deprived of celestial ornament. Even the pagans, when they made statues – I do not mean a clothed Diana but a naked Venus – made her cover with a hand that which should not be seen, and here someone who claims to be a Christian, who holds art in higher regard than faith, considers it a royal spectacle to show indecorousness in virgins and martyrs as well as to show the damned dragged to hell by their genitals, a sight not fit even for a brothel.

Aretino had previously written a letter to Michelangelo containing gratuitous advice on how to treat the *Last Judgement*, and his advice had been ignored. Titian was more receptive of his friend's ideas, and it seems likely that it was Aretino _101_ who thought up the symbolic alibi for Titian's *Venus and the Organ Player*, based on Ficino's neoplatonic doctrine that the senses of sight and hearing were equally noble. With a hand still on the keyboard, the organ player turns to look at the female nude; the picture therefore celebrates the equality of seeing and hearing, through their most exalted expression in painting and music. (One can imagine Aretino cracking a joke about the player, whose eyes are fastened on the naked woman's middle, producing an organ swell.) The fountain in the background with water spurting from a jar on the head of a satyr is not intended to symbolize incontinence, and the fondling of a small dog by the woman is not supposed to refer to the sense of touch because, like the senses of taste and smell, it was merely physical and considered to have no connection with Mind or Spirit. We can be fairly confident, however, that when the music stops, the responsiveness of the organ player and the woman to one another will bring all the faculties of awareness into play; nose, mouth and hands will achieve an equality with eyes and ears – and there will be an emission, that the fountain does not symbolize, from the you-know-what. In other words, this is a painting of a man playing the organ to his mistress as a prelude to intercourse. The naked woman is as good-looking as Venetian women are always said to be, but she is not idealized into Venus, and she will go the way of all flesh. Her belly is already on the heavy side and Titian has not eliminated its natural sag. Her face is that of a woman well into her thirties. That Titian intended the nude to suggest a particular person in an erotic situation seems to be supported by the awkwardness produced in her posture by the propping up of her shoulders with an ill-placed cushion (as if she herself placed it as well as she could without drastically changing her position) and by the abandonment of the convention, started by Giorgione and copied by Titian in the *Venus of Urbino*, of gently and ambiguously shielding the crotch with a hand.

Goya must have known *Venus and the Organ Player*, which was in the Spanish royal collection, and he may have had in mind the propping up of the female _105_ figure when he posed the model for his *Naked Maja* in order to suggest the impending of an afternoon love bout. She is younger than the woman in the Titian, her body more slender and beautiful, and the glimpse of pubic hair and the absence of any mythological or allegorical excuse for painting a female nude was an erotic liberation all the more remarkable for occurring in inquisitorial Spain. After the painting of this picture, the game of idealizing the figure of woman to represent an assortment of virtues began to look ridiculous. The picture has a legendary association with the Duchess of Alba because of Goya's long and passionate love affair with her. The story is that the duke heard that his wife was posing in the nude for Goya and planned to catch them red-handed, but that Goya was warned of his intention and hastily produced a clothed version to account for her presence when the duke paid a sudden visit to the studio. The face in neither the clothed nor the naked version bears any resemblance to the duchess's, but the head in *Naked Maja* joins the body uncomfortably enough to have given some art historians the idea that it was painted later than the body, implying that a more distinguished face was originally intended. Alluring bodies, however, are not reserved for upper-class females, and it is my impression that Goya wanted to suggest that the girl had brought her head forward for a moment, whilst carefully maintaining her voluptuous pose, in acknowledgement of the arrival of her undepicted visitor.

In a burst of Venetian lyricism, Tintoretto during his final period paid loving tribute to the erogenous softness of woman's flesh, and his Vienna *Susanna and the Elders* is one of the first paintings of the female nude in which woman's touchableness is a striking attribute of the form. If he had given the volumes more weight, his *Susanna* would have been a foretaste of the art of Rubens, in which the vision of naked woman as a sublime totality of living warmth, and the technical virtuosity with which the weight, texture, resilience and even the animal smell of plump, healthy feminine substance is conveyed, have never been equalled. The desirability of Rubens's women is of an order in which the prospect of excitement is subsidiary to the promise of the subsequent lying together in utter peace and contentment. Renoir is the only painter who has come near to challenging his supremacy as a painter of flesh, but the fascinating procession of Renoir's nudes discloses an anxious awareness of the claims of classicism and, later, a pursuit of monumentality that turns his servant-girl models into a kind of slow-breathing earthenware. It retards the sense of woman as a haven, and compared with the nudes of Rubens, they are a little too obviously artefacts.

The promise of the warm aftermath of love is in some of Rembrandt's nudes, but they are more complicated beings than the Rubens nudes. They never look radiant and never look quite fresh. His *Bathsheba*, still naked after her bath, looks as if she will be more at ease when she is back in her heavy clothes and giving orders to the servants. Even his magnificent *Danaë* is, one feels, more anxious for security than for erotic adventure. To be ravished by the god will be remembered by her as one of life's little ironies when she goes about her daily chores. Nevertheless, she somehow reminds a man of that first startled encounter with feminine nakedness that is one of the turning-points in his life – that moment in which the sudden confrontation with the physicality of woman gives him no time to suppress a shiver of apprehension.

Visual images of plump women tend to be erotically innocuous. Plump women can certainly make exciting lovers in real life, and it is said that they make successful prostitutes because very young men feel less shy with them than with slim girls, and the sexually jaded scent the promise of grosser pleasure. In drawings and paintings they tend to arouse simply an amused tenderness as in Arthur Boyd's comic painting of plump lovers, or a sense of their 'otherness' that inspires awe rather than desire, as in the superb drawing by Rodin called *Three Boulders*.

104

The popular idea that Ingres was a perennial painter of plump nudes is not borne out by the facts. It is true that he was always careful to provide no sign of the bone structure, but his nudes were reasonably slender before he painted that fantasia of plumpness, *Le Bain Turc*, in the last year of his life. His greatest painting of the nude, the *Bather of Valpinçon*, was painted when he was twenty-eight years old. Degas was the first to point out that Ingres's great virtue was his ability to create soft, mellow spaces within the contours of the figure and charge them only slightly with details, and Ingres himself seems to have realized that the *Bather* exemplified the virtue to perfection, for he copied her twenty years later and put her in the foreground of a small painting called *Interior of a Harem*. She is an exact copy of the original, except that the robe over the left arm is knotted above the elbow in the *Bather*, and that the one defect of drawing – the treatment of the sole of her right foot – has, if anything, become more obvious. The back is as marvellously smooth and bland as before and the striped towelling is still twisted turban-like on the back of her head. Even her bed has been transported to the harem, and the sparkle of the white linen sheet has not been dimmed. The items of apparel and the sheet are given a cool, unstressed erotic value by the mere fact that her flesh is in contact with them. The other girls look like a hasty attempt to provide her with companions. Thirty-four years later, at the age of eighty-seven, Ingres returned to the harem theme, and made a last supreme effort to provide his Bather with suitable company. This time she is seated on the floor, and her left arm has been raised so that her hand can grasp the long shank of a musical instrument and at the same time reveal a breast which is significantly smaller than those of her companions. She is playing for a fantastic assembly of plump nudes, and her own belly now protrudes somewhat, to make her look more like 'one of them'. The picture succeeds as a composition and nearly succeeds in integrating the *Bather* by the young Ingres with the plump nudes of the old one. The music is sending the girls into romantic reveries; they stretch and coil and tangle together like fat cats, to form an astonishing community immersed in carnal longings. It is an old man's vision of feminine amplitude, an old man's solemn vision of Paradise.

107

Baudelaire declared that thinness is more naked and more indecent than plumpness, and although there is no call to describe them as indecent, there is no doubt that the most erotic images of women tend to extreme slenderness and are often unnaturally elongated. There is also a sense in which the concept of original sin is acknowledged, and its value as temptation and fall retained, in the process of creating an erotic ideal.

108

In a sixteenth-century illumination, in the Bibliothèque Nationale, which illustrates Theseus's desertion of Ariadne, the nude is still quaintly medieval, but the artist is struggling in an unsophisticated way and without sufficient objective knowledge of the human form to give seductive credibility to a conception of nakedness imbued with the idea of mankind's fall from grace. It was Lucas Cranach who achieved the perfect solution. His vision of Venus is the Gothic image of shame transfigured by erotic idealization. He was influenced by Italian Mannerism, but only used its elongations to impart dignity and beauty to a Northern tradition signifying the ugliness and indignity of nakedness.

Cranach was a close friend of Luther, and these slender nudes of his last period can be seen as a Lutheran victory over Puritanism, for they spring not from a purification of the senses but from a new-found confidence in them, sanctioned by the Reformation. He did not treat the nude realistically, nor did he turn it into an embodiment of noble proportions, but if there is a fundamental difference between nudity and nakedness, Cranach has somehow bridged the gap. His Venus *63* is as beautiful and unashamed in her nakedness as the classical Venus in her nudity. She belongs to a purely imaginary golden age in European history when women had small breasts which never sagged and soft ovoid bellies which only very slightly protruded; a time outside time when Nordic women walked the earth clad only in hats and necklaces and yet miraculously retained the pallor of a rarely exposed skin. The pale skin carries a deliberate reminder of the secrecy of the bedroom. It also implies that she comes from a secret world of inordinate dreams which involves the image of woman but which no woman can ever satisfy. She secularizes the notion of transcendence.

I think that the only other painter who has achieved an equally magical synthesis of the nude and the naked is Modigliani. John Russell seemed to confirm this view when he referred, in the catalogue of the Tate Gallery's Modigliani exhibition, to the 'majestic fullness' of the last phase – which includes the superb *Reclining Nude* in the Zeisler collection – where 'to be naked is no longer a con- *106* dition of anguish.' These are words which apply no less aptly to Cranach's transformation of the Gothic; it may seem a little strange to be praising a twentieth-century painter for achieving a victory already won in the sixteenth century, but the conquest of anguish is an important aspect of Modigliani's achievement precisely because the intensity of his erotic evaluation of the female figure seemed to clash with his no less compulsive search for pure form and involved him in an anguish of decision-making. His subtle and sumptuous revaluation of female anatomy gives mysterious exactitude to woman's ineffable promise. The Zeisler nude is an image created out of man's despairing eroticism: it is the dominating presence of a being forever absent, and I can think of no other great painting of the nude in which actuality and dream have come closer together.

He painted several versions of this reclining figure, and in most of them his disposal of the figure diagonally across the canvas, with the legs cut off above the knees by the canvas, brings her very close to the beholder and gives him the sense of actually leaning over her. The painter's early death from the effects of drugs and alcohol and the stories of his wild behaviour and his love-making give him biographical equality with Toulouse-Lautrec, but, unlike Lautrec, he did not make an identity for himself out of his milieu, and the most telling of all the anecdotes is the one that recounts his short, sharp meeting with Renoir. The old man had heard about Modigliani's nudes and began to talk to him in a banteringly lascivious manner about the advantages of painting from the living model. It made Modigliani so angry that he turned on his heel and left the room. If Renoir

126 (*Opposite*)
PARMIGIANINO
Pedro Maria Rossi at R

127 (*Left*)
TITIAN
Emperor Charles V

128 (*Opposite*)
URS GRAF
Soldier with two-handled
sword

129 (*Overleaf*)
PIETER BOUT
An amorous pair

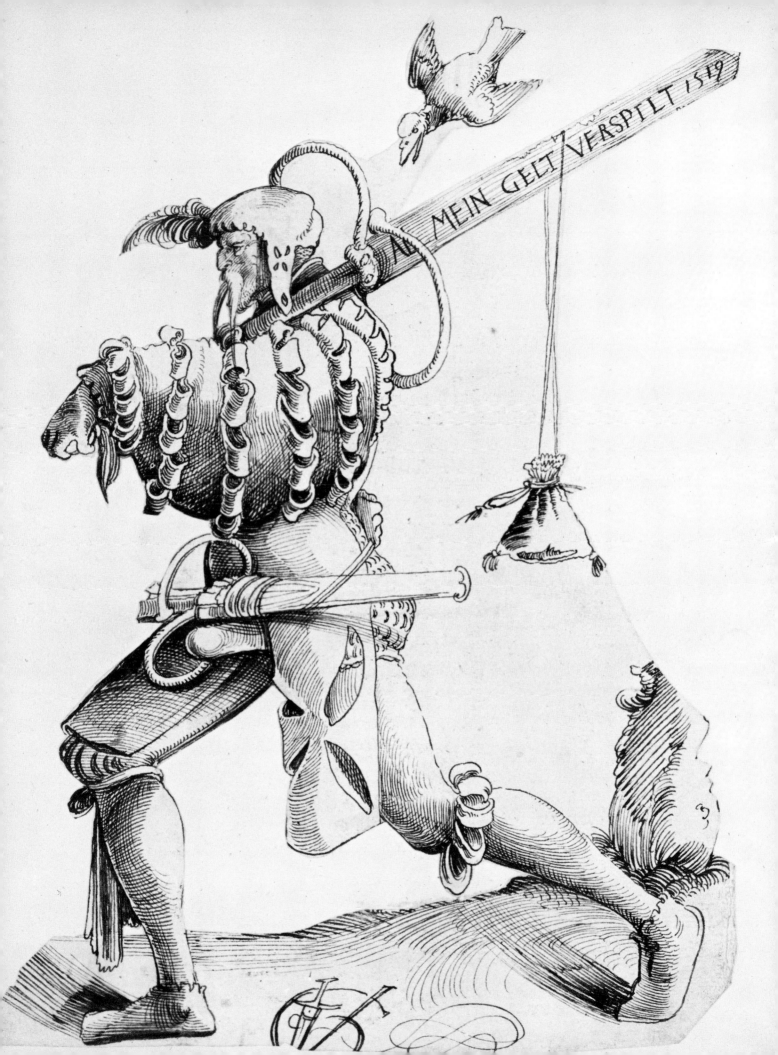

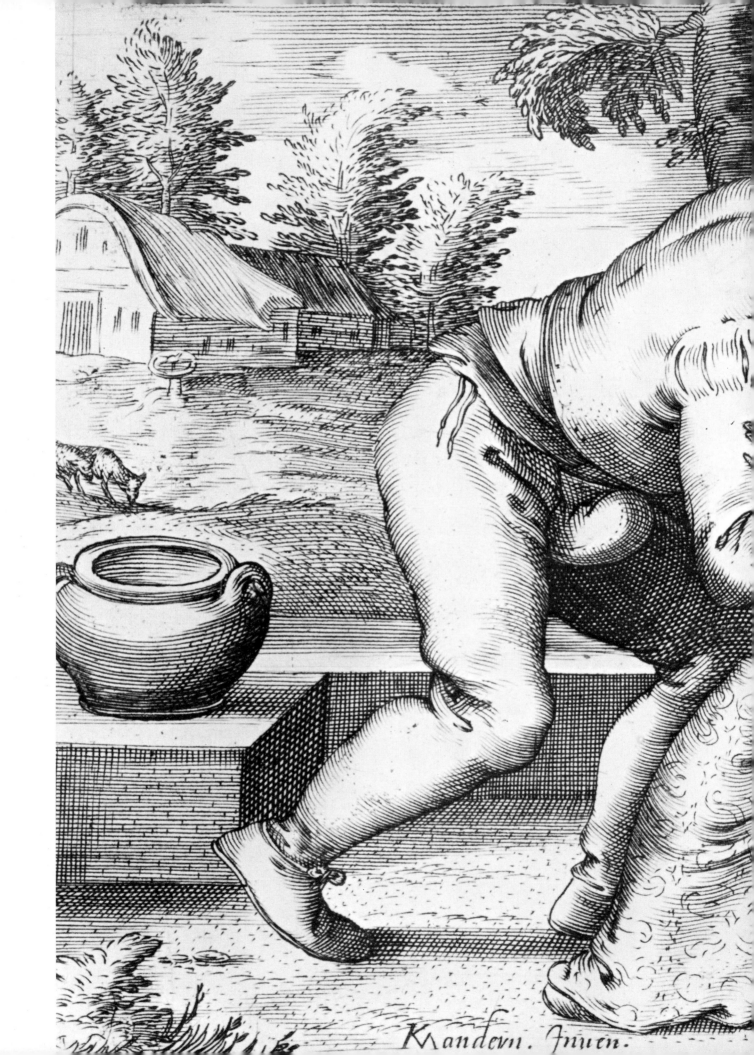

Mandevn. Jnuen.

Bveen. Schulptov.

130 (*Left*)
ROPS
Heart in hand

131 (*Left*)
Artist unknown
'More than half seas over'
'*Un anglais qui ne peut plus*'

132 (*Opposite*)
TITIAN
Allegory (Alfonso d'Este
and Laura Dianti?)

f. Boucher

133 (*Previous page*)
FRANÇOIS BOUCHER
Miss O'Murphy

134 (*Left*)
GOYA
Majas on a balcony

135 (*Opposite*)
VERMEER
At the procuress's

136 (*Above*)
ROWLANDSON
The spy glass

137 (*Left*)
GAYWOOD
Young man, harlot and
beldame

138 (*Far left*)
BROUWER
Tavern scene

139 (*Opposite*)
DEGAS
Monotype illustration for
La Maison Tellier

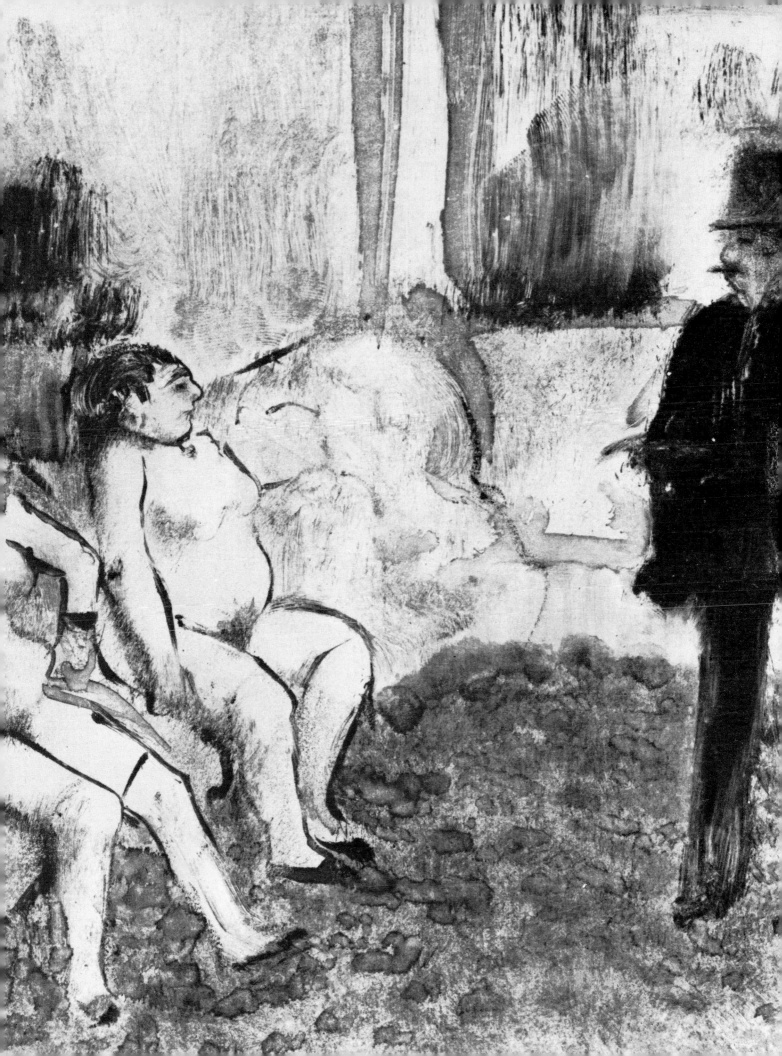

140 (*Left*)
ROPS
Street corner

141 (*Left*)
FERNANDO BOTERO
The house of Mariaduque

142 (*Opposite*)
FERNANDO BOTERO
Rosalba

143 (*Overleaf left*)
BEARDSLEY
Juvenal scourging Woman

144 (*Overleaf right*)
MAX ERNST
The robing of the bride

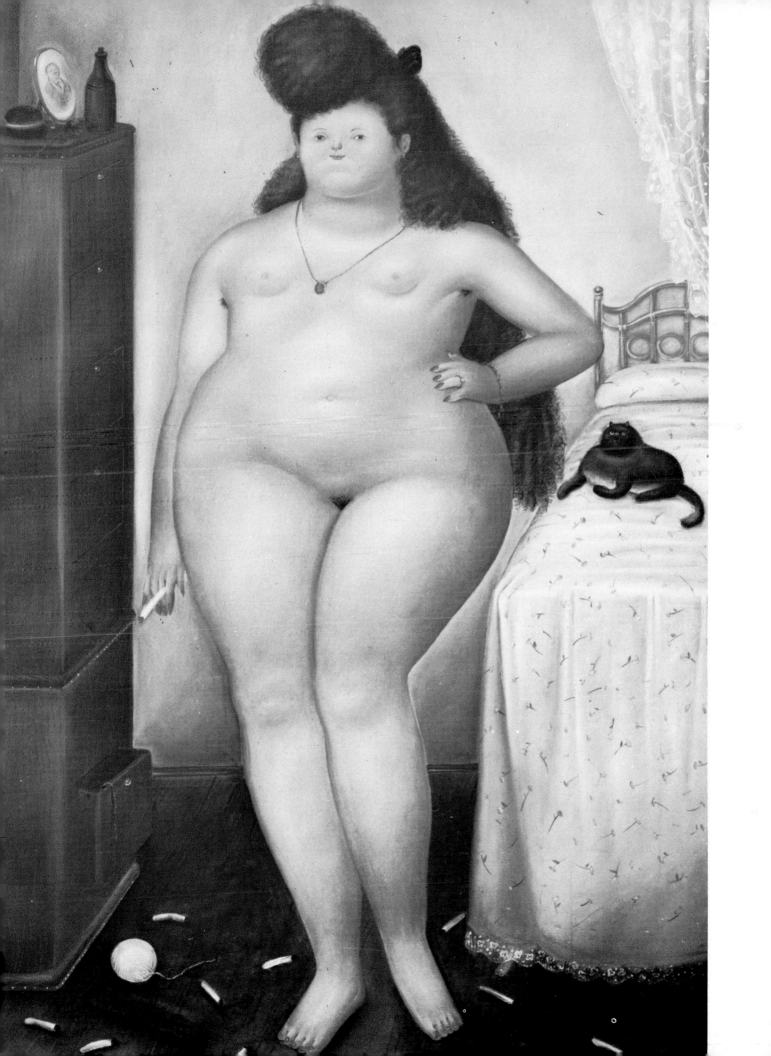

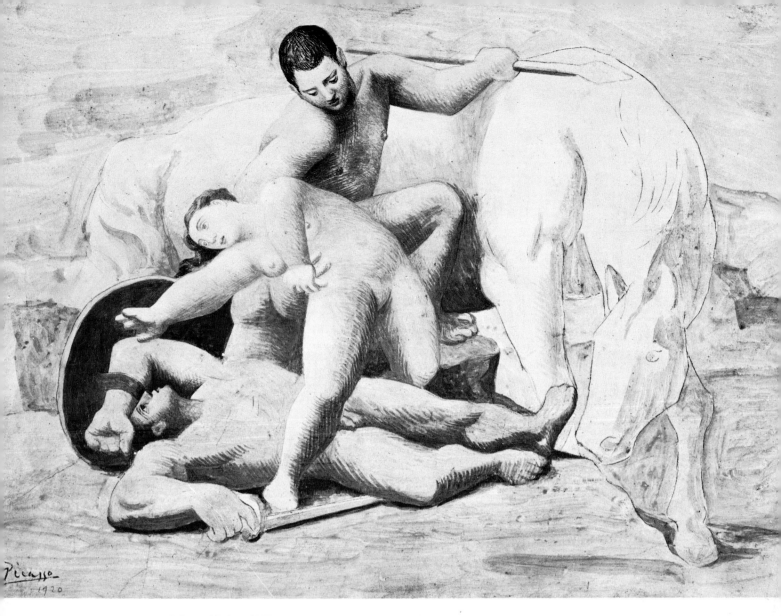

45 (*Opposite*)
ERRE KLOSSOWSKI
he beautiful woman from
ersailles

6 (*Above*)
CASSO
he rape

(*Right*)
GRAF
and the young Woman

(*Far right*)
S BELLMER
raved frontispiece for
nage

149 (*Previous page left*)
DELVAUX
Sleeping Venus

150 (*Previous page right*)
BALTHUS
Nude with cat

151 (*Left*)
CARACCI
Old men surprising a girl

152 (*Below*)
Hellenistic marble group of
a hermaphrodite with an
old satyr

53 (*Right*)
ETTY
Study for Pluto carrying
off Proserpine

54 (*Below*)
Artist unknown
Bacchus, satyr and nymph

55 (*Overleaf*)
School of Fontainebleau
Nymph and satyr

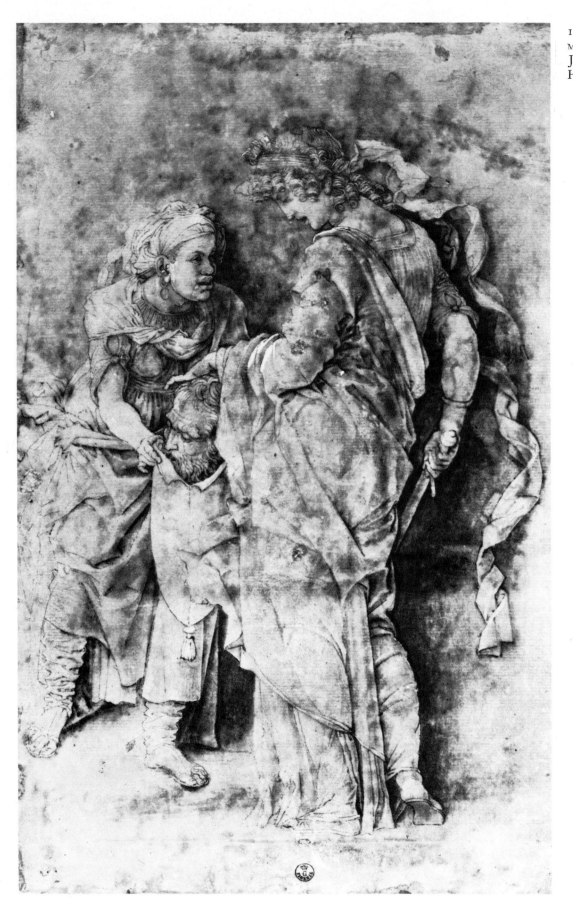

60 (*Opposite*)
AIRO
udith

61 (*Above*)
IERO DI COSIMO
Mythological subject (Death
f Procris)

62 (*Right*)
ERONESE
eath of Lucrece

63 (*Below*)
RANACH
eath of Lucrece

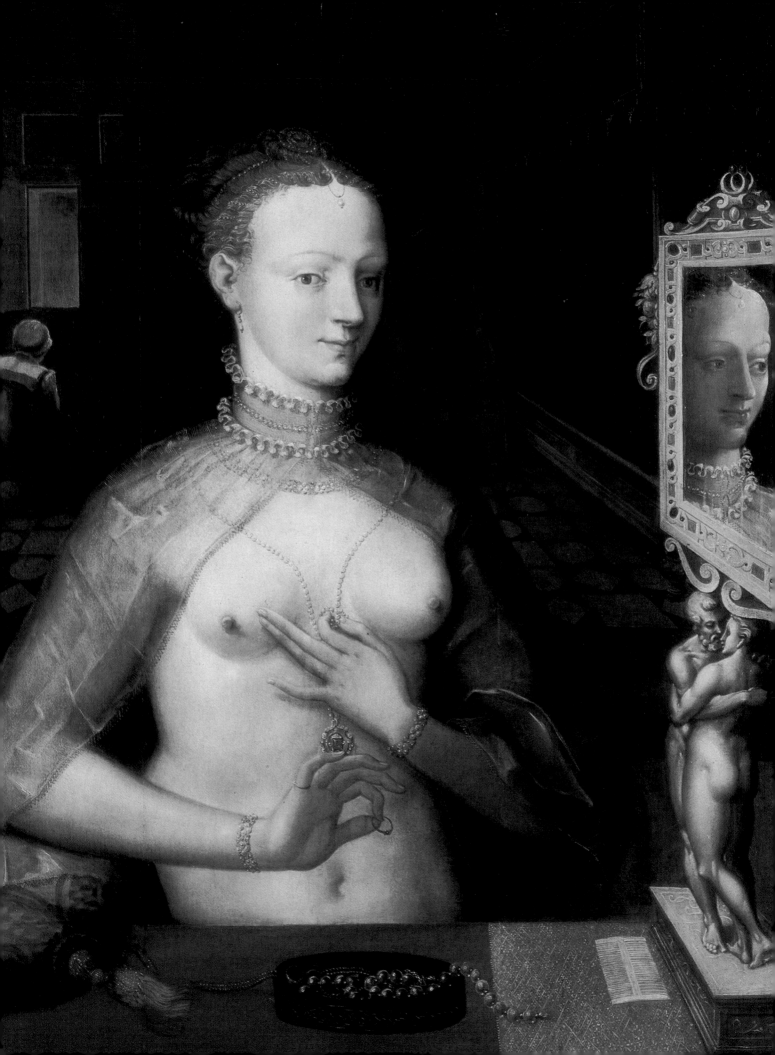

saw some of the nudes he must have been very puzzled indeed by Modigliani's reaction to his line of conversation, for they are more openly erotic than his own, and as one writer has quite justly remarked, they lie 'as if wanting to offer each limb in turn to the beholder'. There is nothing lascivious about them, but they seem to break a taboo because they are characterized by a purity that is totally amoral. They are immensely calm and stable, yet dedicated to vertiginous sensation.

Modigliani wanted to be a sculptor, but he was interested only in direct carving and the work taxed his declining strength too severely. A caryatid and a few stone heads are all he left to us, but they are enough to convince us that we lost a great sculptor. The dealer Paul Guillaume said that it was Modigliani's intention to build a temple in honour of humanity, in which his carvings would have played an integral part. There were to be hundreds of caryatids, which he called 'colonnes de tendresse'. He wouldn't have wanted anything to 'go on' in his temple except a quickening of the pulse, some lovers' meetings and maybe a deepening of the sense of the validity of the will to form.

Among Baudelaire's 'consoling maxims on love' there is this: 'If the fat woman is sometimes a charming caprice, the thin woman is a well of sombre delights!'. He associated feminine thinness with lasciviousness, and when he declared that the certainty of doing Evil was the supreme pleasure of lovemaking, he had in mind a plunge into the 'well of sombre delights'. The Decadents even thought of leanness as the beauty of spiritual corruption, as a sort of basically evil construction that engendered incomparable excitements by virtue of its own intensity. We now have to make love without the spiritual uplift that goes with a sense of wrongdoing, but the association of sin with thinness still lurks at the back of the mind to determine our sense of beauty. Georges Bataille seems especially relevant on this point:

The erotic value of feminine forms seems to me to be bound up with the absence of the natural heaviness that suggests the physical use of the limbs and the necessity for the framework of bone: the more ethereal the shapes and the less clearly they depend on animal reality or on human physiological reality, the better they respond to the fairly widespread image of the desirable woman.

It could be a description of the apparitional images of women in the Art Nouveau of Toorop and Klimt. Klimt's painting of two unbelievably thin and
64 elongated girls illustrates Bataille's continuation of the passage already quoted from his long, sustained study of eroticism: 'The image of the desirable woman as first imagined would be insipid and unprovocative if it did not at the same time also promise or reveal a mysterious animal aspect, more momentously suggestive. The beauty of the desirable woman suggests her private parts, the hairy ones, to be precise, the animal ones. Instinct has made sure that we shall desire these parts. But above and beyond the sexual instinct, erotic desire finishes up by exasperating desire and exalting the animal parts.' Like the extreme aspects of Mannerism, Klimt's two girls bear the marks of perversity, quite apart from any presumption of Lesbianism provoked by the embrace. They are closed off from us by their intimacy, but it is intended as an additional provocation. They do not invite tenderness. They are in a sense a ceremonial offering, but what they have to offer is hidden and they invite transgression. One notes with cold satisfaction

that the arms are too weak to offer resistance. The girls are tempting us to crack them open, as if they are sacred vessels and we their appointed iconoclasts. The effect is supported by Klimt's use of gold in his intricate decorative patterning, which gives the picture an almost Byzantine splendour.

In *Danaë*, which is another of his decorative masterpieces, the figure is not *67* elongated, but her beauty and posture evoke with astonishing intensity the desirability of her undepicted 'animal parts'. She is curled up asleep, all resounding curves and innocent enticement, and the strands of her bright auburn hair fall across her pearly face and shoulder, and lap against her equally pearly breast like lacquered Chinese waves. It is Art Nouveau preciosity at its fantastically inventive best, and although modern painters pride themselves on being the very opposite of the precious, the astonishing thing about Klimt's elaborate decorative detail is the persistence with which it brings to mind the composition and textures of the free abstractionists. An obvious instance is the treatment of the shower of gold in which Zeus hides his identity from Danaë. It has been treated by Klimt as the god's spermatozoa and is an intricate raised pattern of little discs and hooks and twigs which look like a gilded version of Dubuffet's mud language.

Contemporary examples of thinness and elongation taken to perverse lengths are to be found in the art of the German printmaker, Horst Janssen. He com- *110* bines emaciation with ambiguous cruelties to create images of erotic ferocity. He calls them 'lustful little sybils . . . full of decay, yet elegant sketches in sil-houette'. It is a valiant attempt to create a female nude capable of competing with the power of alcohol, LSD, and various kinds of hooliganism to 'send' us.

We can return for a moment to the seventeenth century, to retrieve a sense of the raffish element in normal, natural thinness. In Tiepolo's lovely drawing of *109* nymphs irritating a dolphin, the nymphs with their straggling hair, their delinquent faces and their restless sinister charm look capable enough of snatching the souls of men.

4 The Toilet

The Bath

For most of our waking lives we are heads – eating, drinking, listening, talking, thinking heads, with interferences from below, and if the interferences are intermittent we tend to count ourselves fortunate. The well-known story of the officer in a small Indian regiment who farted on parade and instantly committed suicide is an extreme example of our horror of the body's spontaneities; nevertheless, we are inclined to think of our bodies as, so to speak, mentally backward. 'We' use polite language; our bodies emit only animal noises, and we feel compelled to treat them as cunning and unruly children. They cannot even keep themselves clean! However, it is when we are submitting them to total immersion for the purpose of cleansing them that our bodies appear to belong to our heads. In the bath we look somewhat like a printed page, with a short paragraph of text at the top followed by a very long footnote. If the temperature of the water is right and its smell agreeable, head and body can be lulled into an illusion of oneness. It is this illusion, rather than the act of cleansing, that accounts for the legends and myths in which eternal youth is conferred by immersion in the waters of a magic fountain.

113 Bosch seemed to be making use of this legend when he placed a bathing pool in the centre of *The Garden of Terrestrial Delights*. Every human figure in the centre panel is youthful, and although a side panel is devoted to Hell, to remind us that the artist is only day-dreaming, it evidently gave him great pleasure to imagine a state of being in which erotic excesses had no evil consequences. Bosch's garden had no walls, and to show that his dream embraced the whole world he included some black-skinned figures in the company.

112 The subject of a stilted yet enchanting sixteenth-century illustration, showing a walled garden in the heart of a city, may be the fountain of eternal youth, but more probably it is the treatment rather than the subject that is mythical, for it could be intended as a pictorial description of one of the communal open-air bathing establishments which were already fashionable in the previous century. If, as seems likely, it exaggerates the charm of the place, it possibly served the same purpose as the cover of a brochure advertising the facilities of a private

club. The atmosphere of refined and tender sensuality is certainly appealing.

Hans Bock's open-air bathhouse is much more realistic. An interesting feature *115* is the table for light refreshments placed in the middle of the pool. Surrounded only by a fence, the pool is surprisingly open to the public gaze. It has been sited in a lonely spot in the countryside, but has nevertheless attracted a couple of locals and a travelling man. Their voyeuristic interest in the scene is undisguised, and one of them is drawing the attention of another to the naked man in a turban who is removing the last bit of drapery from a woman. She is putting up a show of shyness by pressing against the naked back of a man who is pouring wine for the woman wearing a hat and a necklace. The turbanned man would seem to be in charge of the bathhouse and is probably its 'leading spirit'. When he has removed the last vestige of clothing from the woman who is being coy, he will no doubt persuade the woman in the hat to dispense with the piece of cloth that covers her pubic hair. The bathers may well be members of a heretical cult of the kind referred to in Fraenger's *The Millennium of H. Bosch*, which advocated and practised nudity and free love as the means by which the human soul could establish a harmonious relationship with Nature. It is evident that membership is not confined to the young and beautiful. Music and the drinking of wine, as in the scene in the walled garden, are inducing the women to relax, and the artist has made obvious use of the musical instruments to symbolize erection. A couple just behind the two foreground figures are examining an open book which is perhaps a collection of love poems or an apologia for the cult. The man takes advantage of his position to fondle the woman's breast.

The indoor bathing establishment illustrated on a page of a fifteenth-century *111* manuscript is possibly a sudatorium, but the massive wooden structure into which most of the figures are crowded appears to be constructed to contain water. A long table runs down the middle, and the animated group of figures gathered round it is enjoying a light repast. The humid and scented air combines with the luxurious service and appointments to provide a perfect atmosphere for sexual indulgences, and it is clear that this is not only a bathing establishment but a high-class brothel. One couple is already in bed, with wine conveniently placed on a side table, and at least four other couples are leaving the bath to celebrate in the same way. A fully-clothed couple has appeared at the far end of the chamber, and the man has the tentative look of someone who has not been there before. If the establishment provides the women, it would seem that there are times when they are sent out to find well-heeled clients.

One would like to know the background of De Bry's anecdotal engraving in *117* which two naked girls are forcibly divesting a jester of his clothes with the intention of making him share the bath with one of them. The fact that his genitals are already exposed leaves one in no doubt that the joke is sexual. The jester has perhaps been boasting of his sexual prowess, and the girls intend to put his virility to the test. He is not a young man, and apart from his possible distaste for washing, the fear that he might not pass the test would account for his consternation. The girls are probably servants at a big house, and the provision of a bathtub for them in the garden seems to indicate that their mistress or master expects them to keep their bodies fresh.

Bathing on one's own, behind a locked door, makes one's own body a peculiarly enigmatic and interesting object, and one would like to be able to emulate the Dali nude who has turned her torso into a chest of drawers and opens one drawer after another to examine its wet and glistening contents. Although the drawers remain open, Dali does not allow us to see what is in them, and one gathers from his own remarks about the very beautiful drawing I have in mind that they do not imply a visceral rummage but illustrate the idea that she is engaged in a systematic sniffing at her own parts. He says that they illustrate 'a certain complacency in smelling the narcissistic odour of each of our drawers'. With the play on words in mind, I think that the drawing, made in 1936, may have been inspired by the scene in *The Blue Angel* (1930) where Marlene Dietrich, halfway up a spiral staircase, took off her drawers and threw them down to Emil Jannings, who rapturously buried his face in them: it could have occurred to Dali that Marlene might have been no less interested in their odour than Emil.

114 The late nineteenth-century painting of a woman in her bathtub, by Alfred Stevens, is not as curious and inventive as the Dali drawing, but it has some peculiarities. To begin with, although she is almost entirely immersed she is still wearing an undergarment. This cannot be due to an excess of prudence on the part of the artist because only the beginning of the rise of her breasts is visible above the side of the bath, but we are certainly expected to notice the straps of the garment still in place over her shoulders. The open book on a pile of clothing beside the bath indicates that at one point she was reading and that she has been in the water for a considerable time. The clock in the soapdish suggests that she has her eye on the time and is taking a bath before dressing to keep an appointment. Yet the final impression created by the roses in her hand and the look of drowsy reverie in her eyes is that the appointment has already been kept, and that she is in no state to notice or care whether she has taken off everything before immersing herself. The oddly shaped waterpipe poised like a muscular invertebrate ready to strike may be intended to emblemize the nature of her reverie.

Underclothes

Images of women in their underclothes became a popular subject of painting during the second half of the nineteenth century. They were a reaction against the absurd bits of classical drapery that came from nowhere to hang round the loins of academic nudes. Long before that, of course, artists were demonstrating that a peep under the dress could be more erotic than nakedness. Urs Graf who was not given to hiding the nature of his interest in women, liked to depict them in the act of drawing up their skirts and found some slender excuses for the display, as in the engraving of a woman raising her dress well above her knees to
122 cross a stream which just covers her ankles. In *Prostitute with Scales*, the woman is presumably raising her skirt to signify her profession, but if some art historian has given the engraving its title I do not know how he can tell that some of the women who pull up their skirts are prostitutes and others are not. The meaning of the scales is obscure. The woman is balancing one of the artist's initials against the other and 'G' for Graf is heavier than 'U' for Urs. The imbalance is keeping

the scale's pointer out of its slot, and if by any chance the pointer represents the artist's penis, it must mean that he will only have intercourse with the woman if the two sides of him come to an agreement; but it is difficult to imagine that this tough and brutal soldier-draughtsman might be in two minds about taking her. In another design, by the same master, the person holding a chalice is obviously *120* emblematic and is said to represent Venus. If this is true, he has turned Cupid into a devil with a tail and has arranged for the wind to blow up the goddess's dress and reveal the part of her that so often before or since has been covered by a hand or a bit of drapery. The wind emerging from her chalice is no doubt rushing off to flap the skirts of female mortals. Venus does not of course wear drawers, nor, it seems, did English women until the middle of the nineteenth century, for if taken short in town or country they could slip into an alley or behind a hedge and relieve themselves simply by standing with their legs wide apart.

Showing a leg was a cliché of the boudoir eroticism of eighteenth-century French painting, and a set of petticoats drawn up high enough to disclose a garter is about all we ever see of what the women wore underneath. But nineteenth-century artists were not as intrepid as one might have expected. Manet's charming *Nana*, in blue stays and white petticoat, looks almost over-dressed, although the painting was refused by the 1877 salon as an outrage against morality. Félicien Rops showed women in various stages of undress, but scarcely touched on the sado-masochistic possibilities of the whalebone corset in his sexual fantasies. By far the most important painting of a woman in a tight-laced corset is Seurat's portrait of his plump mistress, called *Woman Powdering Herself*, where it becomes a noble architectural cladding. It is a painting that tends to confuse aesthetes. Roger Fry, for instance, came to the conclusion that it is a work in which 'the element of illustration drops out altogether and becomes irrelevant', but not before he had been horrified by the image of an 'impossible woman, in the grotesque déshabillé of the eighties'. Seurat, however, painted her as if he valued her as a highly desirable sexual object, and it must have given him infinite pleasure to watch her undress and begin to expand as she loosened the lacing of her armour.

Twentieth-century painters have been given the opportunity of exploiting the erotic charm of underwear in a closer relationship to the natural figure. German painters are particularly sensitive to the arousal value of underclothes, and the effectiveness of some of their images is due to the heartlessness in their treatment of women as sexual objects. George Grosz scarcely bothered to hide the satanic eroticist lurking behind the satirist. Bullet-headed Prussian officers and fat war profiteers infest the drawings in his *Ecce Homo* and are accompanied by young prostitutes. There are no young men and the implication is that they have all been sacrificed to the war machine. Grosz shows his hatred of the whores by giving them cruel, painted faces, but his treatment of their bodies puts them among the champagne and roast chicken as the good things denied the young men, and he makes brilliant use of the transparencies of Cubism and Futurism to present his whores as fully clothed nudes. Horst Janssen's treatment of the female figure always ensures that our response will be purely and unsentimentally sexual. In his print *Efi*, the slack leather belt encircling the loins of a naked girl like the *110* holster belt of a cowboy would be an incitement to attempt monstrous practices if there were an actual confrontation. Beckmann's art has a brutal side to it. He was not averse to thinking up scenes of torture and calamity, and a number of his images – women tied-up, bound to stakes, kept in cages – are fantasies of sexual domination. All his paintings of women are boldly erotic and he somehow managed to convey the impression that the models were his personal property.

118   The woman asleep in a yellow corslet is a notable example of his work, much less violent than many of his paintings, but typical of his style, with its black outlines and the paint gleaming wetly as if freshly licked. The book on the table, beside the apples and the champagne, is Stendhal's *Essai sur l'Amour*. Kirchner's spiky Expressionism achieved equally effective images of undress. His picture of a

121   woman bunched up on a low stool, patting the back of her hair and looking into a tilted mirror that does not reflect her image correctly, owes all its allure to the lovely passage of paint devoted to the flashing white corslet. But it cannot be called a victory of style over content; all that has happened is that the corslet stands in for the woman as an object of desire. The Parisian painter, Kees van Dongen,

119   discloses in his painting of a girl in a black chemise, with eyes blackened to match, a softer, warmer eroticism than that of the German painters.

The American painter William Copley has close connections with the Surrealists and possesses an important collection of Surrealist paintings and objects. As a collector, he is refined and sophisticated; as a painter he has thrown his sophistication to the winds. His pictures illustrate Oscar Wilde's contention that simplicity is the last refuge of the complex. The antecedents of Copley's girls are the wood nymphs, but whereas the nymphs went about naked the girls are at

123   their most natural in their foundation garments. Then again, the nymphs were the natural prey of the satyrs, but when these girls wander into the street they are chased by the cops. And in one way they are more like satyrs than nymphs; they are a new kind of hybrid and perhaps, like Venus who sprang fully formed from the seed of Uranus after his testicles fell into the sea, they came forth in their bras and suspender belts as the issue of a drop of sperm that fell on to an advertisement in a woman's magazine.

The Parisian painter, Leonor Fini, who, like Copley, has strong connections with the Surrealists, has rediscovered the railway carriage as an erotic terrain. In the chapter on 'Crimes against the Person' in his comprehensive account of Victorian sexuality, Ronald Pearsall points out that, before the introduction of the corridor train, the railway carriage could provide ideal conditions for sexually assaulting a girl travelling alone. These were: 'no means of immediate access for rescuers; the fact of a man being alone with a young woman he did not know; the darkness of a tunnel (lit railway carriages were rare)!' By the same token, it was an ideal place of assignation for a couple having an illicit affair, and equally suitable for a love bout between mutually attracted strangers, provided the stations were few and far between and other travellers could be kept out of the

210   compartment. Augustus Egg's two lovely girls were travelling in just such a compartment, and a few years ago, Leonor Fini paid homage to Egg's master-

90   piece in a delightful painting in which two girls of our own time sat facing one another in similar circumstances, although their relationship was rather more ambiguous. The picture takes us into pure fantasy, for the situation is presented in a railway carriage specifically designed for erotic adventures. The blind is

down and reveals a frieze of cupids dancing against a summer sky. The girl, whilst enclosing her unisex lover between her legs, graciously assumes the air of a victim and has neatly freed one breast from her corslet to imply that it has been forcibly uncovered. A set of cool triangles formed by stocking tops and pale skin refers our attention to her secret triangle of golden hair.

The intensity of Egon Schiele's stare at the living model turns into the hungry tangibility of his drawings and rises from the lines and touches of colour like a wave of heat. Looking outwards at the object of desire, and taking entire possession of it in his forms, does not mitigate the expression of his own inner turmoil. Sometimes, in an extravagance of desire, his eyes batter at the flesh until it is bruised or flayed, and when bits of underwear are added they look like a sauce poured over doubtful meat. In the splendid drawing of a woman lying on her back *95* with her knees in the air the flesh is unharmed, and instead her knickers, ignited by the artist's obsessive interest in what they cover, have become a linear conflagration. They are a blossoming of the vagina into a wildness of crisp petals, and he has placed their function beyond any fumble or pry. They are more living than the flesh, and they give the drawing a kind of elevation – but not in terms either of gymnastics or nobility; more in the sense of a bloodstained sword raised in triumph.

Bellmer takes the idea of underwear as an extension of the flesh even farther. By interpreting textures obtained from the automatic process known as decalcomania he has created for a girl in striped stockings a pair of lacy drawers which *124* look as if a series of discharges has formed a cladding of stratified and petrified matter; in a sense it is what Germaine Greer has called 'the great vaginal odour story' transformed into a poetic concretion.

Miss Greer had a strong case when she told the National Press Club in Washington that the vaginal odour joke had been used by deodorant manufacturers to frighten women into squirting all kinds of stuff on themselves 'to stop them from being so offensive'. For some reason, most males are ashamed to admit that the musky smell of the vagina excites them, and the kipper has long been consecrated for Englishmen as a symbol for the vagina. When the International Surrealist Exhibition was held in London in 1936, a well-known composer hung a kipper on a spoke projecting from a Miró relief, and because of the kipper's long association with dirty jokes about women this was the only thing in the exhibition that the intellectuals of the period could appreciate. The painter Allen Jones has created an image closer to the average male's unadmitted association of the vaginal odour with the smell of the musk-rose, by situating the feminine fork at the heart *99* of a canvas shaped like an abstract bouquet.

The Mask

It was on the opening day of the International Surrealist Exhibition of 1936 that a girl with her face hidden by a mask of red roses walked about among the guests, and a photograph of her in this guise, her entire head seemingly replaced by a mass of flowers, was taken in Trafalgar Square and reproduced on the cover of the bulletin issued as a memento of the show. Masks, of course, have been worn at ceremonies and festivals for many thousands of years throughout the world, and in eighteenth-century Venice it became a customary item of wear for the upper classes when appearing in public. The Venetian genre painter, Pietro Longhi, and his followers, painted innumerable pictures of well-dressed men and women, wearing masks at various functions, or in the piazza, or in gambling houses, convent parlours and coffee houses, or mingling with the crowds to listen to the quacks and showmen in the arcades of the Doge's Palace. These masks appear to be of two kinds, more or less standardized: white masks with beakish noses attached to loose black hoods falling over the shoulders, or black masks with flattened features, attached to white hoods. Some writers claim that they served simply to facilitate flirtatious conversations, but it is difficult to imagine that the many courtesans in the city did not take advantage of this fascinating convention to put casual and anonymous meetings to more profitable use.

Two years after the girl in the mask of roses appeared in Trafalgar Square, a corridor of twenty wax models treated by various artists to represent their ideas about sex appeal was included in a Surrealist exhibition held in Paris. The most striking of these exhibits was by André Masson. The head of his wax model was in a wicker cage and the lower half of the face gagged with a band of black velvet. The rest of the model was naked except for a 'G' string of glass eyes.

But the most remarkable outcome of this period of Surrealist mannequins is Max Ernst's *The Robing of the Bride*, which he painted in 1940. The huge red owl-mask of downy feathers looks like a ferocious variation on the mask of roses, and it is attached to a cloak which may have been suggested by the Peruvian mantle of tiny feathers in his own collection. It brings to mind the description in André Breton's essay, *Beauty will be Convulsive*, of a cape called 'The Emperor's Mantle' in the Fairy Grotto at Montpellier, 'whose drapery forever defies that of statuary, and which a spot-light covers with roses, as though determined that it should be in no way inferior to that other, and none the less splendid and convulsive, mantle made of the infinite repetition of the unique little red feathers of a rare bird, which is worn by Hawaiian chieftains'.

One eye of the bride peers out of the mask at a much lower level than the glass eyes set above it and reinforces the impression created by the armed bird-man guard that she is a prisoner and a victim, about to be subjected to sexual practices which will end in her death. Every detail in the picture points to an eretomaniacal ritual which has been repeated many times, always with a new bride. Perhaps the picture inspired the last chapter in *The Story of O*, when O appeared at a candle-lit ball, naked except for an owl mask that entirely covered her head, led by a little girl in black, on a leash slipped through a ring attached to O's genitals.

The Codpiece

In none of the enthusiastic accounts of Titian's first portrait of Charles v have I found any mention of the detail which is so striking a feature of the painting that it is the first thing that meets the eye. It is the emperor's metallic codpiece, gleaming in the very centre of the composition. It has emerged from the shadowiness at the fork of the legs, and its convexity is defined by a pale golden highlight running down the middle. The painting is considered to be a copy of the portrait of the emperor painted by Jakob Seisenegger in 1532, and is much finer than the original. Panofsky has pointed out that full-length portraits were so rarely painted by Italian artists that this full-length by Titian was preceded by only two known examples, one of which is Carpaccio's *Portrait of a Knight* in the Thyssen collection; and, as it happens, Carpaccio's young knight has an equally striking codpiece. He is wearing a full suit of armour, and the codpiece, made of a surprisingly soft material and coloured bright red, comes out from between the metal thigh plates in a way that would make it a conspicuously vulnerable target in combat; a slit in the side provides a space for documents, and the edge of what may be a love-letter is showing.

If the codpiece had a protective function, it survives in modern times as the jockstrap worn underneath the shorts of boxers and players of various ball-games: but the fact that it was worn on the outside meant that a well-dressed Renaissance man expected it to make a contribution to the elegance of his attire and at the same time serve as evidence, true or false, of his virility. The Seisenegger portrait of Charles v was based on direct studies from the life, made when the emperor went to Bologna to meet Pope Clement vii, and the codpiece is likely to have been an exact copy of one that he actually wore. It looks like a plump sausage, and Titian has greatly improved its shape by making it look more like the beak of a large bird. He seems to have retained the vertical and horizontal lines engraved on the surface of the Seisenegger codpiece, but his more painterly treatment partially obscures them. (They are purely decorative but were probably suggested by the seams of the leather specimens which were in more general use.) Titian's codpiece brilliantly conveys the impression that the sexual organs it covers are of very superior quality.

The Mannerist painter, Parmigianino, treated the codpiece rather less circumspectly in his portrait of Count San Secondo. With this portrait in mind, Arnold *126* Hauser has remarked that Parmigianino created 'a new psycho-physiological human type, more delicate, more highly bred, more cultivated, with more highly developed nervous reactions, more thin-skinned and vulnerable by nature than that of his predecessors, but also more capable of and more eager for pleasure'. He makes no mention of the astonishingly belligerent codpiece, and perhaps finds it an acceptable emblem of the count's eagerness for pleasure; but it is a curiously indelicate attachment to a gentleman of such refinement.

The Titian codpiece clearly allows room for the penis to extend, but is designed to hide any sign of stiffening by preventing it from rising. The Parmigianino is quite another matter. It is not a metal shield; it appears to be a bag made of reinforced linen, and one would like to know whether it was made to remain permanently in the position in which it is represented in the portrait, even when the penis inside it was small and limp (in which case, the artist may have been making a reference to the phalluses which actors in ancient Greece strapped round their waists), or whether it was flexible enough to rise and fall in response to the movements of the penis.

If the position was fixed, it is difficult to imagine that it was a usual item of the count's apparel since it amounts in appearance almost to what is called indecent exposure. On the other hand, if it was flexible, it means that the count has been deliberately depicted with his penis in erection. But its grossness is out of character with the painter's preciosity and refined eroticism, and I think its inclusion in the portrait must have been stipulated by the sitter. I think that the portrait was intended either for the boudoir of a mistress or for a private room in which the count entertained a circle of libertines. For everyone's pleasure, it has found its way to the Prado.

The count's codpiece is a beautifully made version of a kind that is familiar enough in studies of the lower classes, especially in northern Europe. They are to be seen in almost all of Bruegel's pictures of peasants, though only as unsightly bulges and never in what might be termed the rampant position. But in Bout's engraving, in which the lady from the big house discloses her taste for the peasantry, the man's codpiece is raised as high as the count's, but less ambiguously. The only question is whether such codpieces ever served as contraceptive sheaths.

Urs Graf's wandering soldiers were never without a leather codpiece jutting out between the plates of their armour. More often than not he drew a head-on view, so that what we see is a knob-like form with a seam down the middle which suggests the mouth of the penis. When he drew the side-view it looked like a club, an additional weapon. He was himself a hardened mercenary soldier; his drawings disclose a delight in infamy and a contempt for women; he was not the sort of man to forgo any opportunity for pillage and rape, and it would be natural for him to think of his penis as a weapon. His taste for emblematic design turned his weapons into emblems of the penis. In the drawing of a mercenary carrying his heavy sword over his shoulder, the worn edge symbolizes a life of slaughter and incontinence, and the bag hanging from it suggests the auto-eroticist's playful use of the hardened penis as a bracket.

5 Sexual Readiness

The Tate Gallery's catalogue of foreign paintings tells us that Paul Delvaux painted *La Vénus Endormie* in Brussels in 1944, when the Germans were attacking *149* the city with flying bombs. This information implies that the picture reflects something of the atmosphere of anxiety in which it was painted and no doubt accounts for the skeleton and for the agitated figures in the background. At the same time, he must have felt that skeletons made a nice contrast to his well set-up girls; a skeleton or two appeared in almost every picture he painted in 1944. Delvaux himself has said that he gave the content of *La Vénus Endormie* 'a certain mysterious and intangible disquiet', which is perhaps another way of saying that he eroticized his anxiety. The sleeping nude is lying on an antique divan in a moonlit public square surrounded by classical temples. A dressmaker's black dummy and a skeleton stand at one end of the divan, and a naked girl stands at the other, raising a protesting hand. Considered as an erotic fantasy, the situation seems reasonably clear. The dressmaker's dummy is a living object and has been given the role of procuress. She is offering the sleeping girl to her client, the skeleton, who has not yet decided whether to accept the unconscious invitation in the posture of Venus asleep or yield to the objections of Venus awake.

The treatment of the encounter between Death and the Maiden is not always so equivocal. Urs Graf drew a skeleton with genitals and the skeleton cups them gleefully in his hand-bones as he creeps up behind the unsuspecting girl. Munch calls one of his prints *Maiden and Death* to underline the fact that the girl is seducing the skeleton; she presses luxuriously against his thigh bones, and covers the teeth in his skull with a kiss. Goya, in his *Disasters of War*, dispensed with a skeleton, and gave top place on a deathcart heaped with carcasses, to a naked girl, spreading her legs to give a macabre invitation of sexual readiness.

The skeletons in Delvaux's paintings do not approach the girls and appear not to be interested in them, but as symbols of Death their presence constitutes a threat. From time to time, a human male turns up among the nudes but never discloses the slightest inclination to interfere with them. The indifference of these males is so marked that the only conclusion to be drawn is that they are impotent, and would not be allowed into the canvases if they were otherwise. Delvaux is as vigilant in this respect as a sultan taking a new attendant into his harem.

Delvaux's attitude to the girls in his fantasies is partly devotional, partly proprietorial. Their sensuality is not moderate, but it usually assumes a protective impassivity. There are many of them but they represent an endless celebration of the face and figure of one woman and bring to mind Rubens's preoccupation with the face and figure of Hélène Fourment, his young second wife, who posed for all the goddesses in his late mythologies. Delvaux too discovered goddesses, or at any rate nymphs, in the spectacle of one woman's nakedness. Her image has populated his paintings since 1936; he must know her physical attributes better than the back of his hand, and it is more than likely that he no longer works from the model, so there is a sense in which this woman has escaped into his canvases to remain forever young. It was much the same with Bonnard: the many dazzling paintings of a woman in a bathroom which he painted in his old age reflect his ageing wife's neurotic fear of not being clean, but the figures in the pictures are images of his wife when young.

At one time Delvaux was a respectable landscape painter, and the predominant influence on his decision to become a painter of the nude was some paintings by Giorgio de Chirico, which contained no nudes. Chirico, working in Paris but nostalgic for the small Italian towns of his childhood, made a series of paintings between 1910 and 1917 in which the squares and arcaded streets of a ghost town seemed to have been created for assignations. The silence and emptiness are deepened into disquiet by the presence of a solitary public statue casting a long black shadow in the sunlight of late afternoon. Sometimes the public statue is a memorial to a nineteenth-century frock-coated statesman, sometimes a draped reclining figure based on a Roman copy of a lost Hellenistic statue of Ariadne in the Vatican Museum. An atmosphere of expectancy reigns supreme as if the town itself were sensitized by desire.

With the example of Chirico in mind, Delvaux created a town of his own. He perceives it in the sharpest detail and it looks rather like a provincial industrial town in his own country. Sometimes it is surrounded by great slag heaps, occasionally it is near the sea. It has handsome nineteenth-century warehouses and a railway terminus. Trams run along some of its long, straight streets. The interiors of the houses, still lit by gas, have an old-fashioned luxuriousness, with long mirrors and wainscoting and velvet upholstery. Even the classical temples surrounding the public square in *La Vénus Endormie* look as if they were planned by an ambitious nineteenth-century town council, and the horses' heads which decorate the building on the right come from the old Royal Circus in Brussels.

Usually it is nightfall before the girls walk out into the town, and they remain quiet and unassuming like the girls of another time who went for a walk after church, prayer-book in hand. They are not the girls we know today, who are as much at home in a bikini as a dress. Their undressing is a secret happening; something that takes place only in the privacy of the bedroom. Their nakedness on the streets is beyond possibility, and they are not really aware of this situation. They have been put into a trance by the painter and sent out into the night after he has cleared the streets. The town is as silent and deserted as Coventry on the day Lady Godiva rode naked through its streets, and the painter is Peeping Tom, spying on his own dreams. (The distant group of agitated people in *La Vénus Endormie* is unique, anomalous and only to be regretted.)

Delvaux's paintings present a strange and powerful account of a man's polygamous desire for one woman, for a woman with big, gentle eyes and heavy breasts and a triangle of pubic hair like one of Cupid's arrow-heads, a woman well-built for love.

The eroticism of Félicien Rops took the form of a highly romantic attitude to female prostitution. He lacked either the intelligence or the integrity to question the conventional moral code of the period, for he confused his fear of syphilis with moral indignation, and treated his lascivious visions of the female nude as evidence that women are instruments of the devil. He was fascinated by the idea of woman as a beautiful carrier of disease and death, but his recipes for turning naked female figures into alluring symbols of Evil were usually farcical. A pair of stockings or a bit of slipping drapery on his handsome naked models, or a sash tied in a bow over their big bottoms, only made them look vulgar or pathetic. But when he was not over-indulging in crass symbolism he could produce splendidly sensual studies of the nude. His drawing of a shivering girl to illustrate 'The Greatest Love of Don Juan' in Barbey d'Aurevilly's *Diaboliques* was good enough to inspire Edvard Munch to paint his masterly *Puberty*, in which the pose evokes the confused mental response of an adolescent girl to the processes of physical change.

Huysmans considered Rops to be superior to Rowlandson, whose work he nevertheless admired. 'It must be admitted,' he wrote, 'however desirable she may be, Rowlandson's woman is altogether animal, without any interesting complications of the senses. In short, he has given us a fornicating machine, a substantial sanitary beast, rather than the terrible she-faun of Lust.' But Rops is at his best when he is closest to achieving Rowlandson's 'substantial sanitary beast'. One of his finest graphics depicts a big, buxom girl with her blouse open and her legs apart to show that she is not wearing drawers. It is quite free from symbolism, but it is hypocritically entitled *Deplorable Attitude*, as if he were disclaiming responsibility for her pose. The print he called *Heart in Hand*, in which an exu- *130* berant peasant girl, lying on her back, seems to be waving her legs at the entire male sex, is one of the most straightforward studies of sexual readiness I have ever seen. Unfortunately, she holds in the hand of her outflung left arm a large and absurdly symbolic flaming heart, with a penis standing up in the middle of it; it is totally out of keeping with the naturalistic drawing of the girl, and one could wish that the idea had not occurred to him; but it is not sufficiently involved with her image to spoil it. It was not as a follower of Rowlandson that he produced such bold and zestful images of woman, but as an enthusiast for the art of Courbet, and especially for such paintings of eroticism in the round as *Woman with White Stockings*, now in the Barnes Foundation collection.

In the present century, two great artists, Chirico and Balthus, have been influenced by Courbet. Chirico's admiration for him was intense; he thought of him as a romantic, and in praise of him wrote: 'The sense of reality is always inseparable from a work of art. The profounder this sense is, so much the more poetic and romantic will be the work of art. Mysterious laws and rules of perspective dominate such facts. Who can deny the perturbing relation that exists between perspective and metaphysics.' The two last sentences really describe his own early work, where he used linear perspective to create uncanny prospects and put simple objects into relationships fraught with meanings beyond rational explanation. When he attempted to emulate Courbet's painterly realism the results were disastrous. The art of Balthus bridges the gulf between Chirico's visionary period and Courbet's warm, down-to-earth approach to woman as he found her. Like Courbet, he is a master of the soft and solid, and like Chirico he has the rare faculty of poetic insight.

Balthus was of Polish descent, but had a Scottish grandmother and was born in Paris in 1908. His brother, an interesting graphic artist, retains the family surname of Klossowski. By any other standard than that imposed by the twentieth-century illusion of 'progress', Balthus is a great painter. The potency of his images makes it difficult to dismiss him, but he is sometimes treated as a reactionary. Picasso put this point of view neatly to Françoise Gilot when he discovered the influence of Balthus in a batch of new paintings by Dora Maar: 'That kind of painting may not be outgrown for Balthus, but it certainly is for someone who has been working against the tradition that Balthus is working in. Balthus began with Courbet and never got very much beyond him.' He is also frequently criticized as a 'literary' painter, simply because he has not hidden his interest in *Wuthering Heights*. It has been left to such writers as Antonin Artaud and Albert Camus to appraise and defend his work – but that could be called his good fortune.

Artaud was profoundly appreciative of his paintings of the female nude:

Balthus paints, primarily, light and form. By the light of a wall, and polished floor, a chair or an epidermis he invites us to enter into the mystery of a human body. That body has a sex, and that sex makes itself clear to us, with all the asperities that go with it. . . . It is an invitation to love-making, but one that does not dissimulate the dangers involved.

Camus has a wonderfully illuminating passage on the Balthus illustrations for *Wuthering Heights*:

Balthus has understood that one of the keys of this book, which expresses the anguish and fury of adult love, is the remembrance of the childish love between Cathy and Heathcliff, and the terrible nostalgia that obsessed these two beings until the hour of their final parting. They were literally on fire with nostalgia, and that suffering which people think of as something out of the ordinary thus reveals its true face, blind and ravaged, the very face of human misery, in its exhausting struggle to return upstream to the source of innocence and joy.

Emily Brontë's *Wuthering Heights*, like her sister's *Jane Eyre*, is a book one reads very early in life and, as George Saintsbury remarked, one 'never seems to have read it for the first time'. Balthus was fourteen when he discovered it, and by the early thirties, when he made a series of pen-and-ink drawings to illustrate it, the story was in his bones. I think they are the greatest book illustrations of our time, and it is quite extraordinary that they have never been reproduced in an edition of the text. The harsh penmanship and the convulsed and angular movements of the two chief characters reproduce all their passion, desperation and cruelty. He never produced anything quite like them again, but Cathy and Heathcliff remain the instigators of almost all his finest paintings, and there is a sense in which Balthus has inherited Heathcliff's desperate nostalgia for the wild young Cathy who roamed the moors with him when they were children. Cathy is everywhere. She pores insensately over books, lunges in her sleep, plays a game of patience as if trying to tell her own fortune, impatient for the future, stands suddenly still in front of her own naked image, poses extravagantly in front of Nelly the maid. The atmosphere is full of invisible stirrings, full of the unease of growing pains and vague expectation. It is strangely close to the atmosphere of Chirico's early paintings. Outside, there could be a deserted square and at the far end of it a statue facing the other way, casting a long shadow. It is Chirico's world of premonitions transferred to domestic settings and centred on a girl approaching adolescence.

Nelly the maid is often there, and never absent when her young mistress is naked. Sometimes she is an old woman, sometimes a girl only a little older than Cathy. In the sombre masterpiece called *The Room* Cathy is naked and has adopted one of her extravagantly shameless poses. It is impossible to tell whether she is asleep or shamming. Camus suggested that Balthus had too keen an appreciation of extremes not to include crime, and claimed that all his sleeping girls have had their throats 'discreetly' cut. The girl in *The Room* presents the strongest case for such a claim, and the maid adds her own fears to the situation by tugging dramatically at the curtains to let the light pour in; but I prefer to think that if any blood has come it shows between Cathy's thighs, and that in her violent way she is celebrating her first menstruation.

The naked girl in the *Nude with Cat* is in a very similar pose to the girl in *The Room*; only in this case alibis have been provided for her nakedness and for the unguarded pose. A bowl on the floor and a towel on the arm of the chair suggest that she has been standing in the bowl for an all-over wash. The cat, who was watching her from a distance in *The Room*, is now close behind her, lying on top of the washstand to give the impression that Cathy is stretching back to fondle him. The drawing aside of the curtain has become an everyday action again. Nevertheless, Cathy's pose remains a disturbing element, undermining the quietness and the domesticity. She is still making her own scene. She is not fondling the cat, but is immersed in an ecstatic premonition of future encounters. Her pose is an expression of an ardent nature; her sexual readiness is a state of mind. Without any undue emphasis, the scene conveys the sense of a return to the past. This is the agonized hindsight of an adult, discovering the desirability of a childhood playmate.

150

(Opposite)
L WUNDERLICH
ining nude

(Right)
. KITAJ
chromy with F.B.

(Overleaf)
ROP
three brides

174 (*Above*)
MAN RAY
Observatory time—the
lovers

172 (*Previous page left*)
LUCIAN FREUD
Portrait fragment

173 (*Previous page right*)
COSIMO
Simonetta Vespucci

175 (*Left*)
MICHELANGELO
Head of Cleopatra

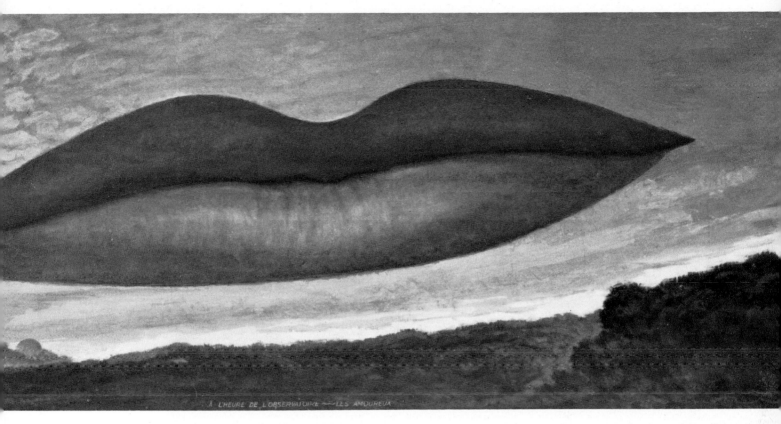

À L'HEURE DE L'OBSERVATOIRE — LES AMOUREUX

76 (*Right*)
EDVARD MUNCH
Summer night at Oslo Fjord

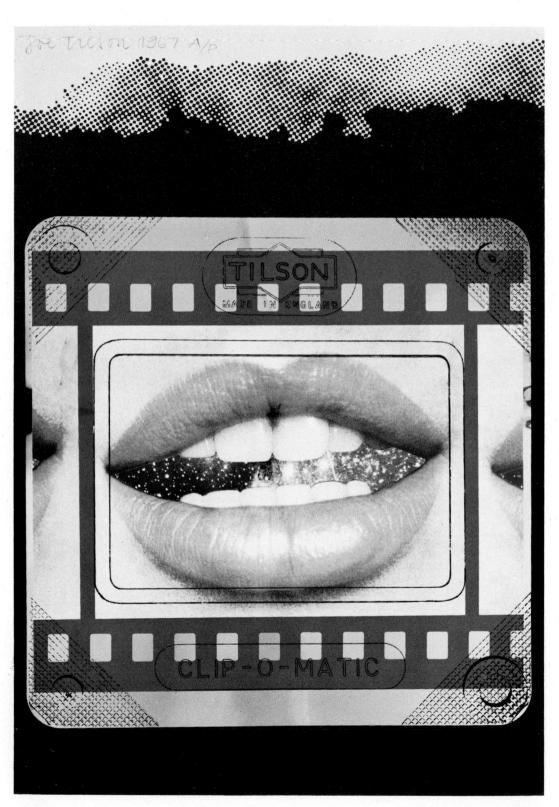

177 (*Left*)
JOE TILSON
Diapositive, mouth and stars

178 (*Opposite*)
PEDRO MACHUCA
The virgin and the souls in purgatory

179 (*Left*)
TINTORETTO
Woman revealing her breast

180 (*Left*)
ROPS
Bourgeoisie

ANET
londe with bare breasts

VATTEAU
ête champêtre (detail)

AVBREY BEARDSLEY.

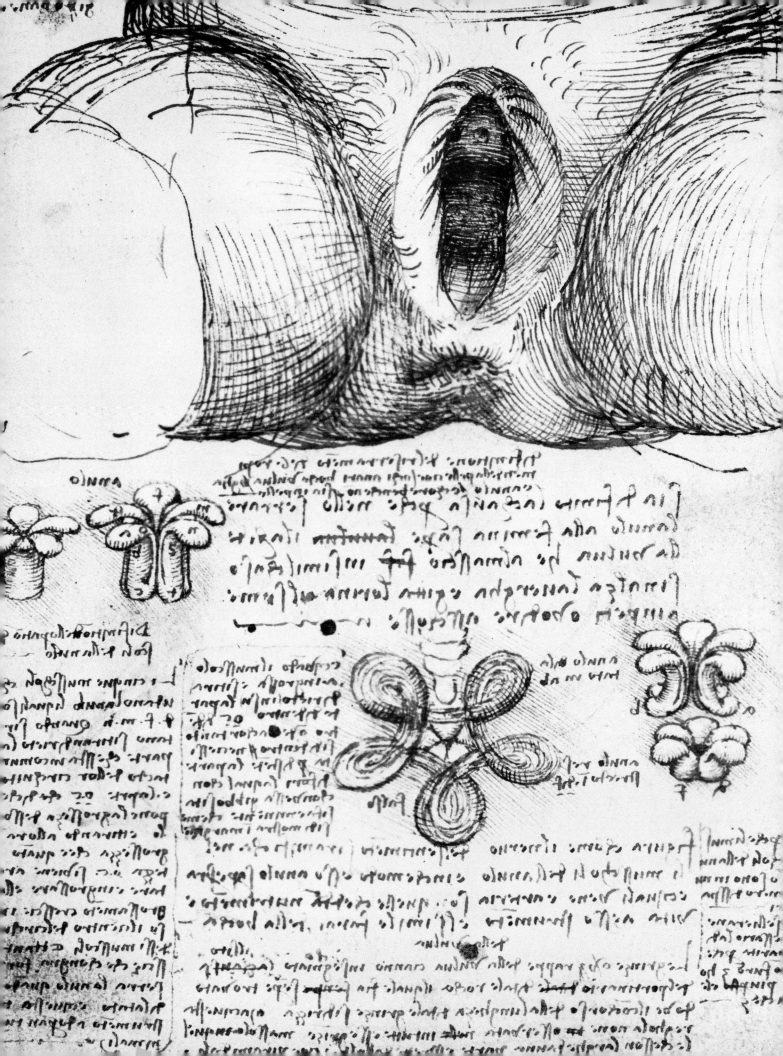

186 (*Previous page*)
LÉONARDO DA VINCI
Anatomical drawing

187 (*Above*)
TINTORETTO
Vulcan surprising Venus
and Mars

188 (*Left*)
ROPS
Girl in chair

THE HAIRY PROSPECT OR THE DEVIL IN A FRIGHT.

Once on a time the Sire of evil
In plainer English call'd the devil
Some new experiment to try.
At Chloe cast a roguish eye
But she who all his arts defied
Pull'd up and shew'd her sexes pride
A thing all shagg'd about with hair
So much it made old Satan stare
Who frightend at the grim display
Takes to his heels and runs away

190 (*Left*)
GRAHAM OVENDEN
Mezzotint

91 (*Right*)
USELI
ady Betty

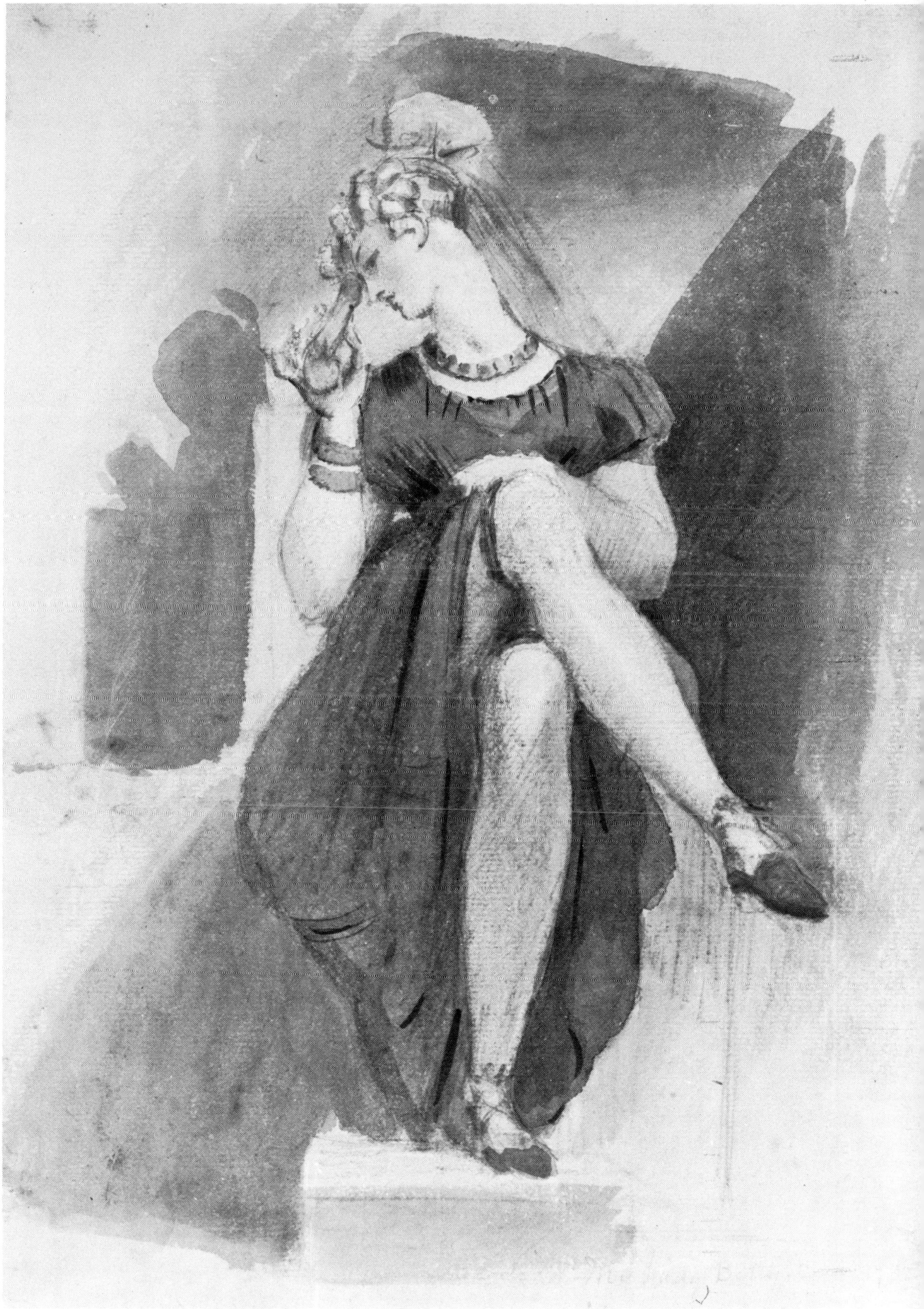

192 (*Left*)
DALI
The erotic life

193 (*Left*)
BEARDSLEY
The stomach dance (detail)
Illustration for *Salome*

6 Mistresses and Courtesans

132 Titian's double portrait of a man and a naked woman in the National Gallery of Art at Washington is sometimes called an allegory because the man is helping the woman at her toilet by holding up a mirror. She appears to be about to apply pomade to one of her long braids of hair. The presence of the mirror could imply that the female figure personifies either Truth or Vanity. If she stood for Vanity, the Renaissance idea that nudity is the noblest form of beauty would go by the board; Vanity is more likely to be richly apparelled. If Truth were the subject, the figure holding the looking-glass would be a maiden; the association of a man with a woman engaged in her toilet implies a sexual relationship which would be inappropriate to high-minded notions about Truth. I much prefer the alternative suggestion that the couple is either Alfonso d'Este and Laura Dianti or Federico Gonzaga and Isabella Boschetti. The man bears some resemblance to Titian's portrait of Gonzaga in the Prado, but not strikingly enough to be evidence. Nevertheless, I find the pleasant if never-to-be-rewarded pursuit of furnishing the couple with cards of identity thoroughly understandable, for I incline to the view that the painting is concerned with two people in love, and that Titian was happy in the commission to commemorate an intimate and tender relationship. All the same, it would be breaking all the rules of propriety governing the conduct of a man of position if he were to commission a double portrait of himself and his wife in which his wife was undraped; the same rules would apply if the woman were promised to him in marriage. So if these are portraits of actual people, the woman must be the man's mistress, and the ring has been placed on the table as an emblem of a warm attachment that is not binding in law. The man takes a subsidiary position in the composition because the primary purpose of the painting is to celebrate the woman's inordinate beauty. I use the word 'inordinate' because I think that the image of this woman is close to the actuality on which Titian's idealizations of the female figure is based. There is a sense in which the generalized version of her type in other works is more prudent. Incidentally, nothing quite like the monumentality of that raised arm and that hand holding the braid of hair happened again in European art before Picasso painted his neo-classical nudes.

But I like to think that it was the memory of this woman that inspired Titian in his old age to paint the wonderfully ponderous figure of Europa on the back of a somewhat intimidated bull. Something that was said, I think, by Hazlitt applies particularly to this woman pomading her hair. He said that the eye acquires an appetite for Titian's painting of flesh, and then adds, rather ambiguously, that the impression made on one sense excites another.

At the libertine court of Charles II, the art of portraiture, although never more popular, came down in the world. The court found its appropriate poet in the Earl of Rochester, whose brilliantly scandalous verses deserved the graphic support of a Rowlandson; instead, it was a period of dull and boring portraiture in which every duchess and countess who went to bed with the king was painted as if butter would not melt in her mouth. The Duchess of Cleveland, who was, so to speak, his official mistress in the first decade of the Restoration, was painted at least a dozen times by Lely, and her portraits were in so much demand that his little factory produced countless copies. He painted her not only as a fine lady but as a shepherdess, as Pallas Athene, as Saint Barbara, and even as the Madonna. Rochester, on the other hand, celebrated her nymphomania, her dissatisfaction with the jaded sexuality of the men of her own class, and her taste for being the paying whore. The 'Knight' in the following *Song* was one of the king's humbler mistresses:

Quoth the Duchess of Cleveland to counselor Knight
'I'd fain have a prick, knew I how to come by 't.
I desire you'll be secret and give your advice:
Though cunt be not coy, reputation is nice.'

'To some cellar in Sodom Your Grace must retire
Where porters with black-pots sit round a coal-fire;
There open your case, and Your Grace cannot fail
Of a dozen of pricks for a dozen of ale.'

'Is't so?' quoth the Duchess. 'Aye, by God!' quoth the whore.
'Then give me the key that unlocks the back door,
For I'd rather be fucked by porters and cowmen
Than thus be abused by Churchill and Jermyn.'

In a long poem called *Signior Dildo* (in which a number of court ladies are named, including the Countess of Southesk, whose husband, suspecting that she was having an affair with the king's brother, the Duke of York, deliberately contracted a venereal disease in order to pass it on to his wife, and soon had the pleasure of hearing that she had infected the duke) Rochester devotes four fearsome lines to the Duchess of Cleveland:

That pattern of virtue, Her Grace of Cleveland,
Has swallowed more pricks than the ocean has sand;
But by rubbing and scrubbing so large it does grow,
It is fit for just nothing but Signior Dildo.

But as the duchess said in the earlier poem, 'reputation is nice', and like all the king's high-born mistresses she was always decently draped or gowned in her portraits. Nell Gwynne, as a woman of the people and an actress, did not have to put up a show of respectability, and in the half-length portrait attributed to Simon Verelst her breasts are charmingly exposed. Some time in the nineteenth century they were covered up, but she has been undressed again by a recent cleaning.

Rochester, in spite of dubbing her 'the countess o' th' Cockpit' (a reference to the part of Whitehall Palace that included a theatre, but probably carries another meaning), was fond of Nell Gwynne and protected her interests, and when she became the king's mistress told her to 'cherish his love where-ever it inclines, and be assur'd you can't commit greater Folly than pretending to be jealous'. When he wrote the poem about Charles that he handed to him by mistake and as a result had to disappear for a time, the king was still in his early forties, but his sexual parts were already worn out; and he has a word of sympathy for Nell:

> This you'd believe, had I but time to tell ye
> The pains it costs to poor, laborious Nelly,
> Whilst she employs hands, fingers, mouth, and thighs,
> Ere she can raise the member she enjoys.

The Verelst portrait of her may have been overcleaned, but her blanched skin (more obvious in the painting than in the colour plate) is very effective, and if it is anywhere near the truth, the sudden whiteness of her body when she stepped out of her clothes must have been startling and impressive.

The disconcerting thing about the erotic content of eighteenth-century French painting is the cold mildness, the almost complete absence of sensual warmth. The amorous scenes, whether they are *fêtes galantes*, mythological love affairs, or genre studies of the initial rebuffs in the indoor recreation of seduction, are calculated distillations of the libertinism of the period. Sex is in one place, kept playfully out of sight, and love is a mechanistic game of hide and seek played with conventionalized poses and gestures which diminish human personality. It is not surprising that this was an age devoted to elaborate and ingenious clockwork figures, and perhaps even less surprising that eighteenth-century France yielded no really great painting of the nude, nothing comparable to the deep, calm sensuality of the nudes of Giorgione, Titian or Rubens, or the sharply erotic studies in formalized nakedness in the art of Cranach and Modigliani.

133   Boucher's famous portrait of Louisa O'Murphy, who for a short while was one of the mistresses of Louis xv, is one of the outstanding nudes of the period. It has been praised to the skies, and is undoubtedly a brilliant technical achievement, but it seems to me to have been painted without any warmth of feeling, and to have been executed to serve a rather squalid purpose. It was evidently commissioned, and the commission probably included specific instructions with regard to the girl's posture. Lying on her belly with her legs splayed, a man might play with the idea of wishing himself between her and the couch, but she looks as if she is awaiting inspection and has been told to arrange herself for a visit from her protector and his friends. I have the impression that it is a variant of the sort of horse picture that is ordered by proud owners, with the difference that in this case the owner's friends would discuss the girl's 'points' with a certain levity.

It seems to be generally agreed that the art of Goya is peculiarly relevant to our time. We feel that he is much closer to us than, for instance, Géricault and Delacroix, as if his art outgrew nineteenth-century Romanticism before it happened; as if the stiff, abrupt gestures of lust and terror so characteristic of his art were a brutal comment upon the heroic gestures of *The Raft of the Medusa* and *Liberty leading the People*. Romanticism was an attempt to recover for man alone the spiritual powers that had arisen from faith in a god. Goya celebrated man's spiritual bankruptcy with a conviction and finality which our time, with its larger horrors more coldly conceived, has tended to confirm. With the exception of Hieronymus Bosch, Goya is the only great painter who told us that we hunger for hell and are more horrible than the other animals. He pointed confidently and exultantly at cruelty, folly and corruption, but scarcely knew where to turn for evidence of their opposites, and in the end it is the dead and outraged human carcass that has to stand for virtue.

Goya was fascinated by the *Majas*, a sort of lower-class demi-monde, whose charms were used to provide money for their opposite numbers, the *Majos*, when these were not living off rich women. In the Metropolitan Museum's portrait of the Duchess of Alba, with a feverish flicker of black mantilla playing round the imperturbably cool face, she appears to be affecting the garb of a *Maja*, but could not be mistaken for a member of the breed. Her finger is pointing down at Goya's name scratched on the ground in front of her, and he seemed not to realize that although it might indicate that he was one of her lovers, it also symbolized the slavishness of his passion for her. The portrait is faithful to her arrogance, and in letting her write his name in the dirt Goya has unconsciously acknowledged his situation. Her gesture can easily be mistaken for a command, as if she were expecting the painter to go down on his knees and lick the pointed shoes which poke out from under her skirts like sharp little rodents. When she had no more use for him, he added an engraving to *Los Proverbios* in which she is depicted as a double-faced monster lying on the ground with other monsters and a sad-looking Goya. In *Majas on a Balcony*, two *Majos* are standing behind the seated *Majas*, *134* wrapped in cloaks, and hooded, with their faces half hidden. They are sinister yet curiously insubstantial, as if they are shadows cast by the women themselves. It could be a way of saying that the women are two-faced, and that the figures behind them represent their hidden rapacity and lust.

It we could tamper with historical sequence, I would put Goya between Daumier and Manet, making Daumier's paintings of Don Quixote the last kindly word about the human condition before Goya's black eloquence brought painting to silence. The silence about the human condition began with Manet, who painted beautiful vacant versions of Goya's *The Third of May* and *Majas on a Balcony*. The killing and dying are ludicrously absent from his *Execution of Maximilian* and all the raffishness is gone from *The Balcony*. Goya's predilections were entangled with his hatreds; connivance mingled with condemnation, and a fierce elation sprang from the cloudy mixture. He revelled in his nausea, and this doesn't put us into conflict with him. The difference is that we are learning to refrain from using the erotic impulse to cast blame.

The casting of blame on the woman taken in adultery, and the unmarried girl who became pregnant and the spurning of these 'fallen' creatures was a major occupation of the Victorians. It was probably one way of ensuring that there were enough prostitutes to satisfy the needs of decent men. Not surprisingly, Victorian painters undertook the illustration of these themes with tear-stained relish. The first to tackle the genre was Rossetti, but he didn't have enough moralistic fervour to really start the ball rolling. The painting he called *Found*, started several years before he finished it, carries no conviction whatsoever. A drover who has come to town to sell a calf finds a Fallen Woman. He knows that she is a Fallen Woman because she is crouching on the ground, in a pretty, flowered gown, with her head against a brick wall. He recognizes her as the girl to whom he had made love years before, and had abandoned in her hour of need. He tries to drag her to her feet, but she turns away in shame from her upright, clean-living seducer. Rossetti was very pleased with the brick wall, which he found in Chiswick, and he painted it direct from nature; this was his contribution to *plein air* painting.

The Awakening Conscience by Holman Hunt was the first of the modern moralities to be exhibited. It was in the Royal Academy show of 1854. The idea was to depict a situation in which the companion of the woman's fall, by sharing an 'idle sing-song' with her, causes her to recall her childhood, repent of her present way of life and make a 'holy resolve' to break out of her 'gilded cage'. It required a lot of symbolic detail (including a cat tormenting a bird under the table) to make it clear that this highly respectable-looking couple were living in sin. According to the critic who covered the Academy show for the *Athenaeum*, most decent people supposed it to represent a quarrel between a brother and sister. He, apparently, was an exception, for he proceeded to explain that the subject was 'drawn from a very dark and repulsive side of domestic life', and that it 'literally represented the momentary remorse of a kept mistress, whose thoughts of lost virtue, guilt, father, mother and home, had been roused by a chance strain of music'. It was left to Ruskin to defend the picture:

The poor girl has been sitting singing with her seducer; some chance words of the song 'Oft in the stilly night' have struck upon the numbed places in her heart; she has started up in agony . . . no one possessing the slightest knowledge of expression could remain untouched by the countenance of the lost girl, rent from its beauty into sudden horror; the lips half-open, indistinct in their purple quivering, the teeth set hard, the eyes filled with the fearful light of futility . . .

Hunt had shown his rough design for the picture to Augustus Egg, who was so impressed by it that he persuaded a Birmingham collector to commission Hunt to carry it out. Four years later, Egg himself exhibited at the Academy a pictorial account of the fate of a woman who had committed adultery. It was a much better example of story-telling than Hunt's, and infinitely more harrowing. Following the example of Hogarth he told the story in a sequence of three pictures, and, following the example of Hunt, included symbolic details that were not really necessary. He introduced them in the catalogue with a hair-raising quotation: 'Aug. 4th: Have just heard that B. has been dead more than a fortnight; so his poor children have now lost both their parents. I hear *She* was seen on Friday last, near the Strand, evidently without a place to lay her head – what a fall hers has been!' The italicized 'She' is spine-chilling.

In the first picture the woman lies sobbing on the carpet; the elder of two little girls has stopped building a house of cards, but she is too frightened to approach her mother; the husband sits at the table, stunned by the contents of a letter he still holds in his hand. The other two pictures represent happenings occurring simultaneously in different places. Egg makes this clear by the simple but effective device of depicting the moon in both pictures with the same little strip of cloud beneath it. In one of them, the children are now in their teens. The younger one has buried her face in the lap of her sister, who strokes her hair and gazes sadly at the moon shining through the bedroom window. The setting of the last picture in the sequence is a gloomy archway by the Thames. The woman crouches on the ground, nursing the child she had by the other man, and gazes hopelessly at the moon.

Alfred Stevens's *Désespérée* is less well-known than the others I have mentioned, but it is a more civilized contribution to the Fallen Woman syndrome, if only because the painter has refrained from inventing a moralistic cause for the woman's state of desperation; but no doubt his contemporaries perceived in this well-observed study of unhappiness a hint of just retribution.

To introduce a lighter note, I recall a print of the period in which two gay and astute Fallen Women have spent a very pleasant evening at the expense of a man who had been expecting to be rewarded. They have got him helplessly drunk, and *131* are stealing away without any intention of looking for a brick wall to crouch against.

7 Prostitutes

Ruskin thought that the two prostitutes in Carpaccio's famous painting were respectable, well-to-do married ladies who were bored because they had nothing to do but dress up and sit about on a balcony in Venice, so perhaps they ought to be called courtesans. But both names describe women who hire themselves out for sexual intercourse and there is no obvious dividing line. James Morris, in his charming book on Venice, says that a sixteenth-century Venetian prostitute became a courtesan when she 'burst the confines of the bordels', although she was compelled by law to carry a red light at the prow of her gondola; but his reference to 'the most famous and cultured of all the courtesans, the prostitute-poetess Veronica Franco', does not exactly clarify the issue. The prostitute-poetess is clearly in a different class from Baudelaire's 'five-franc whore' who accompanied him to the Louvre one day and 'began blushing and covering her face with her hands' at the sight of the marble nudes. Yet after all they simply have different ways of keeping up appearances, and if we change the venue again and glance at Rochester's dithyrambic tribute to St James's Park it becomes evident that their differences are of little account.

> There, by a most incestuous birth,
> Strange woods spring from the teeming earth;
> For they relate how heretofore,
> When ancient Pict began to whore,
> Deluded of his assignation
> (Jilting, it seems, was even then in fashion)
> Poor pensive lover, in this place
> Would frig upon his mother's face;
> Whence rows of mandrakes tall did rise
> Whose lewd tops fucked the very skies.
> Each imitative branch doth twine
> In some loved fold of Aretine,
> And nightly now beneath their shade
> Are buggeries, rapes and incests made.

This vision of a landscape created by human lust is comparable to St John the

Divine's ecstatic vision of Babylon as a whore; and Rochester's St James's Park is an equivalent of the golden cup in her hand, 'full of abominations and filthiness of her fornication'. In spite of knowing the contents of her cup, St John felt 'great admiration' for the scarlet woman, before being corrected by the angel, and his admiration is understandable enough: the golden cup itself is an image of the vagina, the grail for which man desperately searches and is forever finding. When man rages against the prostitute it is because he is under the delusion that it is her wiles that sidetrack his vast vague desire to 'fuck the very skies'. The fall of Babylon, personified as woman on her back with her legs apart – the archetypal posture of irresistible invitation which man pays her to adopt – will continue until the end of time.

The squalid content of those tavern scenes by artists of the Low Countries, so popular in the seventeenth century, only acquires erotic interest when a drunkard whose thoughts have turned to lechery inquires the price of a young woman. The *138* idea that she is prepared to endure the assault of a man so ugly and brutish can start melancholy and confusing reveries, as if the woman in the picture were involved in one's own lost opportunities to descend to the lower depths of sexual pleasure.

The ostensible subject of Vermeer's *At The Procuress's* is the same as such tavern *135* scenes, but the situation has only been visualized by the painter. This is an early work by one of the greatest masters of observed reality; these figures have been looked at separately and with varying degrees of intensity, and only the woman in the yellow bodice has been observed for her own sake. If the picture achieves plausibility, it is due to an element that runs through almost all his finest works – his intense awareness of the mystery of feminine presence. It has been said of this work that the study of facial expressions reveals an interest in psychological situations which he suppressed in later and greater paintings. But the expressions on the faces of the client and the procuress are merely illustrational. The real psychological situation is between the woman in the yellow bodice and the painter. She appears to be a prostitute only because of the circumstantial evidence contrived for an imaginary encounter.

In later paintings in which a woman is alone in an interior, and the act of representation is pure and total – in, for instance, the Rijksmuseum's *Milkmaid*, or the Metropolitan's *Woman Playing a Lute*, or the Louvre's *Lacemaker* – the painting is expressing a relationship, however enigmatic or inscrutable, between the model and the painter. She is as much aware of the painter as he is of her. She does not have to meet his eyes to convince us that she is revolving in her mind something he has said to her, or awaiting his reply to something she has said to him. The seeming absence of a psychological situation is due to the fact that the one to whom she is responding is not in the picture. The extraordinary exception is Vienna's *The Painter's Studio*. The painter has his back towards us, and his model is standing near the end wall, bathed in the light of an unseen window, her face half-turned towards the painter. She is holding a trumpet and a large yellow book. There have been many interpretations of the possible symbolic meaning of trumpet and book, but whatever the model may be personifying – Muse, Goddess, Fame, Fortune, Knowledge – has no connection with the expression on her face. She has veiled her eyes, and her lower lip protrudes slightly as if she may be awaiting the opportunity to speak, but the general impression conveyed by her look and the position of her head is that she is listening; one can even sense her guarded pleasure, as if she is listening to a compliment or to some not unpleasing proposal.

To return to the young woman in the yellow bodice: her equivocal expression yields well enough to an interpretation suitable for the fictional situation; she does not turn her head to look at the young man who is putting a gold coin into her hand; it is the kind of transaction to which she is accustomed; she is neither pleased nor repelled. She is being paid for the temporary use of her body and the identity of the user is a matter of indifference to her. But there are many indications in the composition that the figures are not in a clearly defined space. They appear to have been fitted together collage-wise, and the edge of table and the sumptuous rug are not visually coherent. The young woman is better understood as a woman who posed for the artist with no one else present. Some critics have found in her a likeness to other women in Vermeer's paintings, and Malraux and Goldscheider consider it to be a portrait of his wife. The expression on her face could be a sign of her ambiguous response to his explanation of the use he intends to make of her image.

139   Degas's prostitutes are real. The monotypes he devoted to the inmates of *maisons closes* were made in 1879–80, and several years after his death were used by Vollard as illustrations for his editions of Guy de Maupassant's *La Maison Tellier* and Pierre Louÿs's *Mimes des Courtisanes de Lucien*. These monotypes were made by drawing in diluted oils directly on to metal plates, and the darkest areas were added after the impression had been taken.

Degas would seem to have visited the brothels during periods when the women were resting or just after they had assembled for duty but before the clients had appeared. He discovered a whole new world of form when he began to observe naked woman as if he were an animal painter, and in the late pastels of women washing or drying their bodies he caught them in wonderfully cumbersome or awkward postures and was rarely satisfied until he had given them something of the splendour of a fine shire horse. The prostitutes he depicted were as ugly, coarse, and stupid as their most exacting clients could have wished, but he brought a highly developed sense of the absurd to the study of their relaxed gracelessness and to their shameless display that practice had made habitual and automatic. Some of the postures of the women are deliciously comic and always rather touching. It is usually claimed that these assaults on the convention of the academic nude disclose his contempt for woman, but it would be a mistake to think of the series as a misogynist revel. When he notes that a client has entered he treats him as an intruder edging his way in at the side, and he probably included him merely as an annoying sign that his drawing session was over. He never tired of contemplating the nakedness of woman, and he exercised his right as a privileged voyeur to discover in their naturalness a kind of vulgar innocence.

The woman in Mucha's drawing of a street-walker picked up by the Paris police appears to be either starving or ravaged by TB; but although Mucha could produce effective Art Nouveau designs, his attempts at realism were insensitive. The drawing overstates a case, and one cannot even be sure what the case is. It is possible that he is trying to show that he is compassionate, but one has a suspicion that he is making a crass moral judgement. Rops, inspired no doubt by a real fear of venereal disease, depicted Death strolling the streets as a prostitute, but such *140* symbolism is bearable only if it is treated with the profound solemnity of a Dürer or the cruel gleefulness of Urs Graf. In Rops it is muddle-headed melodrama. Only a very exceptional artist can afford to be solemn. Botero's South American *141* brothel scenes suggest that the comic approach is wiser and nicer, and at the same time lend their weight to Baudelaire's contention that fatness is less indecent than thinness. The group portrait of the inmates of the house decoratively minimizes the heat and staleness of the room by treating the flies as motifs on the wallpaper. The maid who has come in to sweep up the cigarette-ends is reduced in scale, like the portraits of donors in pictures of saints. The last of the clients is forgotten, under a chair. Whores and whoremaster have come together like a close-knit family. The togetherness is emphasized by the fact that the whoremaster is a transvestite and would like to be one of the girls, and he holds the youngest of the girls in his arms to show that she is the baby of the family. The girl on the left is evidently a compulsive and untidy smoker, for in the full-length portrait of her in her cubby- *142* hole of a bedroom the floor is scattered with stubs. Her allurement is dependent upon her tremendous bulk, and one imagines that she draws tiny men to her like a magnet. For them she can provide the rare experience of woman as a total environment; and they need never be entirely lost, for in the course of their wanderings they will come across miniaturized female parts which will give them their bearings.

8 Violence and Violation

Whipping

The vast number of pornographic whipping books produced in the nineteenth-century reflects the popularity of the one erotic pleasure that could be indulged in with open and savage abandon by respectable parents and schoolmasters of the period. Fortunately the flogging of children has abated. There remains, as a sediment, whipping between consenting adults.

One of Aubrey Beardsley's two drawings of whipping illustrates the desire to be whipped; the other illustrates the urge to castigate. The whipping of 'Earl Lavender', the abject male figure kneeling in a Victorian drawing-room, is not as desultory as it appears to be. The woman's poise and elegance have a ritualistic significance; her feet are well placed to enable the body to swing and turn as she strikes, and the fact that the straps of her gown have slipped off her shoulders suggests that she puts considerable force into each stroke. She holds up her gown with her free hand, but if she were being aroused by the performance she would not bother to cover her breasts; there is little doubt that she is executing a commission and is not emotionally involved. The male figure is a grown-up version of the frail, round-shouldered youth who is masturbating in the first version of *The Toilet of Salome* and the drawing may well be a bitterly satirical fantasy on the flagging virility of a consumptive. The man is having himself whipped in the hope of bringing on an orgasm without intercourse, to simulate an involuntary emission.

143   The other drawing, *Juvenal scourging Woman*, is set with exemplary economy in a public square in Ancient Rome, and is intended as a pictorial comment on Juvenal's scathing account in the Sixth Satire of the vanity, treachery, cruelty and promiscuity of woman. Beardsley probably based the female figure on his own superb portrait of Messalina, which remains remarkably close to Juvenal's description of her (I quote Peter Green's recent translation):

> . . . hear what Claudius
> Had to put up with. The minute she heard him snoring,
> His wife – that whore-empress – who dared to prefer
> the mattress

Of a stews to her couch in the Palace, called for her hooded
Night-cloak and hastened forth alone or with a single
Maid to attend her. Then, her black hair hidden
Under an ash-blonde wig, she would make straight
    for her brothel,
With its odour of stale, warm bedclothes, it's empty
    reserved cell,
Here she would strip off, showing her gilded nipples and
The belly that once housed a prince of the blood. Her
    door sign
Bore a false name, Lycisca, 'The Wolf-girl'. A more than
    willing
Partner, she took on all comers, for cash, without a break.

The cylindrical pillar on which Beardsley has sat her, with the top thrusting
into her crotch, is a collective image of all the penises that have entered her, and
to judge from the position of Juvenal he intends to aim the knotted cords at her
belly. She is in no need of sexual stimulation and the whipping is entirely a punishment. But Beardsley's treatment of the flagellant – robe tucked up to expose his
genitals – introduces the idea that Juvenal himself had erotic motives for
scourging woman.

Bellmer's sado-masochistic study of Lesbian whipping may have been influ-   *148*
enced by Beardsley. The height and posture of the woman with the whip is not
unlike that of the woman standing over Beardsley's kneeling man, and the other
female figure, like Juvenal's victim, is tied to a cylindrical pillar. But Bellmer's
linear effects are different. The flagelliform curves of the two figures are variations
on the whiplash snaking out of the standing woman's hand, and the whiplash
itself is like an uncoiling of the flagellant's tightly sprung forms. The more rotund
figure of the victim looks as if it has been formed by encircling lashes from the
whip, and the sense of a cruel and implacable flogging is conveyed without
dependence on a realistic marking of the flesh.

Klossowsky's drawing of a man beating a half-dressed woman with her own   *145*
parasol is an incident in a sexual fairy tale. She was about to go for a walk wearing
only a hat and her underwear. The beating is a pleasure for all concerned, but one
feels that if it goes on too long the girl may well ask when the raping is going to
begin. She can be trusted not to struggle unreasonably, and since the man has an
assistant who is already grasping her wrists, he will not grumble too much if she
kicks him a few times before his ultimate purpose is accomplished.

The Rape

The old man grabbing with demoniacal lust at a young woman in an Urs Graf   *147*
engraving will not accomplish a rape. It is said that it's virtually impossible to
take a woman against her will unless her arms and legs are held, and a man on his
own cannot deal with four thrashing limbs. It is a man's point of view, of course,

and smacks of special pleading, since it does not take into account the blanketing effect of the weight of a man's body when he presses on a woman he has brought down. Nevertheless, it is probably easier to kill a woman than to rape her, and may explain why women are not infrequently murdered before being sexually assaulted. The powerful young woman in the Urs Graf engraving is well aware that the old man cannot take her unless she consents. He is entirely dependent on her whim, and at the moment she is playing with him. As he pulls up one side of her gown she provocatively pulls up the other. The artist is laughing at the plight of old men whose virility is a long time dying and delighting in the contrast between their aching skinniness and the complacent plumpness of his beauties.

Two elderly judges of Babylon who went every morning to the house of Joacim to interview people bringing law suits were inflamed by the beauty of Joacim's wife, Susanna. Every afternoon she walked in the garden, and they took to hiding in the bushes to watch her. One day when she was quite alone and had taken off her clothes to go into the garden pool, they approached her suddenly and said that unless she consented to lie with them they would bear false witness against her and swear that they had seen her in the arms of a young man. Painters and printmakers have usually taken up the theme purely as an excuse for painting a female nude and have relegated the old men to the distant bushes, treating them as harmless Peeping Toms; but in the Carracci engraving they are making their *151* demands and are so sure that she will yield to their threats that one of them is already pulling up his robe to be ready to take her. But there was still justice even in Babylon and the story ends happily with the old men put to death.

146 Picasso's drawing is simply called *The Rape*, and does not put classical names to the figures, but the violence of the scene is conceived with classical serenity. The white horse is one of his personal contributions to myth. It has strayed from the bullring, where, at other times, he has depicted it with head thrown back in a scream as the bull's horn pierces its belly. It always personifies woman and usually stands for hysteria, but when, as in the present drawing, the woman herself is being demonstrative, it represents her passivity. Its mildness is a prediction that the woman, overwrought by her husband's defeat in combat, will soon find her captor acceptable.

The nude is not one of the picture categories in which the English excel, and there is always William Etty to remind us with poignant persistence that we have no Titian or Rubens. At the same time, there are his delightful oil sketches to remind us of the promise he was unable to keep. In the sketch for his *Pluto* *153* *Carrying off Proserpine* the central figures are beautifully conceived as an explosive meeting of milky and sooty bodies but it is all too evident that they are surrounded by a miscellaneous selection of life studies from the female nude.

The Use of Satyrs

It has been a well-used convention through the centuries to replace the male nude with satyrs or centaurs when the subject is the inordinate sensuality of the human male. It has enabled some artists to revel in the animality and Dionysiac energy of the male and treat him primarily as a sexual organism without having to take responsibility for celebrating man's intolerable and shameful lust for woman. And by referring to the female nudes as nymphs – bevies of semi-devine but not immortal creatures, entirely pleasing to the senses, who roamed naked through the woods and bathed in streams and acted as attendants at the banquets of the gods – woman is brought down to the same amoral animal level of the satyrs without losing her human appearance. Usually, the nymphs are taken by surprise, and their struggles are a way of depicting their excitement at the prospect of being outraged. A quite rare example of the explicit treatment of a nymph as a case of nymphomania is in a seventeenth-century Italian engraving: a nymph has waylaid *154* Bacchus and an ancient satyr mounted behind him on an ass; she is already covering the satyr and is grasping avariciously for the erect penis of gross and drunken Bacchus, which is turning a piece of cloth into an indiscreet tent.

Satyrs were frequently given the task of showing the kind of curiosity which was thought to be beneath the dignity of a man. A School of Fontainebleau *Nymph and Satyr* in which a satyr is uncovering the fleece of a sleeping woman is probably *155* based on Tintoretto's popular painting of Vulcan examining Venus for signs of the lovemaking of Mars, whose helmeted head is peeping out from under a valance. Vulcan, however, was an ill-used husband, and the satyr's only excuse was a natural desire to take any opportunity of getting a look at any woman's private parts. By the same token, it is an old satyr who pleads with the herma- *152* phrodite, in a Hellenistic carving, to let him see how the duality of the genitalia is manifested.

A curious feature of Renaissance images of satyrs is the treatment of the penis as an unnaturally long, thin, up-curving appendage, like a feathered earthworm rampant. The penis of the remarkable Mannerist satyr, making himself fearsomely agreeable to one of the charming nymphs at the end of the table in the painting of the *Marriage Feast of Cupid and Psyche*, from Giulio Romano's workshop, does *159* not appear to be feathery, but it is certainly long and thin, and very red; his pubic hair looks as if it is bursting into flower and his huge red scrotum promises the prowess of a supermale. In view of the loving attention paid to the satyr's genitals it is curious that the painter has troubled to mask the fleece of the nymph, who has nothing very sensational to hide; but it is one of the little paradoxes of the convention that although nymphs were so often involved in love-bouts with satyrs, they were given the same modest treatment as the straight female nude.

Satyrs are monsters in the technical sense in which all hybrids – even mermaids – are monsters; but this purple-skinned Romano satyr is monstrous not only because he is horned and goat-footed; the painter has gone out of his way to express the significance of the horns and the cloven hoofs: his face and body disclose a built-in lustfulness which is pure in the sense of being unmixed with any other attribute. He does not have to lay hands on the nymph to reveal himself as a relentlessly lustful presence. Yet he is not evil as men are evil; he represents the innocence of man before man tasted the fruit of the Tree of Knowledge. He personifies man's instinctual sexual drive, unhampered by an awareness of good and evil, and, as such, his monstrousness does not disallow a nostalgic affection for him. In our time, Picasso has replaced him with the Cretan minotaur, and, with an even more obvious affection for this monster with a man's body and a bull's head, has endowed him with the mournful nobility of an outcast.

Decapitation

In European art, the frenzy of woman has usually been expressed as a seductively wild demonstration of grief and despair, but certain classical and biblical characters – Circe, the Medusa, Delilah, Judith, Salome – are the archetypal figures for the presentation of woman as a destructive erotic force. Edvard Munch even re-arranged the circumstances in which Charlotte Corday assassinated Marat, to depict them as nudes in a purely sexual situation, with Marat dead on a bed and the murderess standing complacently in the foreground, looking the very image of self-centred femininity.

The subjects that have provided the most interesting images of murderesses are the stories of Judith and Holofernes, and Salome and John the Baptist. The fundamental difference between the two stories is that Judith herself decapitated Holofernes and Salome only claimed the Baptist's head after it had been severed by the palace executioner.

Beardsley illustrated the kissing of the Baptist's head before he was asked to illustrate Wilde's text, and the version for the book is a simplification of the earlier drawing. In both versions, the blood dripping from the head is in outline and is less convincing as an incontinent bleeding than the illustration for the Wilde play which Beardsley called *The Dancer's Reward*, where the blood is depicted in solid black. The head of the Baptist is being handed to Salome by the executioner who is represented only by an arm held up vertically to support the dish on which the head lies. Arm and dish form a macabre occasional table. Salome takes ecstatic possession of the head, grasping it by a lock of its hair to tilt it back so that she can gaze into the dead face, and her avidity implies that she will do more monstrous things with the head than Beardsley could be expected to depict. She is being intimate with the blood. She dips a finger into it and will suck the finger; and Beardsley has drawn a pair of elegant slippers to indicate that she has uncovered her feet in order to feel the blood splash on to them and to stand barefooted in a slowly spreading pool of it. She is now more intimate with the Baptist than she could ever have been when he was alive. She can do what she likes with him. She can open his eyelids and stare into the glare that's already acquiring a bloom; she can put a finger or a nipple deep into his open mouth. Huysman's idolatrous description of Gustav Moreau's Salome is really closer to Beardsley's conception of her: 'She had become, as it were the symbolic incarnation of undying lust, the Goddess of immortal Hysteria, the accursed Beauty exalted above all other beauties by the catalepsy that hardens her flesh and steels her muscles.'

If the Baptist had responded to Salome's desire for him and if Holofernes had seduced Judith, neither woman would have been a killer. Judith was a beautiful widowed Jewess of Bethulia, who, to save her native city from the armies of Nebuchadnezzar, assassinated his general, Holofernes, in his tent. When she approached his camp she told his soldiers that she had fled from her own people and could show their general a secret way into the city, without the loss of any of his men. Holofernes was impressed by her beauty, and with the idea of making love to her arranged a feast in her honour. After a time the rest of the company, knowing his intentions towards her, left his tent; but he had drunk too much wine and fell asleep on his bed. Judith took his sword in one hand, the hair of his head in the other, prayed to the Lord for strength and smote him twice on the neck. Having parted his head from his body, she called her maid and they stuffed the head into the bag containing their bread and figs and left the camp. The elders of the city put the head on a spike and the people were so heartened by the sight that they rushed Nebuchadnezzar's armies and put them to flight.

Mantegna's fine drawing shows Judith putting the severed head into the bag, *156* and one wonders whether Judith and her maid celebrated their triumph by feasting on the blood-soaked bread and figs. Francesco del Cairo depicts her as a successful head-hunter proudly posing with a memento of the day's bag. She is a *160* *femme fatale* or *homme manqué* who has discovered a way of reducing the anxiety caused by penis envy; her ashen skin has a suitably greenish tinge.

The decapitation scene was a favourite subject of Caravaggio and his followers, and it is not inappropriate that the most ferocious version was painted by a woman, Artemisia Gentileschi, daughter of Orazio, who was among the most notable of the Caravaggisti. Artemisia was deliberately attempting to paint an *159* even more violent version of the beheading than Caravaggio, and although she owed a great deal to his interpretation, she succeeded. Caravaggio's Judith is less convincing than Artemisia's; she is not exerting enough force to make the severing plausible and is not thoroughly absorbed by her task. In Artemisia's version, a close-up of Holofernes's head is in the foreground, and the spurting of the blood is frighteningly realistic. The ruthlessness of Judith is necessary once the throat has been cut, and her efficiency, which suggests that she has had previous experience of cutting into living flesh, increases the horror. But the strangest and most horrifying aspect of the painting is the unconsciously ambiguous treatment of Holofernes's limbs. One can mistake his arms for his raised legs and go on seeing them as legs even after it becomes clear that the clenched hand beyond Judith's sword-arm is joined to one of them and that his knee is raised further down the bed. The result of this ambiguity is that the head looks as if it is being cut from the crotch. It is not likely that Artemisia was practising what Dali calls the 'paranoiac-critical method', but she created a proto-surrealistic image; a decapitation and a castration as a single act.

The Wounded and the Dead

Lucretia's suicide remains a heroic act, even if one finds it difficult to accept the idea that a woman who has been raped but not physically harmed has reasonable cause for taking her own life. If Sextus Tarquin had simply threatened to plunge his dagger into her breast unless she yielded herself to him, her profound respect for the marriage vow would have put his threat to the test, but he also told her that if he had to kill her he would say that he had done so because he dis-

194 (*Opposite*)
EGON SCHIELE
Reclining girl

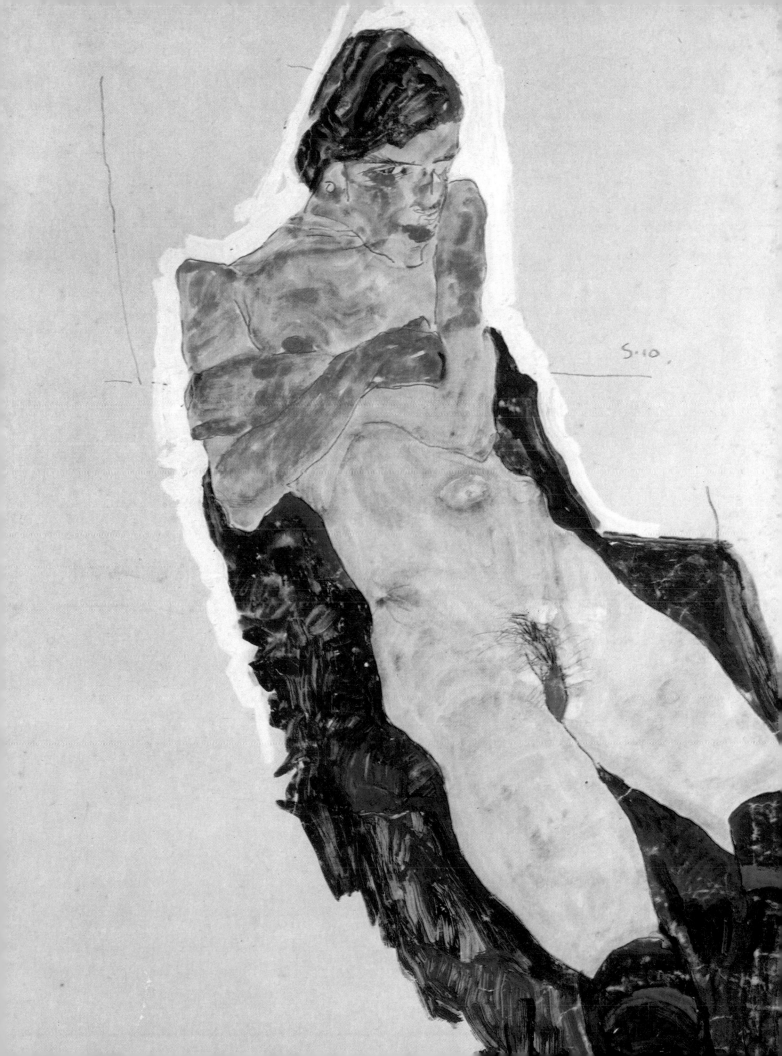

195 (*Left*)
BEARDSLEY
The examination of the
herald. Illustration for
Lysistrata

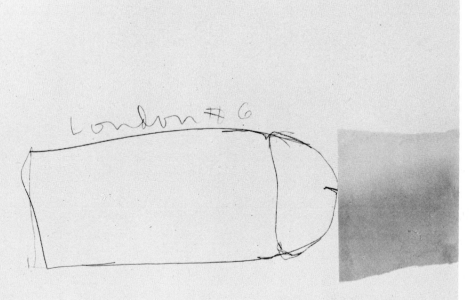

196 (*Left*)
JIM DINE
London no. 6

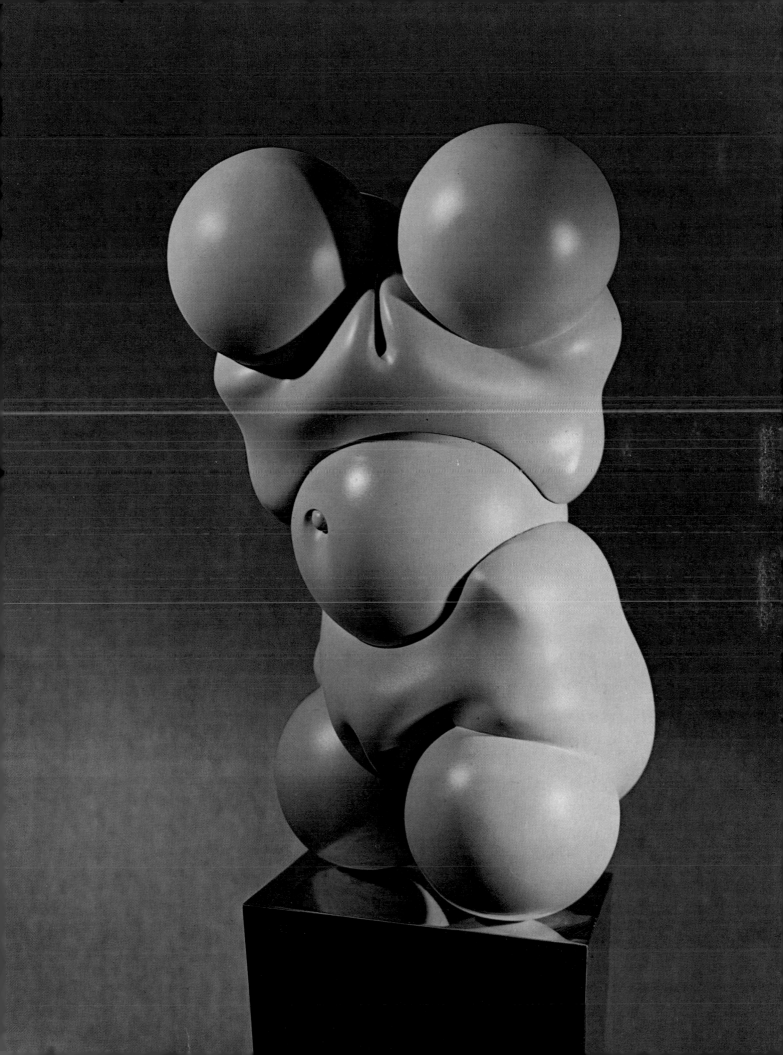

199 (*Previous page left*)
CHIRICO
The uncertainty of the poet

200 (*Previous page right*)
HANS BELLMER
Doll

201 (*Left*)
CORREGGIO
Design for a fountain

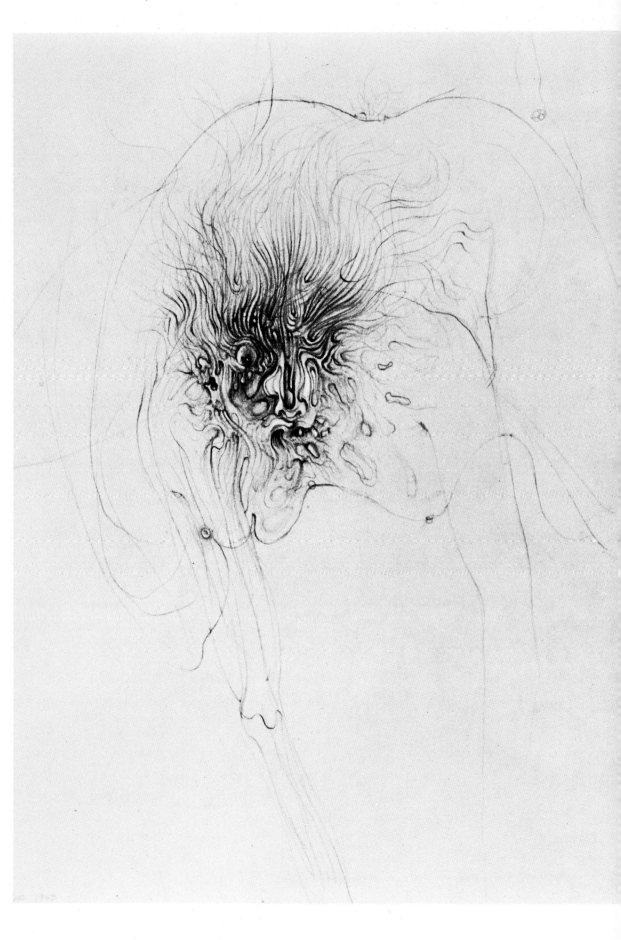

covered that she was dishonouring her husband by lying with other men. So, ironically, the preservation of her good name demanded her consent to his attentions.

In the Fitzwilliam *Tarquin and Lucretia*, Titian tried to be fair to her attitude to the situation, whilst making a totally erotic response to the body of the model. Lucretia's body is not really active in the resistance to Tarquin, and Titian conveys the impression that if it had its way it would be complacent. Her head is small and intense, and its sharply defined features are not in harmony with the large, soft, muzzy forms of her body. The notion of faithfulness and the sense of shame are thus pathetically isolated, and if in these circumstances her body obtained pleasure from the enforced intercourse, she would think that she had been unchaste and
162, 163 find in it a cause for suicide. For Veronese and Cranach, the image of Lucretia plunging a dagger into her own breast has the remoteness of a sacrificial ritual. They are unable to acknowledge that there was any shame in surviving Tarquin's dagger, and in its own way it is admirable that they cannot bring themselves to let her dagger actually pierce her breast. Yet their pictures suffer because of their squeamishness.

I am not wholly convinced by Baudelaire's contention that the pleasure afforded by line and colour is absolutely independent of the subject of the picture. I have no criticism of the line and colour which form the image in either the Veronese or the Cranach. But neither image is satisfactory because there is no piercing of the flesh and no fetching of blood. This is not bloodthirstiness on my part; it is simply that the painters have done less than justice to the finality of the act. Their restraint, their hesitation, is untrue to Lucretia's inflexible purpose.

Botticelli painted the finding of Holofernes after Judith had left the camp, and the headless male body creates an atmosphere of utter desolation; it is an image of absolute impotence. This would not be so if it were the image of a headless woman. The example that comes to mind – George Grosz's *Sex Murder on Acker-strasse* – is a far cry from Botticelli, but the headless body on the bed is still beautiful, potent and desirable. The reason must be that in the conventional sexual relationship between a man and a woman, it is the woman to whom things are done: a dead man cannot act, but a dead woman can receive. If anything, the image of a beautiful woman, wounded, dead or dying increases one's sense of her beauty.

The woman attacked by dogs in the third panel of Botticelli's *The Story of*
166 *Nastagio degli Onesti* is not one of his greatest nudes, but the savaging by dogs makes her seem marvellously beautiful. The story, illustrated in four panels, is taken from Boccaccio. Nastagio, rejected by the daughter of Paolo Traversan, wanders disconsolately in a wood, and a naked girl appears, pursued by a knight and his dogs. The dogs are biting her, but before Nastagio can go to her rescue, the knight tears out her heart and gives it to his dogs. The girl then magically revives and the chase continues. The knight explains that he is an ancestor of Nastagio and that he committed suicide because the girl rejected him. The gods have punished them both by making them enact this chase periodically.
Nastagio invites the girl who has refused him to attend a banquet with her parents in the place where he saw the vision, and in the third panel the phantom chase comes thundering past the banqueting table. After Nastagio has explained its

204 (*Opposite*)
DAVID HOCKNEY
Marriage of styles

significance to his astonished guests the girl agrees to marry him and the fourth panel is devoted to their marriage feast. The panels were designed by Botticelli and carried out for the most part by his assistants, but the nature of the content – the image of the savaging of the naked girl appears in three of the panels – lends to a work which is not particularly distinguished in its line and colour an incalculable charm.

In the painting by Piero di Cosimo which used to be known as *The Death of Procris* but is now cautiously described by the National Gallery as *Mythological Subject*, the woman has died of a throat wound. She was the jealous wife of Cephalos, and had crept into a wood to spy on him when he was out hunting. Hearing a sound of rustling coming from the thicket in which she was hiding, he shot an arrow into it, thinking that a wild animal was lurking there, and unwittingly killed her. Now her death is a mystery. When she was still Procris, D. H. Lawrence wanted to replace Cephalos as her killer. He made a small copy of the Piero but increased the flow of blood and painted it a much brighter red than in the original. His rather detestable defence of his intervention associates the act of murder with sexual plethora: 'I delighted so in painting that bloodstream. I could not resist the urge to make it real red-red, only I couldn't get it bloody enough, the warm slightly steaming, liquid red blood. I wanted to experience the lust of killing in that picture. Killing is natural to man, you know. It is just as natural as lying with a woman. I often feel I could kill and enjoy it.'

I am glad Piero's dead woman is no longer Procris. It frees her from jealousy as the cause of her death. She is still wondrously in the flesh and has become pure feminine comeliness. I think that the myth is Piero's own invention. He is the great poet-recluse of painting and he has conceived this picture as a kind of prodigal's return. She is not being mourned; she is being received back into the animal kingdom with the tenderness due to Nature's loveliest creation. In death she is 'full of fresh delight'.

9 Treatment of the Parts

Hair

Amidst the great series of Deluge drawings by Leonardo, in the Windsor Collection, there is one that is so different from the rest that it has come to be known as the 'Formalized Deluge'. The swirling waters have changed their nature. They have turned into an abstract linear force, no longer recognizable as water. They are slow, sensual, coiling pen lines, destroying a city with cunning. They attack from above with demonstrative spirals, and more insidiously and destructively from below, undermining the foundations with battalions of wire-thin coils that wind more and more tightly as they close in on their objective. We recognize them. The outer ranks are the loose ringlets of the Virgin's hair in the Uffizi *Annunciation*; the inner ranks, massed under the tottering buildings, are the tight curls of the hair of the Angel. The city is collapsing internally: beguiled by the coils (which acquire the power to destroy only by arousing in the city the desire to be destroyed) it falls victim to its own vertigo.

168 If Mary Magdalen had appeared before Christ himself with long serpentine tresses falling as artfully across her naked body as the golden hair in Gregor Erhart's painted and gilded effigy of her, Christ himself might have fallen a victim to vertigo. Erhart, a sixteenth-century German sculptor, carved this figure as part of a group depicting her conversion. The artist relies on the penitential pose to sanctify the sensuality of his conception, and one can only praise his faith in the hypocrisy of his fellow-men and his well-founded conviction that men can arrange a woman's hair more temptingly than she can herself. This is an image that skirts heartlessness in making Mary Magdalen seem full of guile at the very moment of her conversion. Her hair parts to allow her right breast to peep forth and, so to speak, steal the show from the one that is fully exposed. Her hands are clasped together under the right breast, and the arm that crosses her body presses her golden tresses against her belly and spreads them to veil her sex. If and when she raises her arms in prayer her tresses will fall to one side.

The convention of nudity for images of the Magdalen started in the fifteenth century, probably in Italy, and although she was painted only in penitence, her past seems to have provided sufficient excuse for the convention to be tolerated as long as she looks as if she is trying to hide her nakedness with her hair. Titian's *Magdalen*, in the Pitti Gallery, is more straightforwardly sensual than the many *167* copies of it that were made. The facsimile from his own workshop was given to the Ambrosiana by Cardinal Borromeo in 1618. He defended his gift by saying that Titian knew how to maintain the honesty of the nude. It is not difficult to agree with any word meant as praise of Titian's nudes, and 'honesty' is right enough if it covers his deliberately erotic disposition of a woman's luxuriant hair, and his sensuous feeling for the texture of hair and skin. The arm slightly lifting a breast and the hands spreading the lively rippling hair make the Pitti *Magdalen* an unforgettable image of a woman in touch with her own body. The argument for the Magdalen coming naked to the Faith equates nakedness with truth: nevertheless, although Erhart and Titian give expression to her humility and piety in the treatment of her face, they use her hair as an adornment. By doing so, they provide us with a ravishing and peculiarly poignant 'last glimpse' of the beautiful body of a woman who henceforth will be ashamed of it and hide it from sight.

Michelangelo's magnificent drawing of Cleopatra belongs to the period (1532-4) *175* in which he was passionately in love with the youthful, beautiful, highly cultured Tomaso Cavalieri, whose praise and understanding he humbly sought in a series of superb drawings of desperate situations – the Fall of Phaethon, Tityus bound in Hades, with a vulture tearing out his heart – symbolically connected with the torments of love. Cleopatra taking her own life by applying an asp to her bosom is no less involved in the theme of destructive passion. It would seem to be a marvellous variation on Piero di Cosimo's portrait of Simonetta Vespucci, itself a *173* work of intense linear refinement. Piero's Simonetta is impassively beautiful and aware of it; any expression of the convulsions of the soul is in the complicated braiding of the hair intertwined with ropes of pearls. The thickest braid, crowned by a ruby, climbs over the back of Simonetta's head like a slow caterpillar, in sharp contrast to the snake gliding swiftly along a course determined by her gold necklace and darting out its tongue at its tail as if expecting another head to be there. The Michelangelo drawing is a strange and mysterious loosening of the entire conception. The absolute visibility of Piero's image is replaced by ambiguities, equivocations and obscurities which prefigure the Baroque. A hair-band glides down Cleopatra's cheek and one long braid of her hair falls away and slithers round her shoulder like an imitation snake. The snake itself glides in on the air, passing behind Cleopatra's shoulders to sweep down and close round one of her breasts, its tail still far out in space. Cleopatra has been given a face softly and voluptuously mournful, eyes filled with 'perishing dreams and wrecks of forgotten delirium'. The venom is already casting its spell. She has become gentle and patient and estranged from her inordinate beauty.

The Three Brides by the Dutch artist Jan Toorop gathers the hair fetishism of the *171* Pre-Raphaelites and the Symbolist poets into an extraordinary linear fantasia. The ostensible theme is treated unimaginatively. There is a wide-eyed spiritual bride, a weaker, pretty, ordinary bride and an absurdly evil bride wearing a necklace of skulls. They are surrounded by a bevy of floating handmaidens as angular and emaciated as Javanese shadow puppets. One of them gives the spiritual bride a lily, another is running the hem of the ordinary bride's gown through her bony fingers and a third pours a thick libation for the evil bride. But the handmaidens are also the carriers of the real theme. Out of ringing bells pour great streams of wavy parallel lines as if to represent sound, but they turn into labyrinths of hair, and although they issue from the bells they end their rhythmic delirious journey on the scalps of the handmaidens. It is a vision of an expanding universe of hair.

Mouth

The double images which Edvard Munch discovered in natural phenomena leave room for conjecture. To what extent did he intend the moon and its elongated reflection in water to suggest sexual love? The reflection is a form as palpable as the moon itself and in *Summer Night on the Shore*, a painting which once belonged to Alma Mahler, it can be seen as a phallus plunging into the water; an emblem of sexual longings instigated by moonlight. In an earlier drypoint, simply called *Summer Night*, the two forms together can be seen as cup and ball; in this case the moon becomes the male principle and the cup formed by its reflection stands for the female principle, signifying that man is the plaything of woman. All we know for certain is that Munch rarely painted landscape for its own sake, and that whenever these two forms appear in his painting, they intensify the erotic atmosphere. They make a sign, and the sign is more important than the phenomenon ostensibly signified. A lonely walk did not release him from thoughts about 176 woman and his landscapes were an expression of nervous excitement. His *Summer Night at Oslo Fjord* is landscape in collusion with woman, and again the double image or sign or apparition is caused by a moonlit reflection. A long, narrow island with a pale, sandy beach is reflected in the water, and the island and its reflection form a mouth with slightly parted lips. The image as sign remains equivocal; reality and illusion are confused in a single impression, and it really could be a trick of the light seen by the eye and seized on by a mind preoccupied by passion or regret or bitterness or despair.

I do not know if Man Ray knew Munch's picture when he painted a mouth in 174 the sky and called it *Observatory Time – The Lovers*. It looks as if it might have been abstracted from the Munch and put into a simpler, more schematic context. It is a neat, cool, efficient illustration of a charming erotic idea. There is a double image, but it has not been discovered in nature. The mouth is composed of two organic abstractions, pressed together like lovers.

The fashion in mouth-eroticism has changed considerably since Man Ray painted *Observatory Time* in the early thirties. His enlargement of a closed mouth floating across the sky postulates the 'inflatable' as an art object but serves the idea 177 of love as a romantic enormity. Joe Tilson's image of a mouth excised from a laughing girl's face and leaving only the sense of a sexual opening is typical of the fashion of the sixties. It is not an emblem or even an emotive fragment but simply a close-up of a component of the moist machinery of love-making.

Breast

The quietly lyrical, softly luminous study of feminine beauty in Tintoretto's *Woman*

Revealing her Breast seems a surprising work to come from a painter of dynamic and   *179*
tumultuous compositions, yet there is a kind of sacramental boldness in the
woman's gesture that is exceptional in the Renaissance treatment of erotic subjects.
It is something quite different from the 'accidental' emergence of the breasts in
Titian's painting of the penitent Magdalen and confers on the image a grace and   *167*
nobility free from any moralistic concern with right behaviour. It has inevitably
aroused speculations about the identity of the model, but unlike the mystery
surrounding Leonardo's Mona Lisa the nominations for the honour have not
included married ladies. The most pleasantly romantic suggestion is that she was
the famous Venetian prostitute-poetess, Veronica Franco.

A half-length study of an undraped smiling woman at Chantilly was thought
at one time to be a preparatory cartoon for the *Mona Lisa*, and although the attribution to Leonardo was untenable, the possibility remains that it derives from a
lost work by him. There were many rumours and suppositions, during his lifetime, that he had made nude studies of the sitter. Several of the half-length nudes
of women painted for the French court at the Palace of Fontainebleau in the
sixteenth century are variations on the nude *Mona Lisa* by Leonardo's imitators.
The portrait of a naked woman, hidden from just below the naval by a dressing-   *164*
table, is a typical example of the Fontainebleau half-lengths. It is closely related
to Clouet's *Diane de Poitiers*, and like the Clouet exploits the palace convention
of celebrating the erotic virtue of a pair of upstanding nipples. The woman's pose,
the background reference to Titian's *Venus of Urbino* and the ornamental looking-
glass are indicative of the painter's dependence on the Clouet picture, but it is even
more obviously a portrait of a mistress. In the Clouet, the naked effigies of a man
and woman supporting the mirror stand at the opposite ends of the frame, but
have become a central support in the present work to enable the artist to depict
them embracing. The nipples in the portrait are given a transparency suggestive
of precious stones and illustrate the 'conceit' that they are the most valuable and
beautiful gems in her collection. In other examples, the nipples are not made to
look like transparent stones, but their colour is intended to compare favourably with
a display of rubies. Early in the eighteenth century Pietro Longhi painted a
pastoral variation on the theme. A shepherd girl uncovers one of her breasts
to compare the nipple with a little red wild flower. There is nothing to choose
between them; they are dabs of the same colour.

The details of a young woman giving suck to her deprived father through the
bars of his prison is from Caravaggio's *The Seven Works of Mercy*, and in a some-   *165*
what far-fetched way she illustrates either the line in Matthew 25, verse 35: 'I was
thirsty and ye gave me drink', or the line in verse 36: 'I was in prison and ye came
unto me.' It's the only clearly depicted act of mercy in a confused and busy crowd
scene, and it would seem to be the only situation which interested the painter,
for the male angel swooping out of the upper air is concentrating all his attention
on the act. I wondered for a moment whether I should make it a prelude to a note
on incest, but to be the recipient of the freely offered milk of a woman's breast is
one of the universal if rarely mentioned dreams of the adult male.

In *The Virgin and the Souls in Purgatory*, the sixteenth-century Spanish painter   *178*
Pedro Machuca had the delightful idea of giving the souls in Purgatory a real
incentive to expiate their sins and make themselves eligible for entry into Heaven.

In allowing the child Jesus to promise them pneumatic bliss by means of a convincing demonstration on the breast of the Virgin, Machuca is among the few Christian painters who have given us a glimpse of a Heaven that might be fit for human habitation.

The painter Manet was so infinitely more gifted than the print-maker Rops that it seems scarcely possible to make a comparison between them that could favour Rops in any way. Yet in one respect a comparison between Manet's *La Blonde aux seins nus* and Rops's etching of a similar subject seems to me to do Rops much credit. Manet's noncommital attitude to the ravishing subject of his painting is of course more sophisticated and refined than Rops's evident interest in a less beautiful model, and Manet did not need to be interested in his subject to create a telling image as well as a notable example of his free brushwork. All the same, if we can free our regard for the painting from the pleasing erotic associations aroused by the subject it becomes clear that much greater spontaneity and verve have gone into the painting of the girl's headgear than into the painting of her breasts, in which the treatment verges on banality, as if he found them rather uninterestingly bald. The picture lends no support to Baudelaire's contention that line and colour make one think and dream and are absolutely independent of the subject. The outstandingly brilliant treatment of the girl's hat does not in fact make one think and dream. It makes one admire his virtuosity. Rops's treatment of the breasts discloses a more imaginative response. The unusual concentric lines give them something of the whirling and engulfing look of a vortex and a hint of barbaric splendour. They create a sense of that mysterious 'otherness' of woman; and if Manet's treatment of the hat leads to Sargent, Rops's treatment of the breast leads to Picasso, whose art makes Freud's view that civilization has no permanent defence against a vigorous barbarism something to be thankful for.

The Blind and Public Mass

Watteau used the nude in his open air *Fêtes galantes* by introducing garden statuary into the settings. A sculpture group of Venus and Cupid is in *Plaisirs d'Amour*, and the same group seen from precisely the same point of view, but with two extra Cupids, occupies a similar position in the Berlin version of *L'Embarquement pour Cythère*. A naiad reclining on a marble shelf above a miniature waterfall surveys an assembly of exquisites in *Fêtes Vénitiennes*; another is fast asleep in *Les Champs-Elysées*. A group of naked children playing with a goat, copied from a sculpture by Jaques Sarazin, glimmers in the shadowy background of *Assemblée dans un Parc*. All these sculptures are raised above the gatherings of people, and although they are already personifications they seem also to personify the sophisticated pastoralism of the festivities.

The naiad in *Réunion Champêtre* is in a different place in the composition and acquires a different significance. She is in the same plane as the foreground group of elegant men and women, and in this situation she is not so much a personification as a promise, an ideal blossoming of the hidden bodies of the women in the gathering. A man who has detached himself from the group appears to be admiring her. This is not surprising; she is probably the loveliest and certainly the most voluptuous nude painted by Watteau. She has the proportions of a Rubens nude and her forms are so softly rounded that she may well have been based not on an existing statue but on a drawing from the life. A study for her may even have been in the sheaf of drawings of the nude which Watteau, tragically confused by Christian doctrine, destroyed just before his death. The statue presents a back view and is bending forward to disclose a magnificent pair of buttocks. If there were no ladies present, her admirer in the picture would be inspecting this part of her with the same satisfaction as the doctors called in to examine the behind of a young woman in an eighteenth-century French engraving.

Sartre has remarked that 'many women loathe their backside, that blind and public mass which belongs to everyone before belonging to them', but it is probably the most sculptural aspect of a woman's body. There is a painting of the back view of a reclining nude by Courbet, in the collection of the sculptor Henry Moore, which is as beautiful and monumental as the rumps of horses in the paintings of Uccello, and makes a form so self-contained and so seemingly independent of the rest of the figure that it looks like a sensitive boulder that could be rolled away. It reveals unsought-for associations with the smooth biomorphic sculpture of Moore and Arp. Moore himself, explaining the relationship between sight and the sense of touch, has said that a child learns about roundness from handling a ball far more than from looking at it. This could in its turn explain why so many men treat the female behind as a 'public mass' rather than a private part, and it might even provide some sort of excuse for the bottom-pincher. Jordaens seems to have taken this point of view in his treatment of the Bathsheba *183* story. He has not only treated Bathsheba's behind as a monstrous flamboyant, he has made her coquettishly aware that it is a man-trap. Jordaens is on the side of the old men; but his version of the story is not of course the true one, and his Bathsheba would be more suitably employed tempting St Anthony.

Sight and the sense of touch are in perfect accord in Stanley Spencer's drawing *184* of a man's loving approach to a woman's behind. The woman has raised her legs high to afford her lover the best possible view of it. He is lying on his belly, his penis squashed under him and his testicles pressed into view on the carpet. The warmth, smoothness and solidity of the woman's behind are at his finger tips, his nose is lifted to sniff the strong musky perfume coming from it and he is about to press his lips to one of its cheeks. Nothing else is in his field of vision. His organs of sight, smell and taste and his sense of touch are so engaged by its white vastness that it has become his total environment. Adrian Stokes, in *Reflections on the Nude*, makes a plea for an approach to the naked figure which would reconstitute it as an image of bountifulness without the implication of avidity for its parts. Nevertheless, Spencer intended a serious work and it hints at an interest in monumental form and feminine bountifulness, but it needed more than a hint to overcome the anecdotal atmosphere of the drawing and convert the facetious effect of the foreshortenings into pictorial drama. It is a pity that he was given no encouragement to take this idea for a grand composition beyond the stage of a sketch in a secret notebook. I think he might have achieved a work in which he celebrated avidity for the parts as an ineradicable element of eroticism, with only a minimal loss of human dignity. As it is, he has left us a brilliant illustration of what psychoanalysts might describe as an instinctive re-instatement of an infantile condition, with the backside substituting for the feeding infant's total identification with the mother's enveloping breast.

185   Facetiousness laced with irony was intended in Beardsley's sumptuously economical drawing *The Toilet of Lampito*, and the intention is fulfilled. Dying of TB, confined to sex in the head, he sometimes identified himself with Cupid. Sometimes he is the baby boy god, pretty and plump, pissing on a copy of *The Yellow Book* after losing his job as art editor, or trotting off with a gallows for the barber into whose head he has put the idea of cutting the desirable throat of one of his lady clients. He is Cupid old enough to masturbate when helping Lampito with her toilet, and, as promised in Victorian pamphlets about the perils of self-abuse, he has become very thin. It is clear that he is not expecting to make love to her himself and is preparing her for someone else; the position of Lampito's right arm makes it equally evident that she is confidently expecting to receive her lover face to face. Cupid, however, has other ideas, and is gleefully preparing her 'blind and public mass' for an anal insertion.

The Vulva

186   Leonardo's drawing of a gaping vagina has some bearing on his general attitude towards women. His contemporaries had no doubt that he was, at least for a time, a practising homosexual; but art historians who for some reason cannot bear the thought that a handsome boy's anus might be the preferred source of pleasure for so great a genius, lean to the somewhat extravagant view that he endured throughout his life the self-torturing condition described by Freud with ill-suppressed satisfaction as 'platonic, solitary and tragic homosexuality'. But at least no one, as Kenneth Clark has pointed out, can 'seriously maintain that he had the normal man's feeling for woman'.

    The sheet on which the drawing of the vagina appears is number 19095 in the Windsor Collection, and the sheet is described in the catalogue by Kenneth Clark and Carlo Pedretti as follows: 'Above, drawing of external genitalia and vagina, with notes. Below, notes on the anal sphincter and diagrams of suggested arrangement of its fibres and its modes of action.' I do not doubt that the study of the vagina is the result of objective observation, but I very much doubt if the vagina he observed was in a suitable condition for conveying useful scientific information. It is clearly the vagina of a cadaver, and a rather casual indication in the drawing that the legs have been sawn-off above the knees suggests that the carcass has already been much used. Even in a dead body the vagina would be closed unless it had been subjected to too much interference. This is a vulva whose muscular action has been strained far beyond normal limits and may have even been opened to draw out the interior organs, but whether, like Maldoror, Leonardo himself pulled them out, we shall never know. Given the condition of the vulva, it is not surprising that the anus proved to be a better subject for the study of a muscle controlling a bodily opening.

187   When Tintoretto's cuckolded Vulcan lifts the strip of cloth across Venus's loins

to see whether she has just been having intercourse with Mars, he does not expect to find a wide-open vulva; he is looking for signs of their 'liquid raptures', specks of jellified sperm on her fleece, moisture on the sheet. Leonardo's drawing is an ugly travesty of the normal appearance of the vulva, and since its scientific value is negligible, the choice of the carcass from which he made his observations would seem to have served a more subjective purpose. I think that the choice may have been made in a spirit of denigration and that his drawing reflects an aversion to woman little short of horror and disgust. It is like a medieval vision of the mouth of Hell. A yawning cavern 'over whose mouth no bird could fly unscathed, so poisonous the breath exhaled from its jaws'.

Yet one has to admit that there is a hint of the fascination of the horrible in every man's approach to woman. When, in the course of love-making, a man parts a woman's vulva with his fingers he can be taken by surprise and flinch at the sight of the secret pink flesh, glistening with moisture and looking terribly raw as if stripped of skin. Ordinarily, the vulva is veiled by hair, seen in a drawing by Schiele as a natural and attractive camouflage of an important emplacement, and depicted more dramatically and elegantly by Wunderlich from an angle *169* designed to show as much as possible of the vulva without interference. So it is what a man knows rather than what he sees that provides an explanation for those absurd eighteenth-century engravings in which the Devil is frightened out of his wits when a young woman pulls up her clothes and shows him her sexual fleece. In Rowlandson's *The Hairy Prospect or the Devil in a Fright*, the saucy girl has only *189* something very modest to display compared with the Devil's big swag of genitals 'all shagged about with hair'.

The artists of our time when insisting on the sexuality of the naked female figure also tend to paint what they know as well as what they see. In Kitaj's *Symchromy with FB*, the vulva of the girl squatting so anachronistically beside the *170* remarkable image of Francis Bacon as a sort of Dorian Gray on the day of reckoning is treated as a slow-bleeding cut, and in Schiele's nude it has become a creature *194* in its own right, a blood-red beetle with long whiskers, crawling out of the dark. In both cases the redness has the significance of the glow from an interior fire, and one has the impression that the artists are anxious that we should realize that they are not afraid of 'playing with fire'.

If in Leonardo's drawing the vulva is the mouth of Hell, in Lucian Freud's superb *Portrait Fragment* it is the entrance to a secret cave. His foreshortened view *172* of the figure creates a correspondence with landscape, and brings to mind the passage in Beardsley's unfinished novel *Under the Hill* in which woman is described as a promised land:

On the horizon swell two immense snowy white hillocks; these are capped by pink peaks or tips – as if the rosy-fingered dawn itself were playing just behind them. The landscape then undulates gently down to a broad, smooth, swelling plain, its soft, rolling curves broken only in the lower centre by a small, volcanic crater. Farther down, the scene narrows and changes perspective. Off to the right and left jut two smooth snowy ridges. Between them, at their point of juncture, is a dark wood and in its midst is a dark, romantic chasm. In this cavern the wonders of nature abound . . .

Graham Ovenden sees his studies of little girls as Alice, and tends to identify himself with Lewis Carroll. He is not, however, concerned with Alice's adventures. It is Lewis Carroll the photographer with whom he identifies, and his work lends eloquent support to Carroll's passionate contention that there is nothing more beautiful than the naked bodies of little girls, and his admiration for Carroll as a photographer is so great that his art can be regarded as a tribute to Carroll's photographs of little girls in the nude which disappeared, and were probably destroyed, long before Ovenden was born. But in girls too young to have pubic hair the vulva is much more exposed than in a grown woman, and it is unlikely that Carroll would have dared to take the intransigently frontal views of his models that makes Ovenden's paintings and drawings so disturbingly beautiful.

190

The Penis

I have not had the privilege of seeing any of the drawings by Fuseli that are considered to be obscene. When Ruthven Todd published his admirable essay on the artist in *Tracks in the Snow*, in 1946, he reproduced nine innocuous details from six of them 'lately in his possession', and regretted that he was unable to reproduce them in their entirety. He remarks that they 'possess an extraordinary atmosphere, where the faces of the actors are quite unmoved by the strange actions which they perform; Fuseli's hair-fetishism shows in the elaborate head-dresses of the women, whose hair, poured and moulded into fantastic shapes, suffers no disturbance from the static violence of which they partake.' This is a moderate version of Sacheverell Sitwell's approach to Fuseli's drawings in *Splendours and Miseries*, published years earlier. He had evidently seen the same or a similar set of the obscene drawings and said of them that they 'may be characterized as the only really evil drawings ever done'. He finds the same atmosphere of evil in two published drawings, *The Debutante* and *The Fireplace*, and his imaginative interpretation of them is a fascinating supplement to the pleasure afforded by the drawings themselves. He comes to the conclusion that the figures 'are not creatures of flesh and blood but phantoms. The succubi of an ill imagination. In a house in Soho. No! no! in the regions of eternal night.' His reference to their 'static horror' ('the contrast of the finished toilet of his figures and the orgy suggested or realized in their action') becomes in Todd's study the somewhat milder 'static violence'.

I do not doubt Todd's assertion that 'the obscene drawings are among the finest of Fuseli's works', and if they are as fine as the half-length of a courtesan with an elaborate head-dress and an armband bearing an emblem composed of a penis and a pair of testicles slightly conventionalized to suggest a Cupid's arrow, published by Paul Ganz, they are truly magnificent. But I doubt if they create an atmosphere of 'horror', let alone qualify as the most evil drawings ever done, and I have more than a suspicion that what Todd calls 'static violence' is simply the act of penetration, with the penis only partly inside the vagina, a well-established convention for conveying a sense of the rhythmic thrust and return of the penis in action. The imperturbable girls in the details published by Todd bring vividly to mind the fragments of Marcantonio's engravings in the British Museum. The coiffures by Marcantonio are elaborate, and although less fantastic than Fuseli's they are equally undisturbed by the 'static violence' going on below. And it is quite clear in both the Marcantonio fragments and the Fuseli details that the girls have adopted various positions for intercourse. In fact, it is evident that Fuseli was able to examine a set of the Aretino Postures during the eight years he lived in Rome, the city in which Marcantonio worked and in which Nollekins purchased the set which he was later persuaded to destroy. One of the Fuseli details is a full-length study of a standing middle-aged woman who is so absorbed by whatever she is watching that her hands are imitating the motions. She is a procuress or brothel-keeper, and in one of the plates of the Aretino Postures based on Marcantonio's engravings, there is also an older woman watching the coupling.

The nearest thing to an obscene work by Fuseli that I have seen is a charming wash drawing, but not comparable in quality with two drawings analysed by Sitwell or the portrait of the courtesan with an armband. It is inscribed very faintly in pencil 'My Lady Betty' and dated 1785. He was then forty-four years old and still a bachelor. He did not marry until three years later, and in 1785 was probably consorting with prostitutes. He was capable of falling passionately in love but was more in love with the act of love. According to Allan Cunningham, who wrote a life of Fuseli first published in 1829, he never tired of recounting how he spent day after day and week after week lying on his back in the Sistine Chapel, staring at the Michelangelo ceiling; sometimes adding that such a posture of repose was necessary 'for a body fatigued like his with the pleasant gratifications of a luxurious city'. In 1779, when he was spending a few months in Zürich, his home town, before settling permanently in England, he fell in love with the niece of his friend Lavater, the author of a famous book on physiognomy. He failed to arouse her interest but was still infatuated with her when he reached London and he wrote a feverish letter to Lavater in which he confessed to having fantasies of possessing her: 'Last night I had her in bed with me – tossed my bedclothes hugger-mugger – wound my hot and tight clasped hands about her, fused her body and *soul* together with my own – poured into her my spirit, breath and strength. Anyone who touches her now commits adultery and incest!' A little later he was imploring Lavater for news of her, to save him 'from Polly, Nancy, and Peggy'. But he was not saved from Polly, Nancy and Peggy, and it is clear that 'My Lady Betty' belonged to the same profession.

Betty is a very pretty girl, and it is a pretty drawing. The grey washes are relieved by some effective little touches of colour; her necklace, bangles and garters are golden; her cheeks, the fichu draped from her curls, and the male genitals she holds in her hand are pink. It is a study made with admiration for the model's agreeable girlishness, and with delight in the disposition of her gown which provides a provocative glimpse beyond the garters. It does not help me to appreciate Ganz's view that Fuseli's studies of prostitutes express contempt and moral indignation.

Fuseli devotes a quaint paragraph to the provocation of feminine garments in his *Remarks on Rousseau*: 'To know that stays paint to the eagle eye of love here their luxuriance of bosom and milky orbs of rapture and there the slender waist and rising hips; that with the perfumes of their toilet contagion spreads, that aprons will invite Hamlet to build tabernacles between Beauty's legs, and petti-coats appear to Romeo the gates of Heaven – What will be the consequence of all this? They will open them.' This is eroticism pure and simple, but Fuseli was a better draughtsman than writer, and the drawing of Lady Betty is a study of impersonal sexuality. The male sexual parts in the girl's hand have not been conventionalized into a symbolic device. They are drawn naturalistically; they look as alive and fresh as if they were still between a man's legs, and they undoubtedly symbolize her role as receiver (the penis is still in erection), but they are not bloodstained, and there is nothing in their treatment to suggest that someone has been castrated. Nor is there anything in the atmosphere of the drawing to suggest that the girl is a harpy or a succubus. She delights in intercourse; it is the genitals in good working order that matter to her, not the man's identity, and Fuseli has depicted her as a day-dreaming voluptuary. What she holds is not a sinister trophy but a symbol of sexual pleasure. If, as I think, Fuseli himself was in love with the act of love, he has bestowed on the girl his own sexuality. In view of the nature of the gift, I wish that Fuseli could have given it greater visual impact. It could have been larger, a bit out of scale, and although it looks fresh enough, it should look more precious, and perhaps more succulent, like the sacred meal that Dali made of it in one of his most exquisite drawings – and served up

192   on a mouth-shaped dish to celebrate fellatio. One would not of course expect in such a context anything as consequential as the giant penises in Beardsley's

195, 197   illustrations for *Lysistrata*, which are probably the most refined, meticulous, decorative and reverential drawings of the human penis ever devised.

Brian Reade has suggested that in some respects Beardsley was 'an amateur St Anthony' and if one equates the saint with Bosch's version of him, they can both be said to be cases of sex in the head; but I wonder how the word 'amateur' came into the comparison. If Reade thinks of Anthony as a saint by profession he is probably right, but Beardsley had no pretentions to saintliness and was certainly not an amateur in any other sense. Bosch's St Anthony led a life of intense excitement based on his ability to see importunate orifices at every turn; he preserved his saintliness, in spite of his erotomania, by breaking off a sexual daydream when it threatened to bring on an emission, and some might think that his knife-edge exercise of the will entitled him to canonization. Beardsley's drawings of Messalina brilliantly disclose his interest in nymphomania, but he was fascinated by any kind of sexual extremism and was not haunted by female orifices. A horribly effective brake on actual sexual adventures was the threat of tubercular haemorrhages; it was a threat that dogged him throughout his brief life, and it would seem to have given him a compulsive and contemplative interest in his own genitalia. I think the giant penis in the foreground of the frontispiece to *Lysistrata* and the fantastically disproportionate genitalia of the young man in the drawing called *The*

195   *Examination of the Herald*, from the same book, are mirror images.

Borges maintains that mirrors have something monstrous about them, and he is not thinking of distorting mirrors but of those ordinary useful looking-glasses that provide you with an exact, ungetatable duplicate of yourself. They are monstrous because the image they throw back at you is purely imitative. If you put out your tongue at your mirror-image, he will put out his tongue at you. If you show him your penis he will show you his. If you turn round and put your head between your legs to spy on his anus, you will find him looking at yours with exactly the same degree of interest. He raises narcissistic hopes that cannot be fulfilled. If only he would stop imitating you and come out to join you, you could do things together that you could not do with anyone else in the world. It could have been the artist's concentrated stare at the mirror image of his own penis that has imparted to the Herald's huge appendage its strange air of sadness. The Herald himself is not at all sad; but he is not a mirror image; he is invented, not observed. The penis belongs to another world, a world of biological sorrow. It has something of the intense and serious gaze that meets our eyes when an artist paints a self-portrait. In a self-portrait there is a subconscious intention to persuade us that the artist has powers of observation more penetrating than an ordinary man's; the presence of such an intention reduces the objectivity of the portrait, and there is invariably a hint of aggression mixed up with the gravity.

It is no more possible to be neutral about your genitals than your face, and in Beardsley's treatment of the Herald's penis there is a touch of idealization; it is closely observed but the erection has a kind of remote stateliness, and in his study of the testicles he has refused to acknowledge that the skin of a man's scrotum is wrinkled. The element of aggressiveness in a self-portrait here takes the form of an unnatural magnification.

The author of *My Secret Life*, to whom one so often has to turn for discussion of a man's anxieties about his private parts, worried a great deal about the size of his penis, and although he was continually being assured by prostitutes that it was perfectly normal, he was never free from doubt. The same doubt has probably troubled man throughout the ages. There is evidence that certain primitive tribes have gone to the trouble of actually lengthening them or of using devices to make them appear longer than they are. In one African tribe, it used to be the practice to hang weights on the penises of the boys to stretch them. The extensibility of the penis is given a tragi-comic treatment by Martin Van Maele in one of the etchings in his portfolio, *La grande danse macabre des vifs*. A man has managed to stretch his penis until it is long enough to wind round his neck and knot to a hook in the ceiling. A woman and another man, startled out of their love-making, have burst open the door, and the woman is so upset by the sight of a man hanging from his own penis that she might have lost her balance if she had not clutched her friend's penis, which fortunately was still in a state of erection. The British Museum has photographs of a Sepik River tribe in which there are very striking exaggerations of the codpiece. The tribe's isolation in the central highlands of New Guinea is said to have kept its culture intact, but the photographs show that whites have had some influence for a number of tribesmen are wearing frayed and torn shorts which give them a poverty-stricken look. The others wear penis-covers made of long, narrow gourds attached by a string round the waist. Some of the gourds are straight and project at right angles to the crotch; others describe a graceful upward curve. They are protective, aggressive and celebratory. The men who wear them look prouder and infinitely more decent than the men in ragged shorts. Nevertheless, these penis-covers lend support to the idea that if in the beginning was the word, the word must have been 'anxiety'.

I have not forgotten that the Beardsley drawings are witty illustrations of a comedy by Aristophanes. Athens and Sparta are at war, and Lysistrata has brought the Athenian and Spartan women together with a plan to enforce peace. They occupy the Acropolis, and deny the men any intercourse with them. The Herald has come from Sparta with the offer of a peace conference. The old man with a small drooping penis who is examining the Herald's enormous genitals with undisguised admiration is one of the old men who tried to storm the Acropolis but were driven off by a concourse of old women. (In Beardsley's version of this scene, the women are young matrons and the old men retreat before a shower from chamber pots and some well-directed farting.) The Herald's penis is of course too large for practical purposes and is for exhibition only. It is intended as a demonstration of the effect of enforced continence and as a display of virility designed to show the women what they are missing. In the frontispiece, Lysistrata celebrates her victory by placing an olive branch on the magnificent phallus in the foregound, recognizable as the tabernacle, mentioned by Fuseli, which men build between the legs of Beauty.

193   In one of Beardsley's drawings for Oscar Wilde's *Salome* (a drawing of a girl doing a 'stomach' dance) the dwarfish musician in the foreground is a superbly decorative invention. He is the very spirit of lasciviousness, with his tongue hanging out of the corner of his mouth and his plump little penis in erection. The penis is pretending to be one of the folds in the dwarf's tunic, and it escaped the sharp eye of the publisher, who had deleted the male organs in the title page. It must have pleased Beardsley very much to get away with an indecent exposure.

Apart from an exaggeration of the length of the penis, artists rarely take liberties with the form of the male genitals. Dali's penis lolling over the side of a dish, and reminding us that many cannibal tribes considered it the tastiest part

196 of a man, is in a class by itself. Jim Dine has produced an interesting series of variations ranging from short, fat ones, to very long thin ones that would have to be coiled when not in use, but there are no really radical distortions. The artist's conservative approach to the genitals is well exemplified in a life-size male nude by the sculptor Ipousteguy. The figure is a brutally poetic joke against academic personifications of Health and Strength. It has two and a half legs. The extra half emerges with anatomical plausibility from the knee of the left leg, an idea based on those familiar life drawings in which the artist draws an arm or leg in a new position without rubbing out the first. The chest and belly have the look of close-fitting armour plates and bring to mind both the Dürer and the Ionesco rhinoceros, but whilst conveying the sense of an iron physique, they are riven by cracks and deep fissures and are beginning to come apart. The head is peculiarly fearsome: the nose is split, the shaven pate makes nakedness more naked and the tiny round holes for eyes give it the look of an automaton. The genitals have been conceived as a separate entity. The pubic hair is like a shape cut from a bed of moss. The penis rides free, neither limp nor erect, but alertly poised; raised just enough for the testicles to be totally visible. The general effect is of a large intricate badge attached to the body, and the badge is perfect in the sense of being free from blemish; but since it is attached to a body dedicated to the monstrous, its discreetly formalized realism is like a quotation from another kind of work. Another outstanding twentieth-century work treats the naked male figure with entrancing gravity. It is a carefully realistic three-quarter length bronze relief of the painter Arman by Yves Klein, who died in 1962 at the early age of thirty-four. The colour transforms it into an icon. The figure is painted a marvellous matt blue of incalculable depth and attached to a gold panel. It has the dignity and presence of Byzantine sacred portraiture, but having no religious significance it glorifies the

difference between man and woman. Considering the extraordinary distortions to which Picasso has subjected the forms of the female figure, admitting no part of it to be sacrosanct, it is curious that he has not invented disturbing forms for the male genitals. In one of the plates in *The Dreams and Lies of Franco*, he gives Franco an extravagantly large penis and very hairy scrotum, but only to show what a beast he is. Otherwise he is quite solemn when depicting penis and testicles, and in some drawings of Minotaur, emblematic of ferocity, they are as beautifully sedate and serenely limp as the most puritanical aesthete could wish.

One presumes that the male genitals held by My Lady Betty couldn't find their way to the vagina without a helping hand. In the art of Hans Bellmer they achieve complete autonomy and find their way to a woman of their own accord. Most of the length of the penis is usually hidden inside a vagina, and it is only when a woman happens to be transparent that it is seen in its entirety. But we are always given a full view of the scrotum, and this is perhaps the only aspect of human anatomy in Bellmer's work that is the pure fruit of observation. No one has delineated it with greater realism. There are likely to be times ahead when his work will have to go underground again and if ever his name should be forgotten he might be known, in the periods in which his work re-emerges, as the Master of the Scrotum. There is a stubble of short hairs on the wrinkled skin of the pouch, and the skin, somewhat slack and creased towards the centre, fits more tightly over the testicles. It looks very ancient. It leaves the impression that it was created before man himself.

226

Sperm

In his remarks on *Titian's Bacchanal of the Andrians*, Erwin Panofsky mentions that 'all the participants are young adults able to enjoy a life enhanced by the gift of Bacchus and the concomitant allurements of Venus – except for two cases: the infant in the foreground . . . who can do nothing but pass water; and the lonely old man in the background . . .' Boys who are not old enough to pass anything but 'water' are fascinated by their golden streams of urine and take great pleasure in raising the limp penis to make the stream describe a high curve. They are so curious about their genitals that they almost always have their first ejaculation as soon as the semen is ready; they perform their first act of masturbation without knowing what they are doing and the sudden jet of milky substance would frighten them if it were not accompanied by a miraculous sensation of pleasure. Before they reach the age of puberty they sense – or are told – that an intimate physical relationship with girls is established by means of the penis, and some of their play with urine reflects this half-apprehended knowledge. In old schools where the unroofed lavatories are in the farthest corner of the playground because of the pungent smell and only a partition separates the boys from the girls, the forward boys try to force their urine over the top of the partition. Another game, played by gangs of boys when no one else is about, is competitive; they stand in line and see who can expel the longest stream. (The fierce jerking of the more ambitious boys is an unconscious mimicry of the sexual act.) It was probably a childhood

205 (*Opposite*)
EDVARD MUNCH
Madonna

272

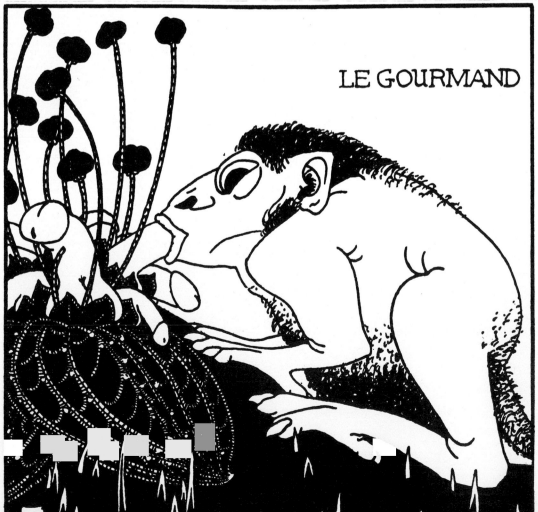

LE GOURMAND

206 (*Above*)
BOSCH
Garden of terrestrial
delights (detail)

207 (*Left*)
BESNAUX
The gourmand

208 (*Opposite*)
BESNAUX
Cinderella

Ө BÄVMCHEN · BÄVMCHEN · SCHÜTTLE · DICH ! Ө

209 (*Left*)
DALI
Autumn cannibalism

210 (*Below*)
AUGUSTUS EGG
The travelling companions

211 (*Opposite*)
HANS BELLMER
Death and the maiden

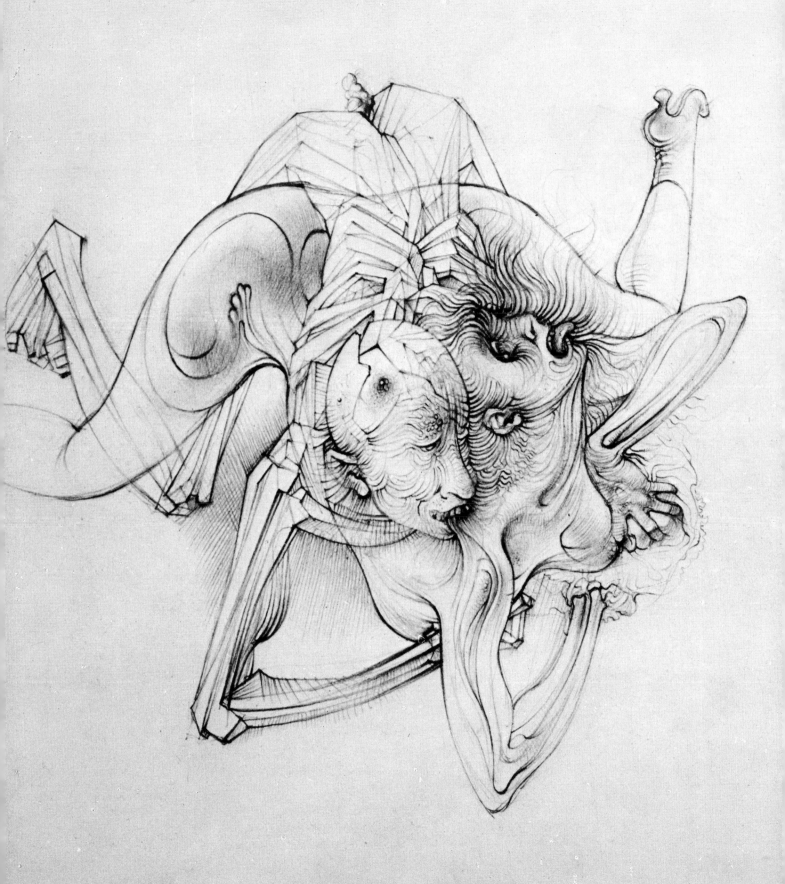

212 (*Opposite above*)
MAGRITTE
Collective invention

213 (*Opposite below*)
DELVAUX
The mermaid

214 (*Right above*)
MAX ERNST
Garden aeroplane trap

215 (*Right below*)
ALLEN JONES
Chair

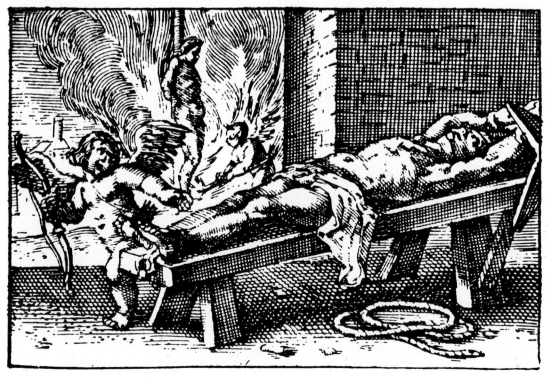

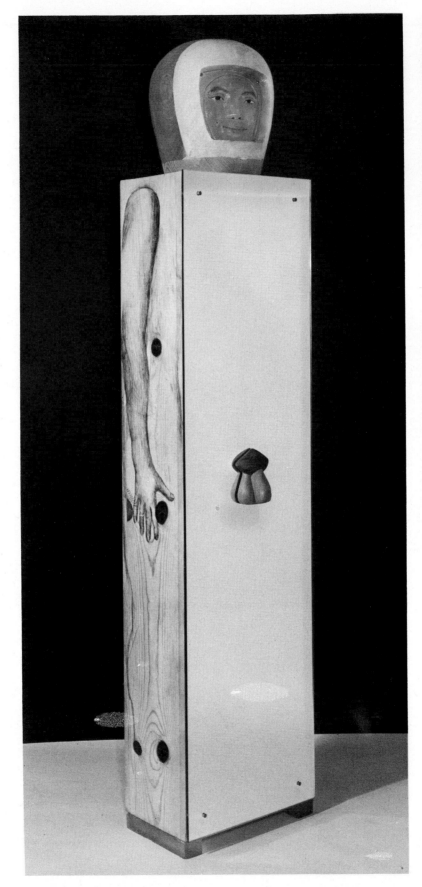

220 (*Above*)
Eighteenth-century
enamelled lockets

221 (*Left*)
MARISOL
Space man

222 (*Opposite*)
BEARDSLEY
Design for title page of
Salome

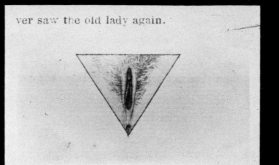

ver saw the old lady again.

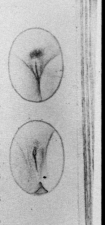

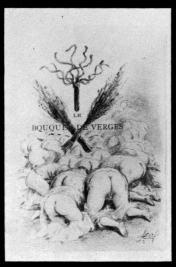

224 (*Right*)
BLAKE
The whirlwind of lovers

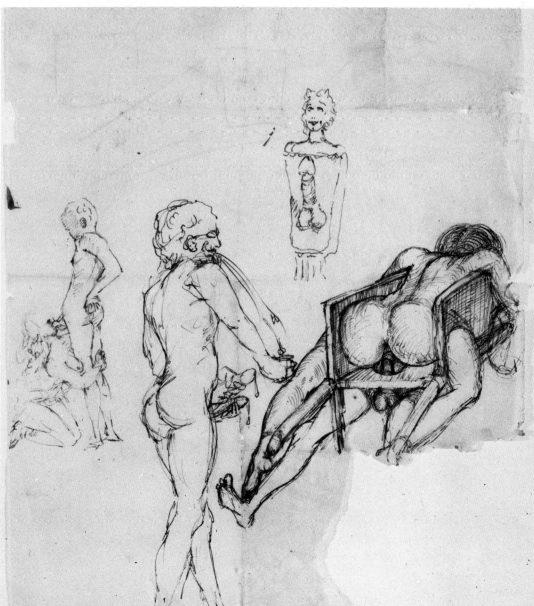

225 (*Right*)
DALI
Untitled drawing

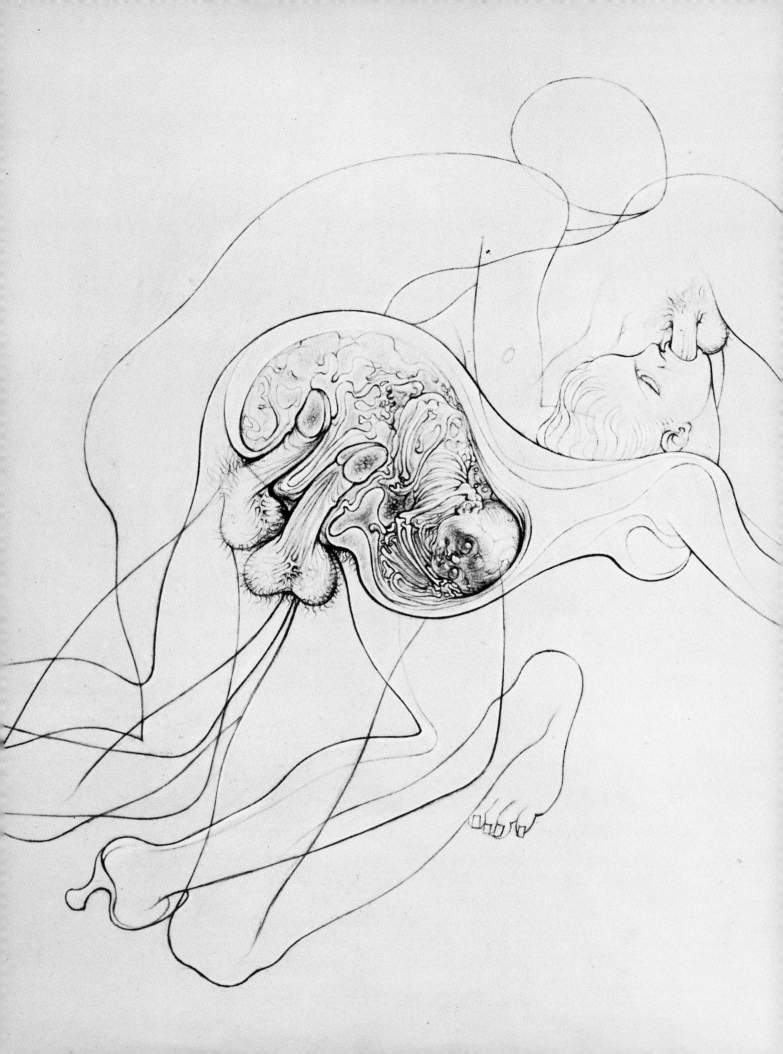

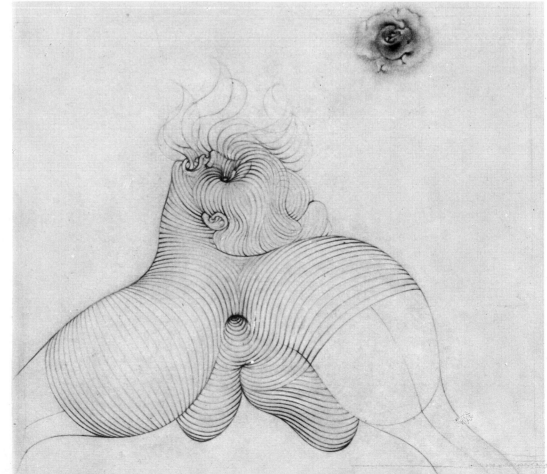

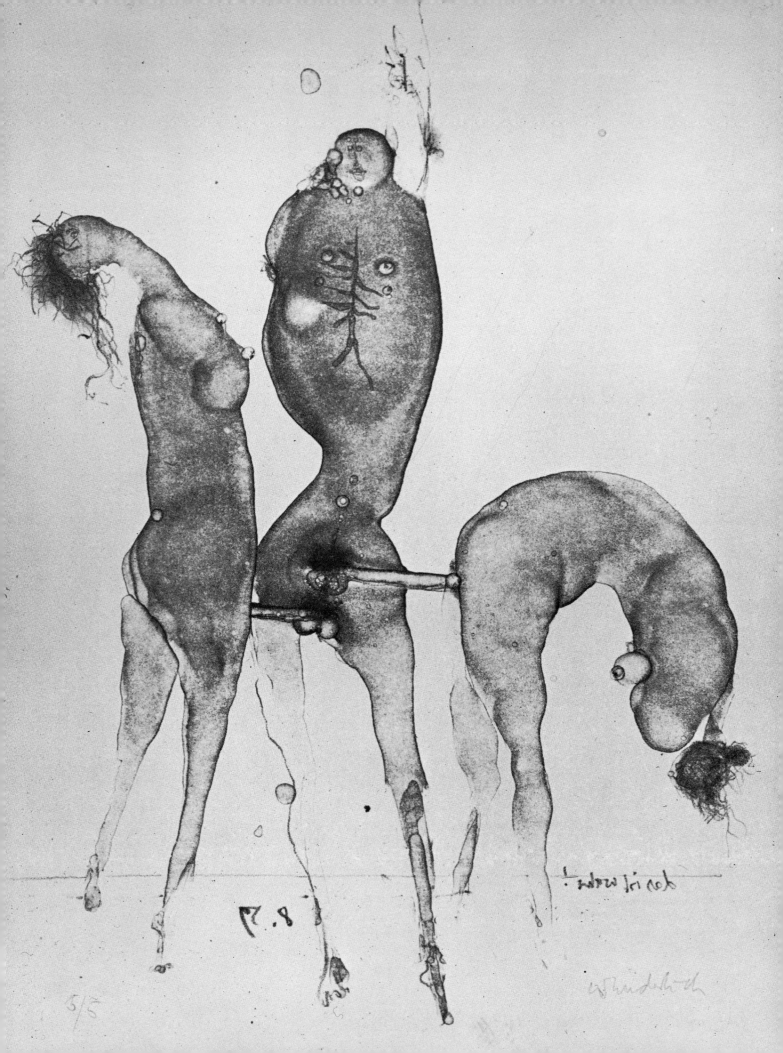

201 memory of this kind that inspired Correggio's lovely design for a fountain: a circle of boys as pretty as Cupids lift their penises to jet long thin streams of water through the air; but they are not in competition, and the even pressure of water passing through the little spouts makes for symmetry in the curve of the jets.

Because of the pissing games of childhood it is not only homosexuals whose nostrils flare when they scent a public urinal. The act of urinating loses a lot of its fascination after puberty, but it remains a disturbing influence on the adult male's feelings about sperm. The seminal spurt does not jet as far or last as long as a stream of urine, and few men could honestly claim that they have not at some time or another desired to urinate inside the beloved. The virtues of the urinatory jet combine with the richer virtues of semen to produce those fantasies of ejaculation in pornographic novels in which the semen is in extraordinarily plentiful supply and regularly spouts from the hero in torrents. This vision of a Niagara of semen 202, 203 can nevertheless serve a poetic vision of sexual intoxication. If Huysmans could have seen the two engravings by Hans Bellmer of women who have just received an impossible flood of semen full in the face and await another drenching in a torment of avidity, he would have been inclined to call them holy images of lust, for he could not have failed to realize that they are 'a plea for those convulsions which elude the flesh, rebounding into a spasmic beyond'. He would have appreciated the illusory actuality of the situation, and whilst noting that the viewer occupies the position of the invisible being who has had the supernatural ejaculation, and that the donees have elected to withdraw their mouths and refrain from drinking, in order to be spattered, he would have understood that the image of plethora represents vertiginous sensation at its wit's end. Craving has found its way to the edge of being. The female figures are the St Teresas of Fellatio, humble before the Lord, and sperm (which the author of *My Secret Life* likened observantly but prosaically to gruel) has become a sovereign's gift of soft jewellery.

Zeus showed his metal as a lover when he possessed Danae in a shower of gold, but in the mineral world, sperm is more effectively represented by the moonstone, and it is not perhaps surprising that many women think of it as unlucky. It is a beautiful and mysterious stone, with delicate colours coming and going under a milky bloom, and it was much favoured by the designers of Art Nouveau jewellery. They were less concerned with the monetary value of stones than with their evocative and symbolic associations, and persistently used moonstones to represent soft, moist substances. Moonstones are used very effectively in the famous 'Medusa' pendant made by Wolfers just before the turn of the century. The Medusa's head is carved out of ivory and encircled by a scarf of the same substance. Her hair is a knot of enamelled snakes. Her glaring eyes are moonstones. One of the snakes has been interlaced with the scarf and its head emerges under the Medusa's chin to spit out a moonstone as a dropper: there is no need to dwell on its sexual symbolism.

I have argued elsewhere that the decorative border round Edvard Munch's 205 *Madonna* lithograph could serve as a rough sketch for the quintessential Art Nouveau necklace and pendant. It could only be carried out in moonstones and a thin silver chain. Munch has conceived his *Madonna*, with a typically *fin de siècle* hint of blasphemy, as a *femme fatale*. With her long tresses, simmeringly half-closed eyes and swoon of abandonment, she subscribes to Art Nouveau's ideal of femin-

229 (*Opposite*)
PAUL WUNDERLICH
Three figures

inity; but Munch thought of woman's magnetism as an actively evil force, and depicts it as an emanation from her entire being by echoing the waves of her long black hair in curvilinear strokes of colour spreading through the darkness around her. In this context, the curvilinear lines have become the pictorial equivalent of erotic vertigo. A few copies of the lithograph were printed with a decorative border composed of magnified sperms trailing long wriggly filaments. They meander round three sides of the lithograph and end in a pendant depicting a foetus. The nature of the pendant brings to mind Beardsley's drawing of a young lady paying a social call on an old abortionist in order to show off her own bouncing little foetus; but the foetus in Munch's lithograph is shivering with apprehension, and I take it to be a male in the making, doomed to suffer under a woman's evil spell.

There is a curious and interesting reminder of the border of magnified sperms in Delacroix's first salon picture; its subject comes from Dante's *Inferno* and he depicts some of the figures of the damned clinging to the boat in which Dante and Virgil are being ferried across the infernal lake. It was painted in 1822, when he was twenty-four years old, and he said that the drops of water on some of the figures were his starting point as a colourist. These drops are composed of strokes of white, green, yellow and red, laid side by side without mixing, and each drop trails a long thin thread of green, possibly to suggest that the water is beginning to slide off the flesh. But they look more like magnified sperms than drops of water, and they are mainly on the two central figures – on the flank of the male figure and the belly of the female figure. The man's foot is lunging spitefully between the woman's thighs, and the situation leaves a strong impression of a violently interrupted act of sexual intercourse. I sometimes wonder whether Delacroix was making a reference to Paolo and Francesca, condemned to make love for ever.

10 Erotic Symbolism

My concern here is mainly with erotic symbolism which is consciously intended by the artist. Once one starts looking for unconscious motivations one can discover symbolism everywhere. Nevertheless, there are certain works in which a mildly sensual intention is carried out with a fullness and richness that belongs to a far more positive attitude to the subject, so that what might be called the excessive solution carries a content which is manifest to everyone except the one who created it. A literary example of the innocently over-explicit occurs in Henry James's first novel, *Watch and Ward*, in which a very honourable young gentleman who has adopted a little girl entertains the secret hope than when she is old enough she will become his wife. He is wondering whether a show of affection that might prepare her for his far-off proposal of marriage would be permissible, and has in mind nothing more than an embrace a little tighter than would be expected or a slight lingering over the goodnight and goodmorning kiss, and this is how James expresses the young gentleman's thoughts on the matter: 'The ground might be tickled to receive his own sowing; the petals of the young girl's nature, playfully forced apart, would leave the golden heart of the flower but the more accessible to his own vertical rays.'

A picture painted eight years before James wrote *Watch and Ward*, Augustus Egg's *The Travelling Companions*, is almost a pictorial equivalent. One of the loveliest of Victorian paintings, it depicts two well-bred sisters, dressed alike as if they might be twins, seated in a railway carriage and possibly doing the grand tour, for, as Graham Reynolds has noted, the view out of the window is of the coast near Mentone. Egg was obviously fascinated by their voluminous satin dresses which half fill the compartment, although it is not likely that he thought of them as creating a rousing impression of tumescence. Raymond Lister has drawn attention to the fact that in an illustration by Tenniel for Chapter 3 of *Through the Looking Glass*, Alice is sitting in a railway carriage, wearing exactly the same kind of hat as the one lying on the lap of each of Egg's girls. The guard leaning in at the window is examining Alice through opera glasses and seems to be taking a particularly good look at the little feather on the front of her hat. It would be interesting to pursue the voyeuristic implication of his image in relation to the significance of the feathers painted by Egg, but I can only mention here that Lister thinks that Tenniel may have intended a parody of *The Travelling Companions*. (Incidentally, Francis Bacon seems to have noticed the swinging tassel of the blind in Egg's painting, for a swinging tassel appears in more ambiguous circumstances in a number of his works.) It is surprising that neither Reynolds nor Lister mention the feathers that are so striking a feature of the girls' hats. They are in pure vermilion, and nowhere else in the painting is a primary colour used at full strength. The hats are black and make an effective contrast to the purity and brilliance of these vermilion accents. Corot made frequent use of a spot of red in his small landscapes, and it became a popular device in nineteenth-century painting, but Egg places the accents conspicuously in the centre area of his composition as if determined to make us admire the two little feathers for their own sake. One girl is asleep and the other absorbed in a book, but the erect little red feathers on their laps are disturbingly alert, and they bear an astonishing resemblance to the bright red vulva in Schiele's *Nude*. Egg's delight in the appearance of his charming models must have inspired thoughts about them that went far beyond what could be observed. *95*

In the twentiety-century Chirico's *The Uncertainty of the Poet* is an example of a *199* painting in which the latent content must have become manifest immediately it was seen by someone who had a broader frame of references and associations than the artist. The picture was painted in all innocence as an enigma, by a man who passionately believed that art had to rid itself of 'all familiar subject matter, all traditional ideas, all popular symbols'. In a note, written in 1913, which is one of the most remarkable statements ever made by a painter, he proclaimed that 'it is essential that the revelation we receive, the conception of an image which embraces a certainty, which has no sense in itself, which has no subject, which means *absolutely nothing* from the logical point of view, I repeat, it is essential that such a revelation or conception should speak so strongly in us, evoke such agony or joy, that we feel compelled to paint, compelled by an impulse even more urgent than the hungry desperation which drives a man to tearing at a piece of bread like a savage beast.' *The Uncertainty of the Poet*, in which a plaster torso of a woman, characterized by emphatic contrapposto, is placed as if turning towards a great bunch of bananas, was painted in the same year, and at that time Chirico was unworldly enough to be quite unaware that the banana is a popular image for the penis. It is said that the pictures which he painted between 1910 and 1917 were given their present titles by André Breton and his Surrealist friends, and that Chirico had simply called *The Uncertainty of the Poet* 'a metaphysical still life'. The present title solves a riddle that was scarcely propounded; the poet is the banana that has broken away from the bunch, and is too shy and too proud to join the clamour for the female nude. It seems certain that if Chirico had known that the banana vulgarly symbolized the penis the picture would not have been painted. It is fortunate that he did not know, because the picture is a masterpiece.

In Maurice Besnaux's drawing of Cinderella kneeling under an unusual version *208* of the Tree of Knowledge, praying to be sent if not a prince at least a man, the fruit hanging from the branches of the tree bears some resemblance to both the banana and the apple. This is because it takes the shape of the complete male genitalia. It is a useful tree for the garden of a deprived girl, for even if it failed to grant her wish, its fruit, if picked and put into storage while still firm, would

provide enough natural dildoes to last through the winter. Another drawing by
207   Besnaux depicts the penis as a member of the family of quick-growing, fleshy, edible fungi, and the unidentifiable creature who is caught in the act of eating one, and values it only for its edibility, nevertheless diverts us with a vivid imitation of fellatio.

Bosch's *Garden of Delights* represents the grand re-opening of the Garden of Eden after the Fall. It has become a kind of rectified Pornotopia, and at the same time has something of the formality of Renaissance gardens. The architectural features are more fantastic than any English builder of follies ever dreamed of,
206   but they are symmetrically arranged with an elaborate fountain in the centre and two summer houses on either side disposed in a strictly uniform distance from it. The separate oval bathing pool, nearer to the foreground than the fountain, is also carefully centralized. Charles de Tolnay's surmise as to the meaning of the picture seems highly plausible. He suggests that it is 'neither a simple didactic sermon nor a positive apotheosis of free love ... it is an encyclopedia of love and at the same time a representation of the sweetness and beauty of mankind's collective dream of an earthly paradise that would bring fulfilment of its deepest unconscious wishes, while at the same time it shows their vanity and fragility'. Even more interesting is his suggestion, based on Virgil's belief that the substance of dream is either ivory (deceptive dreams) or horn (daydreams), that Bosch has built his world out of these substances, 'the crags to be made of horn, and the sinuous figures of ivory'. What he calls the 'crags' are the architectural motifs, and although I agree that the 'crags' look like horn and that the men and women marvellously resemble ivory figures, they raise a problem in relation to Virgil's notion because the horn 'crags' are extraordinarily fantasticated (deceptive) and the human figures purely representational (true).

The giant fruits and plants that flourish in this garden serve a partly instructional purpose. They are there both to stand for and to stimulate the appetites of the naked men and women who are depicted by Bosch with evident discretion. They are examples of nature's unashamed display; they are there to be touched and tasted and penetrated; they represent the moist interior substance of woman, the erections of man and his spouting forth of seed. Compared with these botanical fantasias the apple from the Tree of Knowledge has minimal visual impact, except in certain paintings by Magritte, where the apple fills the bedroom or replaces a man's head. But the apples in an Urs Graf engraving are symbolically well-placed in the folds, just below the belly, of a woman's lifted gown.

In Christian iconography, the apple has always stood for the knowledge (which God vainly tried to keep to himself) that the conscious exploration and excitation of the mucous membrane surrounding bodily openings can provoke states of exaltation analagous to the raptures of the saints. The idea that this knowledge was communicated by the biting, tasting and consuming of the flesh of an apple acknowledges the cannibalistic element in erotic relationships, which is com-
211   memorated with passionate simplicity in the art of Hans Bellmer and with rather more regard for democratic and civilized behaviour in the art of Salvador Dali.
209   In Dali's *Autumn Cannibalism* the love-making is an entwinement of two gourmets intent on consuming one another, but conducting their mutual assimilation with a deliberation that allows for a full appreciation of texture and flavour.

The painter Magritte sometimes applied the practical man's approach to problems raised within the realm of the impossible, and came up with useful solutions without betraying the daydreams which created the problem. Of all the hybrids born of imaginary acts of bestiality, the mermaid is the most alluring; but she presents a problem for the would-be lover, and in this connection I recall a comic drawing – by a graphic artist whose name I never knew – of an Eskimo who has caught a mermaid by the waist and is holding her up to examine the place where her tail meets her torso; he is saying 'How?' Magritte has solved this problem by a simple act of reversal, and although the result is not pretty, his *212* mermaid is at least accessible. In another and even more startling work, appearances are not improved by his gratuitous solution of a non-existent problem. Or at any rate if he invented a problem of accessibility, his solution appears to be eretomaniacal, and he himself entitled it *The Rape*. But it seems also to refer to *219* the fearsome biological jokes that nature sometimes plays on living creatures. The girl, whose eyes, nose and mouth have been replaced by the main features of the torso, stares at us sadly with her nipples and if laughter fits the case it has to be hysterical, for although she has turned into a monster she retains, heartbreakingly, her girlishness. Bellmer's male figure with a penis for a nose and an anus for a mouth would be a not entirely unsuitable bridegroom for Magritte's girl, but he is quite revolting, and it would be a marriage purely of convenience.

In 1935–6, Max Ernst created a series of landscapes closely connected with the *femme fatale* theme which he described as 'voracious gardens in turn devoured by a vegetation which springs from the debris of trapped aeroplanes', but his interpretation does not seem to me to be quite correct. The title given to each of these paintings is *Garden Aeroplane Trap*, and the garden has a fatal attraction for *214* aeroplanes because it gives the illusion of providing small landing strips in mountainous country. But the vegetation is an intimate aspect of its attractions and doesn't emanate from the aeroplanes. It grows in the garden, like the hair that grows on a woman's head and under her armpits and over her vulva. If the parts of aeroplanes brought down by the garden's allure are now lying languidly across the landing strip half buried in the vegetation, it is because they are exhausted by love-making. The paintings are landscapes of sexual enticement, and, like Ernst's many forest and swamp landscapes, are capable of arousing in the spectator the idea of places of assignation for violent and dangerous love-making. This is the secret attraction of the forest drawings of earlier German masters, Dürer, Altdorfer and Huber, and of many of the fairy tales of the brothers Grimm.

I do not know whether to call the life-like effigies of girls by Allen Jones which serve as tables and chairs symbols or emblems. They symbolize man's tendency to treat women as an object, and from one point of view imply a disregard of human dignity which has the effect of intensifying the disturbing efficiency of the mimesis. But they also emblemize man's limitless concern with woman and his desire to live in a totally erotic environment. Female furniture is not of course a new idea. At the turn of the century Art Nouveau produced some curious examples, but I suppose the immediate predecessor of Jones's objects to be the stool, made by the Surrealist, Kurt Seligmann, which was supported by life-like models of the nether limbs of girls, clad in stockings and high-heeled shoes. Jones's *Table* is a girl on her hands and knees supporting on her back a glass table-top. She wears black lace-up boots and tight yellow lurex pants, and gazes into a mirror placed on the floor which provides her and the spectator with a view of her breasts. *Chair* is a girl lying on her back with the top part of her legs doubled back on to her belly and pressed down to make a support for a sponge-rubber seat. Her boots, arm-length gloves and pants in black leather are the kind of equipment romantically associated with perverse activities. She is the most disturbing of the two girls. A broad leather strap attached to the seat encircles her body and has been unmercifully tightened to flatten breast and belly. If the seat were not there she would present an image of a girl trussed up.

The Cupid in a painting by Lucas Cranach is the love-child of the tall, slim fraulein who to my northern eyes is one of the most seductive Venuses ever imagined by poet or painter. He has stolen a honeycomb from a hive in the bole of a tree on the edge of one of those dark forests where children fall into the hands of witches and where André Breton hoped one day to meet by chance a naked woman. Cupid is complaining to his mother because the angry bees are stinging him, and at the same time he is holding out the honeycomb to her as if he obtained it at her behest. One bee still clings to it to emblemize the pain that accompanies the sweet pleasures she personifies. The two figures are under a tree laden with scarlet apples, and if Cupid were not present, the lovely fraulein could be mistaken for Eve awaiting the approach of the Serpent. Venus takes over the Tree of Knowledge as an attribute because it reinforces and enriches the meaning of the honeycomb.

Cupid is transformed into a harmless angel child in Christian iconography; but the face of a little boy so surprisingly given to the Serpent in Titian's *Fall of Man* cannot be intended as the face of an angel child and must be intended to remind us of Cupid. The task of instructing Eve in the art of seduction could not have been in better hands. For that matter, it would not have been out of character if he had put it into God the Father's head to take up with a married woman, and it is just possible that some such thought flashed through Raphael's head when he was painting the two delightful winged boys in the foreground of the *Sistine Madonna*. They appear to be playing a secret game (like Sylvia Plath's poems, 'their little foreheads bulge with concentration') and one of them, looking Heavenwards, may well be saying, 'I spy with my little eye someone beginning with G'.

The scene on the right of the relief on the fountain of Titian's *Sacred and Profane Love* depicts a naked boy being unmercifully beaten by a man, and two other figures appear to be erecting a stake for the infliction of further punishment. Panofsky says that it represents the chastisement of bestial love, which seems to be a harsh way of referring to Cupid. The boy-god was roughly handled in the popular prints of the period and it remained one of the favourite themes of the seventeenth-century emblem books along with some of the exploits for which he was punished. He is shown scattering seed haphazardly and producing a crop of illegitimate babies, and, in pursuit of the pleasures his darts have promised, women burn at the stake and men are stretched on the rack. By way of retribution Cupid is persistently stung by bees, burned at the stake, with a woman tending the fire, and sometimes even crucified. In the following century Reynolds painted Cupid as a link boy, an angel-faced urchin with wings; and to make certain that we realize that he is a young pimp guiding men through the dark streets to bawdy houses, he places the flaming torch so that it rises straight up from the boy's crotch.

The Hermae, the quadrangular pillars surmounted by a bust of the god Hermes, which were set up on highways in Ancient Greece, made his sex peculiarly conspicuous by carving the genitals as a projection on the flat surface of the pillar below the point where the bust ended. Modern variations on the herm exploit the emblematic isolation of the genitals in different ways. The herm designed by Beardsley for the title page of Wilde's *Salome* made the male genitals conspicuous *222* because they terminated an otherwise female torso. The intention to glorify Hermaphroditus instead of Hermes was frustrated in the printed version, from which the genitals were deleted. The youthful male angel gleefully playing at the foot of the pillar has the same slender build as the seated youth who appeared in the first version of *The Toilet of Salome*. Beardsley had to design another version for the book because the publishers noticed that the seated youth was quietly masturbating. It is not unreasonable that confirmed auto-eroticists should worship Hermaphrodite; but a plausible hybrid capable of entering and receiving itself has defied the ingenuity of designers. It is a problem to which Marcel Duchamp might usefully have applied himself after the satisfactory non-completion of his Large Glass, which was devoted to the emblematical representation of nine masturbators aiming their ejaculations in the general direction of a woman and deliberately missing. The science fiction herm devised by the American sculptress, Marisol, appears to treat the sexual organs as the last natural means of com- *221* munication left to human beings, but she may be taking it for granted that her own sex has long since ceased to receive sperm direct from the male, and out of the kindness of her heart has left the arms of her space-man free to defend himself at milking time.

The emblematic use of the sexual organs as head and tail pieces in some of the libertine literature of the eighteenth and nineteenth-centuries was quite often *223* ingenious, witty and decorative. The candle-snuffer clapped over the head of a penis to signify that it is time for bed brings one tale of sexual prowess to a charmingly paradoxical conclusion.

11 Beyond the Possible

Francesca, daughter of the Count of Ravenna, was given in marriage to the deformed son of Malatesta of Rimini in return for military services. She loved Paolo, her husband's handsome brother, and sometimes, if the husband was away, they spent the afternoons reading stories to one another; but when they came upon Guinevere's declaration of love for Launcelot, who had been sent to woo her on behalf of King Arthur, they read no more that day. Discovered in the act of love, they were both put to death. Dante recognized them when he descended to the First Circle of Incontinence in the Second Circle of Hell, where, with other pairs of lovers, they embrace forever, tossed on a howling black wind.

William Blake was horrified by the Christian doctrine of an eternity of bliss for the righteous and eternal damnation for the rest, and when he was illustrating Dante's *The Divine Comedy* he introduced the blessing of light into his study of the Whirlwind of Lovers. It took the form of a sun-like medallion on which was engraved the image of Paolo and Francesca on the day they first embraced. The medallion is emitting shafts of light and it lends the helpless gyrations of the figures, caught in a great curvilinear sweep of wind, a kind of ecstasy. Rossetti, no less concerned for lovers, painted a three-part watercolour devoted to the story of Paolo and Francesca, and his treatment of the wind in the Circle of Incontinence is curious. It is signified by a steady rain of bright flecks against a dark background, and the lovers pass across them in a state of blissful happiness. We will never know exactly what Rossetti had in mind when he painted in the flecks, but they look like a shower of separate little flames with little tails, and appear to serve the same idea as the Hilliard miniature in the Victoria and Albert Museum, which is catalogued as *An Unknown Man against a Background with the Flames of Passion*. The punishment devised by Dante for errant lovers contains the dream of an orgasm sustained forever, and there are few men who have not felt at one time or another that its impossibility shuts them out of paradise.

In Herbert Read's novel, *The Green Child*, based on a folk tale about two children who wandered from nowhere into a Suffolk village and looked like other children

224

except for the colour of their skin, which was of a green tinge, the man who married Sally began to torment her after discovering that she had no interest in human beings and no understanding of the emotion of love, but he remained desperately attracted to her because of 'the mystery of her flesh, the possibility of discovering in her a different mode of love'. It is perhaps this possibility that attracts a man of one race to a woman of another, and causes many of us to wonder what it would be like to make love to a woman of another time. David Hockney's *Marriage of Styles* in the Tate lends such daydreams vividness and actuality. The painting represents the wedding photograph of a twentieth-century businessman and a woman of Ancient Egypt, and although the woman is highly stylized in the Egyptian manner, she wears the conventional modern bridal veil. The idea came to Hockney in a Berlin museum when he saw an American friend standing beside a wooden Egyptian figure; but the painting was executed in London and by that time Elizabeth Taylor's Cleopatra was very much with us. The artist was given the opportunity of looking over the sets that were used in the film, and the painting is a bit reminiscent of a film still. The theme itself could be rationalized to accommodate a PR-slanted marriage between a film producer and his star. Nevertheless, if money could bridge the gap of time and buy a night with Cleopatra herself, Queen of Egypt, born 68 BC, who would not wish to be rich?

In literary and theological usage, to have carnal knowledge of a woman is to have sexual intercourse with her. It is a rather splendid way of putting it, and I am sorry it's acquired a rather old-fashioned ring. All the same, it makes too grand a claim for normal acts of penetration. It refers to aspirations rather than achievements. A man in the throes of passion is only too well aware that his penis has very limited access to the body of the beloved, and behind every desperate thrust is the desire to plunge deeper. Some aspirations are fiercer and more grotesque than others, but all of them are devoted to getting more of one human body into another. In its simplest terms, a man may feel it a deprivation that his testicles have to hang about outside, like children who are not allowed inside a place that serves intoxicating liquor.

Frustration turns the penis into a weapon, but fortunately it is an insignificant battering ram, and, if considered as a dagger, the plunge up to the hilt means at best a snug fit in the sheath Nature has provided for it. More preposterously, a man will sometimes bend backwards during intercourse, as if preparing for his entire body to follow his penis, like a great ship following a pilot-boat into harbour. The fantasies come unbidden; but any attempt to turn fantasy into reality by resorting to a practical means of deeper penetration is criminal assault. (A terrible surrogate was used against a Plantagenet king when his murderers made him bum-boy to a red-hot poker.) But among those who take to murder, it is the pervert, fascinated by the idea that his penis might break through to the intestines of a child, and the disemboweller, running his hand through the female body like a tomb-robber dipping into the treasures in the burial chamber of a queen, who come closest to having carnal knowledge of another.

Drawing is probably the best medium for erotic fantasies which arise when exorbitant desires and illusions of superabundance make the physical equipment for love-making seem inadequate. Drawing allows for obscurities and ambiguities in the representation of biological impossibilities which might lose all plausibility in a less spontaneous medium. Women tend to be amused by a man's concern with the size of his penis and are not slow nowadays to point out that its length has nothing to do with the pleasure it might afford her. But perhaps women take too much for granted when they assume that their pleasure is a man's primary concern. Certainly he wishes to impress, but not necessarily to please. If he had a choice, he might elect to be a freak and expose to her a penis large enough to send her crouching into a corner. Beardsley may have had this dream of power in mind when he gave his handsome messenger genitalia so enormous that the old men of Athens were filled with envy and awe. Artists of our time still take 'poetic licence' when depicting the penis, but they seem more interested in a dream of virility that demands a duplication of the genitals, and I suppose it is not entirely impossible that someone some day will be born with two sets. But if it had already happened, the rumour of it would still be with us however long ago the miracle occurred. After all, our interest in Verrocchio's equestrian monument in Venice is not entirely reserved for its monumentality; as a study of excessive masculinity it lends credence to the rumour, likely to last as long as the effigy itself, that the subject, the condottiere Colleone, had three testicles.

225   In an untitled drawing by Dali of a man with two penises, one is set just below the other. They are depicted in simultaneous ejaculation and are presumably intended for simultaneous penetration of vagina and anus. The artist has not had to decide whether they are served by one pair of testicles or by two because the figure is turning away and the view presented to us does not require them to be drawn. This is a pity. By avoiding the problem of fitting each penis with an exclusive source of sperm he has missed the opportunity of adding another piece of 'tender, extravagant camembert' to his œuvre. In other drawings, he has shown himself to be a sensitive observer of the scrotum in its dangling state, with the testicles visibly at the bottom of the pouch, like a couple of potatoes in a string bag, and in view of the fact that the two penises are in close proximity, and of course eternally erect, the scrotum for the upper one would recline gracefully, when pendulous, on the lower penis, and thus provide an interesting variation on the theme of the limp watch dangling from the branch of a tree in the most famous of his pictures, *The Persistence of Memory*. Incidentally, the sheet on which the man with two penises is depicted includes a study of a woman lying face downwards in a wheelbarrow and receiving, through a conveniently placed hole in its floor, the penis of a man lying face upwards underneath the barrow. This comment on the human desire to make love in extravagant positions and situations also contains a reference to the wheelbarrow in Millet's *The Angelus*, a picture which he subjected with remarkable persistence to his 'critical paranoia', often with brilliant results. The wheelbarrow in Millet's picture is an attribute of the honest toil of his humble and pious peasants, and in Dali's drawing it has been converted to serve the pleasure principle. Dali's great talents have too often centred on self-aggrandizement, but he has painted masterpieces and has had influential insights. His definition of Art Nouveau as 'the undulant-convulsive style' has never been bettered, and he was the first to perceive that Ingres's *Le Bain Turc* is 'a pre-eminent unconscious expression of the intra-uterine paradise'. He pays Millet the compliment of treating his two peasant figures as living human

beings, and reminds one of Hieronymous Bosch, kindly demonstrating to St Anthony the Hermit that any common object can be put to erotic use.

Wunderlich's design for a double penis is rather less plausible than Dali's, 229 though no less ambitious. Each knobbly, stick-like penis is fed by its own pair of testicles, clinging like a burr to the crotch. The penises erect themselves sideways in opposite directions, and are intended to enable a man to take two women at once. An evident drawback is that he would be entirely dependent on the women. He could not propel himself in opposite directions at one and the same time; the penises would be motionless, and all the coming and going along each shaft would have to be undertaken by the women. It is possibly for this reason that the approach to insertion is depicted as peculiarly desultory. Wunderlich was probably less concerned to lend conviction to the sexual apparatus than to create a powerful atmosphere of sexual collusion, and in this respect the drawing is extremely effective. The curiously spurting draughtsmanship and the freakish figuration, which suggest that the collaborators are verging on dissolution, evoke that longed-for state of total sexuality that Bataille called 'wallowing in blindness and oblivion'.

The twin penises in drawings and engravings by Bellmer convey a scarifying conviction. The visualizations are so intense that they look like documentary evidence of materializations, records of hungry abstractions that have put on an excess of human matter. I doubt if any other draughtsman in the history of European art has drawn the plunge of the penis into the vagina with anything approaching the disquieting authority of this artist. All the muscular energy of Bellmer himself seems to have been summoned to the task of depicting the inexorable and exultant thrust. He so impressively creates the impression that the entirety of being has been absorbed into the convulsive action of this outriding stick of male flesh that when penis and scrotum are depicted as if they formed an autonomous biomorph unattached to a human body, the body is scarcely missed. It has yielded itself to the purposive animality of its erectile tissue, and soul and spirit are compelled to acknowledge that paradise may be a plethora of sensation, and they leap with the sperm.

A fascinated loathing may be our first instinctive reaction to these images of the male genitalia, for they are as realistic as Dürer's drawing of the wrinkled face and scrawny neck of his mother. When we look more closely we are allowed to think that our fascination is due to the beauty and poetry of the draughtsmanship, to those flickering pen lines that not only do exquisite justice to the crinkled and hairy skin of the scrotum but refer in busy hieroglyphs to the propulsive tails of the sperms inside. The depiction of the penis is particularly persuasive when the head is buried in the vagina and only part of the swollen stem, corded and veined, is visible, and when the expended semen returns along the stem in a slow opalescent trickle there is no promise of quiescence, only an assurance of unappeasable ferment.

Bellmer uses the transparencies of his linearism to cast light into the interior darkness of the female body and depict exploits beyond all reason and all limits prescribed by custom, in order to express his contempt for the utilitarian compulsions of the sexual instinct and put in a claim for free will and the imagination. In one drawing, a pair of free-riding penises break into a womb, and while one 227 of them seeks out the sexual parts of an unborn child, the other ejaculates into the fluid in which the child is suspended, the tails of its sperms turning and twisting like fish in a pool. In another, a penis projects from inside a woman's vagina as if she has been occupied by an entire male figure, giving a twist to the idea of possession. His drawing of a woman who can open her flesh like a seething mantle to enfold a man is in the same spirit. To disappear inside a woman never to be seen again would be for many men an ideal way of taking leave of the world. Bellmer's art constitutes a sustained rebellion against the natural order; an experiment in transgression resembling Lautréamont's *Chants de Maldoror*, and an exercise in draughtsmanship comparable to Rimbaud's 'alchemy of the verb'. It shares the fervour of Henry James's sentence-making when the words fit situations not consciously intended. A sentence from one of his letters fits the art of Bellmer like a glove: 'It only looms, it only shines and shivers, too beautiful and too interesting, it only hangs there too rich and too full and with too much to give and to pay: it only presents itself too admirably and too vividly . . .'

Acknowledgments

The author and publishers wish to record their gratitude for permission received from owners, agents and photographers to reproduce the following illustrations (numbers refer to pictures; italic numbers to colour illustrations):

Albertina (11, 138) Carlos B. Alemany (66) Antikensammlung, Munich (152) Archives Photographiques (114) The Arts Council (121, 153) Ashmolean Museum, Oxford (129, 137, 151) Bibliothèque Nationale (77) Birmingham City Museum and Art Gallery (210, 224) Hedi Böck (67) British Museum (26, 96, 109) Brompton Studio (25, 59, 78) William N. Copley and A.D.A.G.P., Paris (174) Edward James Foundation (209) Léonor Fini and Galerie Lambert Monet (90) Fogg Art Museum, Harvard University (157, 193, 222) Françoise Foliot (57, 80, 111) Galerie André-François Petit (70, 200, 225) Galleria Galatea, Turin (61) Peggy Guggenheim Foundation (144, 214) Hanover Gallery, London (photos John Webb) (141, 142) Institute of Contemporary Arts (123) James Kirkman (172) Kröller-Müller Museum, Otterlo (171) Kunsthalle Mannheim (118, 176) Kunsthistorischen Museum, Vienna (14, 18, 86, 103, 162) Kunstsammlungen, Dresden (62, 73, 135, 182) Mme René Magritte and A.D.A.G.P., Paris (212) Manchester City Art Galleries (16) The Mansell Collection (93) Marlborough Fine Arts (London) Ltd (19, 54, 110, 119, 178, 179) M.A.S. Barcelona (20, 56, 88, 101, 105, 113, 126, 127, 166, 178) George Melly (219) Metropolitan Museum of Art, New York (102 bequest of Benjamin Altman, 134) Musée du Louvre (7, 24) Museo Capitolini, Rome (52) Museo de Arte de Ponce, Puerto Rico (87) Museum of Art, Sarasota (160) Museum of Fine Arts, Boston, Purchased Picture Fund (4) Museum of Modern Art, New York (146, 205) National Gallery, London (3) National Gallery, Oslo (1, 12, 81, 91, 92, 100, 161) National Gallery of Art, Washington D.C., Samuel H. Kress Collection (132) National Gallery of Victoria, Melbourne (150) Nationalmuseum, Nuremberg (120) Nationalmuseum, Stockholm (183) National Museum, Naples (9) Collection of Mr and Mrs Morton Neumann (99) Öffentliche Kunstsammlung, Basle (115, 122, 128, 147, photo Hans Hinz 164) Österreichische Galerie, Vienna (64) Photographie Giraudon (168)

Redfern Gallery (*169*) The Reynolds Morse Foundation, Cleveland, Ohio (*46*, 65) Robert David (68, 145) Robert Fraser Gallery (17, 98) Rodin Museum, Philadelphia Museum of Art (104) Royal Academy of Arts (13) The Royal Library, Windsor Castle, by gracious permission of H.M. the Queen (48) Scala (*5*, 6, *63*, 107, 112, *159*, 173, 181) Sidney Janis Gallery (221) Mr and Mrs Peyton Skipwith (*53*) The Tate Gallery, London (*149*, *204*) Uffizi Gallery, Florence (156, 167, 175) Wallraf-Richartz Museum, Cologne (133)

Chronological List of Artists

ROMANO, GIULIO (1492 or 1499–1546)
26–45. *Sedici Modi* prints after
158. (School of) Marriage Feast of Cupid
and Psyche

BANDINELLI, BACCIO (1493–1560)
76. Hercules and Anteaus

LEYDEN, LUCAS VAN (1494?–1533)
57. Lot and his daughters

CORREGGIO, ANTONIO (1489 or 1494–
1534)
81. The Madonna of the basket
201. Design for a fountain

ROSSO, GIOVANNI BATTISTA (1494–1540)

MANDIN, JAN (1500–?1560)

ERHART, GREGOR (*d* 1540?)
168. Mary Magdalen

CLOUET, JEAN II ('JANET') (*d* 1540/1)

MACHUCA, PEDRO (*d* 1550)
178. The Virgin and the souls in Purgatory

PARMIGIANINO, FRANCESCO (1503–40)
126. Pedro Maria Rossi at Roscio

BRONZINO, ANGELO (1503–72)

PRIMATICCIO, FRANCESCO (1504/5–70)

SEISENEGGER, JAKOB (1505–67)

ABBATE, NICCOLÒ DELL' (*c* 1512–71)

TINTORETTO, JACOPO (1518–94)
103. Toilet of Bathsheba
179. Woman revealing her breast
187. Vulcan surprising Venus and Mars

VITTORIA, ALESSANDRO (1525–1608)

BRUEGEL, PIETER (*c* 1525/30–69)

DE BRY, THÉODORE (1528–?)
117. The jester's bath

VERONESE, PAOLO (*c* 1528–88)
162. Death of Lucrece

SPRANGER, BARTHOLOMEUS (1546–1611)
14. Vulcan and Maia
18. Hercules and Deianira

HILLIARD, NICOLAS (*c* 1547–1619)

BOCK, HANS (*c* 1550–1623)
115. The bath at Leuk

CARRACCI, AGOSTINO (1557–1602)
151. Old men surprising a girl

GOLTZIUS, HENDRIK (1558–1617)

CARAVAGGIO, MICHELANGELO MERISI
DA (1573–1610)
52. John the Baptist
165. The seven works of mercy

RUBENS, SIR PETER PAUL (1577–1640)

SARAZIN, JACQUES (1592–1660)

JORDAENS, JACOB (1593–1678)
183. Candaules shows his wife to his
favourite, Gynes

POUSSIN, NICHOLAS (1594–1665)

GENTILESCHI, ARTEMISIA (*c* 1597–1651?)
159. Judith and Holofernes

CAIRO, FRANCESCO DEL (1598–1674)
160. Judith

BERNINI, GIANLORENZO (1598–1680)

BROUWER, ADRIAEN (1605/6–38)
138. Tavern scene

REMBRANDT VAN RYN (1606–69)
80. Ledikant
102. Toilet of Bathsheba

LE SUEUR, EUSTACHE (1616/17–55)

LELY, SIR PETER (1618–80)

LE BRUN, CHARLES (1619–90)

VERMEER, JAN (1632–75)
135. At the procuress's

VERELST, SIMON (1644–1721)

GAYWOOD, ROBERT (*c* 1650–*c* 1711)
137. Young man, harlot and beldame

DE TROY, JEAN-FRANÇOIS (1679–1752)
87. Lot and his daughters

BOUT, PIETER (1658–1702)
129. An amorous pair

WATTEAU, JEAN ANTOINE (1684–1721)
182. Réunion champêtre

TIEPOLO, GIOVANNI BATTISTA (1696–
1770)
109. Nymphs

HOGARTH, WILLIAM (1697–1764)

LONGHI, PIETRO (1702–85)
125. Meeting of dominoes

BOUCHER, FRANÇOIS (1703–70)
133. Miss O'Murphy

FALCONET, ÉTIENNE-MAURICE (1716–91)

REYNOLDS, SIR JOSHUA (1723–92)

FRAGONARD, JEAN HONORÉ (1732–1806)
8. After eighteenth-century engraving

NOLLEKENS, JOSEPH (1737–1823)

CLODION, CLAUDE MICHEL (1738–1814)

FUSELI, HENRY (1741–1825)
191. Lady Betty

GOYA, FRANCISCO (1746–1828)
105. Naked maja
134. Majas on a balcony

DAVID, JACQUES LOUIS (1748–1825)

GILLRAY, JAMES (1757–1815)

CANOVA, ANTONIO (1757–1822)

BLAKE, WILLIAM (1757–1827)
224. The whirlwind of lovers

Select Bibliography

Balthus. Exhibition Catalogue. (Arts Council of Great Britain, London, 1968)

BATAILLE, GEORGES, *Eroticism* (London, 1962)

BAUDELAIRE, CHARLES, *Intimate Journals* (New York, 1930)

BAUDELAIRE, CHARLES, *The Painter of Modern Life and other Essays* (London, 1964)

BELLMER, HANS, *Die Püppe* (Berlin, 1962)

BELLMER, HANS, *Oeuvre Grave* (Paris, 1969)

BENESCH, OTTO, *Edvard Munch* (London, 1960)

BERENSON, RUTH AND MUHLEN, NORBERT, *George Grosz* (London, 1965)

Bilder-lexikon (Institut für Sexualforschung in Wien, Hamburg, 1961)

BRISON, CHARLES, *Pornocrates, an introduction to the life and work of Félicien Rops* (London, 1969)

BROPHY, BRIGID, *Black and White, a Portrait of Aubrey Beardsley* (London, 1968)

CLARK, KENNETH, *The Nude* (London, 1956)

CLARK, KENNETH AND PEDRETTI, CARLO, *Leonardo da Vinci, Anatomical Drawings in the Royal Library at Windsor Castle* (London, 1969)

COLLIS, LOUISE, *A Private View of Stanley Spencer* (London, 1972)

COMBE, JACQUES, *Jérôme Bosch* (Paris, 1946)

DALI, SALVADOR, *The Secret Life of Salvador Dali* (London, 1968)

DEKNATEL, FREDERICK B., *Edvard Munch* (Boston and London, 1950)

DESCHARNES, ROBERT, *The World of Salvador Dali* (London, 1962)

ENGLISH, PAUL, *Geschichte der erotischen Literatur* (Stuttgart, 1927)

FOXON, DAVID, *Libertine Literature in England 1660-1745* (London, 1964)

FUCHS, EDUARD, *Geschichte der erotischen Kunst* (Munich, 1928)

FRYER, PETER, *Forbidden Books of the Victorians* (London, 1970)

FRYER, PETER, *Private Case—Public Scandal* (London, 1966)

GANZ, PAUL, *The Drawings of Henry Fuseli* (New York, 1949)

GEISSBUHLER, ELIZABETH CHASE, *Rodin, Later Drawings* (London, 1964)

GENET, JEAN, *Our Lady of the Flowers* (London, 1964)

GERSON, HORST, *Rembrandt Paintings* (London, 1969)

GORSEN, PETER, *Sexualitat im Spiegel der Modernen Bildenden Kunst* (Hamburg n.d.)

GRALL, ALEX AND JELENSKI, CONSTANTIN, *The Drawings of Hans Bellmer* (London, 1972)

GROSZ, GEORGE, *Ecce Homo* (London, 1967)

HAUSER, ARNOLD, *Mannerism: The Crisis of the Renaissance and the Origin of Modern Art* (London, 1965)

HUYSMANS, J.-K., *Against Nature* (London, 1968)

JEAN, MARCEL, *The History of Surrealist Painting* (New York, 1960)

JOUFFROY, ALAIN, *Hans Bellmer* (Chicago n.d.)

KRONHAUSEN, EBERHARD AND PHYLLIS, *A Presentation of Walter's 'My Secret Life'* (London, 1967)

LÉVI-STRAUSS, CLAUDE, *The Savage Mind* (London, 1966)

LISTER, RAYMOND, *Victorian Narrative Paintings* (London, 1966)

LYKIARD, ALEXIS, *Lautréamont's Maldoror* (London, 1970)

MAJOR, EMIL AND GRADMANN, ERWIN, *Urs Graf* (Basel n.d.)

MARCUS, STEVEN, *The Other Victorians* (London, 1966)

MARCUSE, HERBERT, *Eros and Civilization* (London, 1969)

MASON, EUDO C., *The Mind of Henry Fuseli* (London, 1951)

NADEAU, MAURICE, *The History of Surrealism* (London, 1968)

PANOFSKY, ERWIN, *Problems in Titian, mostly iconographic* (London, 1969)

PEARSALL, RONALD, *The Worm in the Bud* (London, 1969)

PIRCHAN, EMIL, *Gustav Klimt* (Vienna, 1966)

PRAZ, MARIO, *The Romantic Agony* (London, 1933)

PRAZ, MARIO, *Studies in Seventeenth-Century Imagery* (London, 1939)

READ, HERBERT, *The Green Child* (London, 1935)

READE, BRIAN E., *Aubrey Beardsley* (London, 1967)

REAGE, PAULINE, *Story of O* (London n.d.)

REYNOLDS, GRAHAM, *Victorian Painting* (London, 1966)

Salvador Dali: oeuvres anciennes (Galerie André François Petit, Paris n.d.)

SITWELL, SACHEVERELL, *Splendours and Miseries* (London, 1943)

SOBY, JAMES THRALL, *Giorgio de Chirico* (New York n.d.)

SOBY, JAMES THRALL, *Salvador Dali* (New York, 1941)

TODD, RUTHVEN, *Tracks in the Snow* (London, 1946)

TOLNAY, CHARLES DE, *Hieronymus Bosch* (London, 1966)

WEINTRAUB, STANLEY, *Beardsley: A Biography* (London, 1967)

WHITE, CHRISTOPHER, *Rembrandt as an Etcher* (London, 1969)

WILMOT, JOHN, Earl of Rochester, *The Complete Poems* (New Haven & London, 1968)

WIND, EDGAR, *Pagan Mysteries of the Renaissance* (London, 1958)

YOUNG, WAYLAND, *Eros Denied* (London, 1965)

Index

phallic symbols—*cont.*
　moth as (Holman Hunt) 62;
　musical instruments as
　(Bock) 196; *115*; pillar as
　(Beardsley) 244; *143*; plant as
　(Bosch) 107; serpent as
　(Gothic) 14, 151; woman as
　(Picasso) 23, 30
phallus *see* penis
Picasso, Pablo Ruiz y (*b* 1881)
　29–30, 233, 246–7, 263; on
　Balthus 207; *Crucifixion* 23;
　The Dreams and Lies of Franco
　272; *Guernica* 147; *Naked
　Man and Woman 198*; *The
　Rape* 245; *146*; *The Three
　Dancers* 30; *Two Figures* 70;
　55
Piero della Francesco (1410/20–
　92): *Madonna del Parto* 64
Piero di Cosimo (*c* 1462–1521?):
　*The Battle of the Lapiths and
　Centaurs* 18, 150, 151–2;
　91–2; *The Death of Procris* 18,
　258; *161*; *Simonetta Vespucci*
　260; *173*; *Triumph of Death*
　150
Pitti Gallery, Florence: *Mary
　Magdalen* ('Titian) 260; *167*
Plato 12
Poling: *National History* 16–17
Pollaiulo, Antonio (*c* 1432–98):
　Battle of the Naked Men 117;
　St Sebastian 114
poltergeists 108
Pompeii, frescoes at 13, 71
Pop Art 31
Portnoy's Complaint (Roth) 105
Poulet-Malassis, publishers 25
Poussin, Nicolas (1594–1665):
　Acis and Galatea 20
Prado, Madrid: *Charles V*
　(Titian) 201–3; *127*; *The
　Garden of Terrestrial Delights*
　(Bosch) 63, 64–5, 148–50,
　195, 293; *20, 58, 88, 113,
　206*; Pre-Raphaelite
　brotherhood, the 26–7 *and
　see* Holman Hunt, Rossetti
Praxiteles (4th Century BC):
　Cnidian Venus 16–17
Priam 71
Priapus 13
Primaticcio, Francesco (1504/5–
　70) 19
Procris 258; *161*
Proserpine 245; *153*
prostitutes 69–70, 71, 112, 159,
　197–6, 237, 239–40, 268; *51,
　122, 135–42, 191*; *and see*
　courtesans
Proust, Marcel 113, 117
Prud'hon, Pierre Paul (1758–
　1823): *The Union of Love and
　Friendship* 61–2; *13*
Przbyszewski, Dagny Juell 58

Psyche and Cupid 17, 59, 61; *7,
　13, 159*
pubic hair, treatment of: by
　Dine 271; *196*; by Giorgione
　110; Gothic 15; by Goya 22,
　158; Mannerist 246; by
　Rowlandson 266; *189*; by
　Schiele 266; *169*; by
　twentieth century artist 117;
　74
purgatory 262–3; *178*
Pyne, W. H. 24

railway carriages 199–200, 291;
　90, 210
Raimondi, Marcantonio *see*
　Marcantonio Raimondi
Ramos, Mel 31
rape 119, 203, 244–5, 248;
　146–7, 151, 153
Raphael (1483–1520) 18–19, 62,
　68; *Galatea* 62; *5*; *Sistine
　Madonna* 295
Ray, Man (*b* 1890): *Observatory
　Time – The Lovers* 261; *174*
Read, Herbert: *The Green Child*
　297–8
Reade, Brian 66, 269
Realism 24–6
red figure painting, Greek
　11–12, 66–7; *24, 47*
Reflections on the Nude (Stokes)
　264
Reformation, the 160
Reims Cathedral 14
Rembrandt van Ryn (1606–69):
　'Ledikant' ('The Great Bed')
　20, 118–9; *80*; *Joseph and
　Potiphar's Wife* 20; *Toilet of
　Bathsheba* 158; *102*
Rembrandt, Saskia 119
Renaissance art 15, 16–8, 147,
　153–6, 246, 262
Renoir, Pierre Auguste (1841–
　1919) 58, 110, 158; and
　Modigliani 160, 193; *Dance
　at Bougival* 58; *4*
Restoration, the 234
Reynolds, Graham 291–2
Rimbaud, Arthur 301
Rochester, John Wilmot,
　second earl of 111–12,
　234–5, 239–40
Rococo art 21–2
Rodin, Auguste (1840–1917):
　The Kiss 26; *Three Boulders*
　159; *104*
Roman art 11, 12–13, 150
Romanesque art 13–14
Romance of Lust, The 147
Romano, Giulio (1492 or 1499–
　1546) 19; *Sedici Modi* prints
　after 19, 67–9, 70; *26–45*
Romano, Giulio, school of:
　*Marriage Feast of Cupid and
　Psyche* 246; *159*

Romanticism 15–16, 22–4, 31,
　206, 236
Rops, Félicien (1833–98) 25,
　113, 198, 206, 242;
　Bourgeoisie 263; *180*; *Girl in
　Chair 188*; *Heart in hand* 206;
　130; *Street Corner* 242; *140*
Rossetti, Dante Gabriel (1828–
　82) 23, 26, 27, 237; *Found* 27,
　237
Rosso, Giovanni Battista
　(1494–1540) 19
Roth, Philip: *Portnoy's
　Complaint* 105
Rowlandson, Thomas (1757–
　1827) 24, 65–6, 67, 69, 206;
　A Country Outing 24, 65; *22*;
　The Hairy Prospect 266; *189*;
　The Miser 146; *A Music
　Master Tuning his Instrument*
　24, 70; *50*; *Soldiers and a
　Prostitute* 69–70; *51*; *The Spy
　Glass* 24; *136*
Rubens, Sir Peter Paul (1577–
　1640) 20, 21, 158, 205;
　Danae 158; *La Kermesse* 20,
　57–8
Ruskin, John 26, 237, 239
Russell, John 160

sado-eroticism 18, 23, 29, 114,
　149, 198–9, 245
St Ambrose 114
St Anthony 107–8, 269, 300
St Jame's Park 239–40
St Jerome 107
St John the Baptist 116, 247;
　52, 56, 158
St John the Divine 239–40
St Mary Magdalen 259, 262;
　168
St Mary the Virgin, *see*
　Madonna, the
St Paul 117
St Peter's, Rome 17, 18
St Sebastian 114–15; *73*
saints and martyrs 18, 20, 106–8,
　114–15 *and see* individual
　saints
Saintsbury, George 207
Salai, Giacomo 116
Salmacis 13
Salome (Wilde) 23, 271
Salome 18, 247; *158*
San Secondo, Count 202; *126*
Sappho 112
Sarazin, Jacques (1592–1660)
　263
Sargeant, John Singer (1856–
　1925) 263
Saradanapalus 23, 112
Sartre, Jean-Paul 115, 117, 264
Saturnalia 14
satyrs 11, 199, 245–247; *152,
　154–5, 159*
Savonarola, Girolamo 151

317